Here and Now!
The Autobiography of Pat Martino

Here and Now!

The Autobiography of
Pat Martino

Pat Martino

With Bill Milkowski

Backbeat
Books

An Imprint of Hal Leonard Corporation

Published in 2011 by Backbeat Books
An Imprint of Hal Leonard Corporation
7777 West Bluemound Road
Milwaukee, WI 53213

Trade Book Division Editorial Offices
33 Plymouth St., Montclair, NJ 07042

Photo of Pat Martino in Powelton Village and photo of Pat Martino with George
Benson are by Len DeLessio. All other text illustrations and insert photos are
from the author's collection.

Appendix III, "Pat Martino Master Class: Sacred Geometry, Simplifying the
Fretboard with Pat Martino" by Jude Gold, used by permission of *Guitar Player*
magazine.

Book design by Mayapriya Long
Printed in the United States of America

Library of Congress Cataloging-in-Publication Data
Martino, Pat.
  Here and now! : the autobiography of Pat Martino / with Bill Milkowski.
    p. cm.
  Includes bibliographical references and index.
  ISBN 978-1-61713-027-4 (alk. paper)
1. Martino, Pat. 2. Guitarists—United States—Biography. 3. Jazz musicians—
United States—Biography. I. Milkowski, Bill, 1954- II. Title.
  ML417.M36A3 2011
  787.87'165092—dc23
  [B]
                                2011033311

www.backbeatbooks.com

To

Carmen Azzara, Genoveffa Orlando, and Ayako Asahi

Special thanks to Anthony Creamer

Who looks outside, dreams.

Who looks inside, awakes.

—Carl Jung

Contents

Preface

I've often asked myself, "What am I?" I'm not a guitar player; I'm not a musician. Because I don't really seem to find that of any interest in the long run. I'm more interested in what this whole phenomenon of life is really all about. All of the events that took place throughout my life that came from AVM (arteriovenous malformation) and all of its side effects, amplified this mystical dream world where I resided. I lived within quite an illusion during that time I was dealing with AVM, and the intake of drugs only added to that deceptive state. But these are not the things I am. In fact, the words *I am* are enough for me. They're the words of God. And that to me is the essence of definition. The greatest truth comes right back down to the central part of what a person truly is—life itself. And when you reach such a conclusion, it's so spiritual that it overcomes as well as transcends any of the crafts, like guitar playing. Maybe that's what art eventually leads us to discover, however long it takes.

As far as the music, its performance, being a bandleader . . . all of that is second nature. That *has* to be second nature so that I'm not subject to a distortion of any of the daily facets of living, such as a greater understanding of other people, living just as valid an experience that may have nothing to do with music.

I think that no matter what has taken place, I've always longed for something that remained in common with "all things," that I could enjoy no matter what the situation was, so at least the end result had some type of realistic continuity that moved toward enlightenment.

That's my intention—to gain more insight into what I am and why I am. Not to be something I'm not, but to take advantage of all the things that the use of this bodily vehicle will allow . . . and to respect, admire, and cherish realistic opportunities under any circumstance. Similar to the old saying

"Everything's gonna be all right," the love of life in such a state is truly a cure for suffering.

I've known people who fear death, because they're totally consumed by the encasement that they believe themselves to be. They're not consciously alive within their vehicle as of yet. That, to me, is truly the issue. As far as biography, profession, accomplishment . . . these things are very elusive. And when we really come down to the true nature of what these things represent and how they are valued, they fail to meet up to what's really taking place within . . . when always in the moment, at the nexus, the core of the moment, the point that meets all points, the neutralization of endless elusive dichotomies occurs. Not in a dream, hoping that it comes true somewhere in the future. And not in something that no longer exists—the past.

It was recently conveyed to me by a great yogi, B. K. S. Iyengar:

> The seer is pure consciousness and witnesses nature without being reliant on it. Nature and intelligence exist solely to serve the seer's sole purpose—emancipation. The union of the seer with the seen is for the seer to discover its own true nature. Right knowledge destroys ignorance and breaks the link binding the seer to the seen. All of this you know. I look forward to you and your music.

This is the bottom line of my existence, being in the HERE AND NOW, the place where perceptive decisions are made.

—Pat Martino

Introduction

This is a story of triumph over incredible adversity. That Pat Martino is still here is astonishing in itself. The man has had so many brushes with death that he stopped counting, a long time ago. That he overcame the debilitating effects of a brain aneurysm and life-saving surgery back in 1980 and ultimately returned to his former glory as one of the greatest jazz guitarists on the planet is nothing short of miraculous. That Pat continues to play, at age sixty-six, with such unparalleled drive and staggering facility, such an unquenchable sense of swing and such heart, is both exhilarating and inspiring to me and hordes of other guitar aficionados all over the world. On a nightly basis, with remarkable regularity, he continues to channel a lifetime of experiences—the bitter and sad along with the joyous and ecstatic—through this tool, this toy, this guitar.

Having always been impressed by Pat's impeccable technique and blazing chops on the instrument, I have come, with the wisdom of advanced age, perhaps, to appreciate his exquisite ballad playing on a much deeper level. Suddenly, his darkly alluring expression on forlorn, melancholic pieces such as Thelonious Monk's "'Round Midnight," Bill Evans's "Blue in Green," or Horace Silver's "Peace" register with greater meaning for me. But he can still burn with the best of them, as he demonstrated recently at Birdland in New York City by surprisingly pulling out John Coltrane's "Impressions," which also happened to be the opening track from his classic 1974 album *Consciousness*.

It was *Consciousness* that first pulled me to Pat Martino. I was nineteen years old in that summer of 1974 and back then spent a lot of my free time perusing the bins at Radio Doctor's record shop in downtown Milwaukee, always on the lookout for new jazz guitar albums. I was coming out of a rock phase of worshipping guitar heroes like Jimi Hendrix, Jeff Beck, Johnny Winter, and Frank Zappa and was gradually beginning to embrace jazz through such players as Charlie Christian and his direct disciples Herb Ellis, Barney Kessel, and Tiny Grimes. Hearing Joe Pass on Oscar Peterson's 1973 album *The Trio* (with bassist Niels-Henning Orsted Pedersen) was a major revelation, as was his solo guitar album that came out later that year, *Virtuoso*. I was primed for someone like Pat Martino. And when I spotted *Consciousness* in the bins, with its striking black-and-white photograph of Pat sitting cross-legged on what appeared to be a lily pad, staring directly back at me with an intense Rasputin-like gaze, I was absolutely transfixed. I took it home, dropped the needle (remember that process?) on the first track—his blazing rendition of Trane's "Impressions"—and was instantly blown away. And I've been a Pat Martino devotee ever since.

When Pat came out with *Joyous Lake* in the summer of 1977, it fed right into my fusion inclinations (I had been heavily into the Mahavishnu Orchestra, Weather Report, and Return to Forever during the early 1970s). Apart from the incredibly powerful music within, there remained a mystical vibe to this extraordinary guitarist, as shown in the depiction of the fifty-eighth hexagram of the *I Ching* (formed by the doubling of the trigram *tui*) hovering over his head on the album cover. That particular hexagram not only symbolized the smiling or joyous lake, it stood for perseverance. Little did I know then how much meaning this hexagram would have in Pat's later life.

That fall of 1977, when I heard that Pat would be performing in Madison, about ninety miles away from my hometown of Milwaukee, I made the pilgrimage with my best friend and fellow guitar enthusiast Ric Weinman. Determined to see this mystical six-string guru in the flesh, we drove to Wisconsin's capital city to get enlightened. Pat was appearing in a duo there at an intimate restaurant/club with fellow Philadelphian Bobby Rose, and as we entered the joint after our ninety-minute drive, the two were engaged in a burning rendition of Wes's "Four on Six." We stood in awe of Pat's facility and inventive lines during that set and afterward sought him out for a chat. Surprisingly, he was not only approachable and forthcoming (gods rarely are), he invited us back to his hotel room to continue our conversation. What followed was a rather freewheeling, esoteric rap that lasted into the wee hours and touched upon aspects of guitar as it relates to sacred geometry, twelve-pointed stars, and the sixty-four hexagrams of the *I Ching*, along with myriad other mind-blowing topics ("Music is food; the guitar is merely a fork") that were way over my head at the time. I left that encounter inspired and determined to elevate my own game as a novice guitar player.

By 1980, after moving to New York, I was already fully immersed in the jazz scene as a freelance scribe. And as both a fan and critic, I watched with amazement as Pat made his heroic comeback following his near-fatal aneurysm—first with an October 12, 1984, performance at the Bottom Line (on a split bill with fellow Philadelphian Stanley Clarke) and then with a weeklong engagement in February 1987 at Fat Tuesday's (documented and released by Muse Records in 1989 as *The Return*).

My own personal connection with Pat Martino was rekindled some years later when on the afternoon of December 12,1995, I received a phone call from Blue Note Records president Bruce Lundvall. "Bill, lad," he began in that jolly jazz-Santa manner of his, "we just signed Pat Martino and we'd like you to produce his first record with us." Then he laid out a plan for a prospective all-star assemblage of guest guitarists paying homage to Pat, each one appearing on a separate track playing alongside the master. It would be his debut for the prestigious label and usher in a new era of greater visibility for the legendary guitarist, but the overly ambitious project was doomed from jump. Throughout his career, Pat was used to recording whole albums in one or two days with well-rehearsed ensembles. This bloated affair was strung out over a full year and required that Pat create instant chemistry in the studio with musicians whom, in some cases, he had never met before. (Props to co-producer Matt Resnicoff for handling the lion's share of duties throughout that prolonged and often painful process.) It did, however, produce a couple of gems in Pat's delightfully engaging collaboration with Les Paul on "I'm Confessin' (That I Love You)" and his stirring duet with Cassandra Wilson on Joni Mitchell's "Both Sides Now."

Phase three of my interactions with Pat—I guess you could say that my boyhood trip to Madison to see him play back in 1977 and followup interview was phase one and the Blue Note debacle of 1996–97 was phase two—is this book. In a series of several sit-down sessions at his South Philly home (which bears the unmistakable upbeat signature of his wife, Aya, whose passion for stuffed pigs is apparent throughout the house), Pat revealed insights into his life as well as his philosophy about the nature of life itself.

The narrative arc of the Pat Martino story is epic and compelling, the stuff of legend and Hollywood movies. It's the story of a small, skinny son of a Sicilian laborer in South Philly (family name Azzara) who becomes a guitar prodigy, makes it to the *Ted Mack Original Amateur Hour* TV show with his rockin' combo at age twelve, then heads out on the road at age fifteen as the only white musician in the eighteen-piece Lloyd Price Orchestra before undergoing important apprenticeships with bandleaders Willis "Gator Tail" Jackson and Jack McDuff in Harlem. By 1967, he joins the band of forward-thinking alto saxophonist John Handy during the Summer of Love. That same year, the twenty-two-year-old phenom cuts his own first recording as a leader, *El Hombre* (the title itself carries an air of swagger, though the formula doesn't stray too far from his own organ-group roots). And while his early 1968 release *East!* implies a bit of mystique in the title and the depiction of Buddha on the cover, the program is steeped in hard bop with the occasional foray into more modernist modal territory.

With Pat's next recording, there is a definite stylist break from his previous outings as a leader. From the cryptic title alone—*Baiyina (The Clear Evidence): A Psychedelic Excursion Through the Magical Mysteries of the Koran*—it is obvious that Pat is now courting a very different muse on this late-1968 release, one that is more informed by Ravi Shankar and Owsley Stanley than Jack McDuff and the chitlin' circuit. From the mind-blowing cover art to the provocative music within (two guitars executing intricate lines over tabla and tamboura drone, nearly four years before Miles Davis charted this Indo-jazz territory on his groundbreaking 1972 album *On the Corner*), *Baiyina* is a daring stretch by a serious artist in transition. In his liner notes, Michael Cuscuna called the work "an astounding suite which signifies a major step for Martino as a player and composer." (Approximately thirty years later, Pat would record a kind of companion piece, *Fire Dance,* with tabla master Zakir Hussain, flutist Peter Block, and sitarist Habib Khan.)

Pat followed with a string of potent and highly influential recordings through the mid-1970s for the Muse label—1972's *Live!* (which yielded a radio-play hit with an instrumental version of Bobby Hebb's "Sunny"), 1974's *Consciousness* (featuring a blistering "Impressions" and a solo guitar version of Joni Mitchell's "Both Sides Now"), 1976's *We'll Be Together Again* (his dreamy ballads project with Gil Goldstein on Fender Rhodes electric piano), and the quartet offering *Exit*—would have a lasting impact on a generation of musicians, and guitar players in particular. That incredibly productive year of 1976 culminated with the recording of Pat's major-label debut on Warner Bros., the adventurous *Starbright,* and the trailblazing fusion follow-up, *Joyous Lake,* which was recorded in September and released in early 1977.

And then at the peak of his powers and popularity, the lights went out.

In 1980, following some years of experiencing headaches and occasional seizures, the legendary guitarist suffered a near-fatal brain aneurysm. The emergency surgery that subsequently saved his life left him with total amnesia. As a man without a past—unencumbered by the baggage of history—Pat was now forced to live strictly in the moment, a prospect both horrifying and liberating. He struggled for the next few years through a process of reclaiming memory and gradually reacquainting himself with the instrument he had formerly mastered with such precision and unparalleled facility, until finally reemerging on the scene in 1987 with the aptly titled *The Return,* a live document of an engagement at Fat Tuesday's in Manhattan. The deaths in fairly close proximity of his mother (in 1989) and father (in 1990) caused an immediate paradigm shift in Pat's world, or, as he reflectively refers to it now, "a time of responsibility and realization." It was during this period when his parents were literally dying before his eyes that Pat privately recorded at home the profound though little-known orchestral work *Seven Sketches,* which he performed solely on guitar synthesizer triggering symphonic sounds. Included in that collection of works composed between 1987 and 1998 is the darkly dissonant "Mirage," which sounds like it may have been written by Pat as a kind of requiem for his father, Mickey.

Pat got back on a career track in 1994 with *Interchange* and *The Maker* and 1996's *Night Wings,* then rebounded from that aforementioned *All Sides Now* debacle with a triumphant reunion of his Joyous Lake band on 1998's *Stone Blue,* which created new visibility for him as a major attraction at jazz festivals and nightclubs all over the world. He followed with 2001's Grammy-nominated *Live at Yoshi's* with organist Joey DeFrancesco and drummer Billy Hart (who had appeared on 1976's *Exit*); 2003's *Think Tank* with tenor saxophonist Joe Lovano, pianist Gonzalo Rubalcaba, bassist Christian McBride, and drummer Lewis Nash; and 2006's popular and acclaimed *Remember: A Tribute to Wes Montgomery.*

In 2008, British filmmaker Ian Knox released the intriguing documentary *Unstrung: A Brain Mystery,* which examines the details of Pat's aneurysm, surgery, and struggle to recover his memory, with neuropsychologist Paul Broks acting as intrepid tour guide. Three very insightful interviews with Pat Knox and Broks regarding this powerful documentary, originally written by Victor L. Schermer for *All About Jazz,* are included here in the appendix section.

Working as Pat's Boswell on his very revealing autobiography has allowed me to step outside my usual journalist-critic mode and view him not as a guitar hero but as a heroic, inspiring figure. He has defied all odds . . . come back from the dead, so to speak. Back in 1980, he was given two hours to live . . . and he's still here. He has rebounded from multiple surgeries, electroshock treatments, the debilitating effects of COPD (chronic obstructive pulmonary disease), and a laundry list of other maladies. As his manager Joe Donofrio put it,

> I've watched him get in situations that would really defeat most people, and he just bounces out of them. I love his attitude. He's incredibly strong-willed and even at his lowest point he manages to bounce back.

I've seen this over and over again with him. That's something he wants people to know about him, and I also think that is something that can help other people. People will call him because they read about his aneurysm and his fight, and he'll talk to them and counsel them. He really wants to be able to help people. He likes to talk to people about how they can get through these tough times.

Donofrio is also quick to point out, "Pat has nurtured his demons in order to understand their pain. And over the years he developed self-discipline. Where once he would explode, he now defuses through self-imposed bouts with reality. In that sense, he became his own guru by conveying a strong spiritual sensibility to his existence."

Pat Martino's story is also much more than a tale of perseverance, just as Pat himself is much more than just a guitar player. Perhaps Kirk Yano, Pat's road manager and engineer since 1998, put it best when he said: "It is a beautiful love story, when you look at the big picture of everything. It's totally about musical love. And you think about all the people that he's touched in five decades . . . I mean, it's amazing."

—Bill Milkowski

Exit and Return

Let's be honest. When you don't remember something, you have no idea of its existence. And upon awakening after the surgery, I remembered nothing.

But it wasn't a disorienting feeling. If I had known I was a guitarist, if I had known those two people standing by my bedside in the hospital were in fact my parents, I then would've felt the feelings that went along with the events. What they went through and why they were standing there looking at me then would've been very painful for me. But it wasn't painful, because to me they were just strangers.

The lack of my career from the aneurysm and surgery to save my life? I had no idea there was a career. The only thing I knew upon opening my eyes was . . . now. Here I am. I am. Why are these people looking at me?

Did I remember my own name? I can't recall. And what name would that have been? Pat Martino, or Pat Azzara? Which of the two is my name? Which is the mask? There's always two sides . . . there's always the opposites.

I think the first event that I can actually recall was a significant difference regarding one thing that has always been latent within me—my interest in my own appearance as an individual. I remember a moment when . . . and it seems to be one of the first things that I remembered . . . I raised my hand to my cheek and I felt the beard that was protruding. And I asked for a mirror and I looked in the mirror, and I didn't care for what I saw. And then at that moment my first objective became to be able to make it to the restroom and shave. And it took a number of days to be allowed to do that.

And once I was allowed to do that, I made it there . . . I was guided there, watched over by hospital personnel . . . and I shaved for the first time. That much I remember.

When I finally left the Pennsylvania Hospital here in Philadelphia, I came to my parents' house, this very house I live in now. I was placed upstairs in a two-bedroom facility—one bedroom was very small, the other was medium. In the medium bedroom were just a bed and a dresser and a closet. And in the small one was just a desk where eventually I began teaching guitar when the guitar became active again in my life. I resided in that bedroom. And I heard through the floors, every Saturday, my father playing all of my records that he treasured so much. And since I was told that that's what I did, from time to time I would pick up an album cover and bring it into the bathroom and hold it up to the mirror and look at it and say, "Yeah, he's right. That's who I am," without really remembering what that was. I didn't like having to do that. And it was futile because of the condition I was in. For my father, it was sheer disappointment and turmoil. And my mother, of course, with her rosary in hand, constantly in prayer . . . praying for this to come to an end. It was a very difficult time. And that was only a scratch on the surface.

After my brain operation, I wanted to give up music. It meant nothing to me anymore. And I wanted to die. The reason I didn't was not because of any courageous act on my part, but the very opposite—because of the lack of courage to commit suicide . . . the innate fear of all of the religious implants from childhood on up, suicide being a mortal sin in the Catholic religion. And as the pain of my dilemma became more and more, less and less did I see any fruition from the outer world, from social interaction, from friendship. And finally, throughout stages of it, looking for answers to it, the psychiatrists that I would see as part of the therapy to recover from this dilemma would give me different types of antidepressants. And nothing worked. Periods of therapy were highly affected by prescribed medication, as well . . . very heavy chemicals, very heavy drugs. And what was the heaviest reality of all was that they were not working.

I was given lithium and other drugs that began with Z, others that began with S, others that began with R. I went through the whole alphabet with drugs based on this misdiagnosis. And with each of them I was given preparatory descriptions of, "It'll take two weeks before it'll become active, so don't expect too much too soon. Have patience." Two weeks later, nothing was going on . . . I'm still suffering, like so many individuals in our society suffer.

So that's what it came down to. The drugs were failing to be of any service to me. In fact, the depression and the anxiety and all the frustration, the suicidal tendencies, were leading to havoc. And that's where the guitar came in. It became my distraction from it. The pain and misery became so intense and so magnified that I looked for a way out of it. And there was the guitar. And my attitude was, "Let me pick that up and see what that does." And when I did that, some innate powers were ignited. Little by little, just a minute here and there . . . and I was back to the kid again, exploring the instrument with the kind of playfulness and openness that I had as a child. And this toy would become the escape route from the pain I endured. I was drowning in a sea of misery, and the guitar, in effect, became my life preserver.

2

Mickey and Me

My father was Carmen Azzara, but everyone called him Mickey. His father was born in Palermo, Sicily, and he grew up in South Philadelphia at Ninth Street and Montrose, just off of Passyunk Avenue, which at the time was strictly an Italian neighborhood. Now it's primarily Cambodian and Vietnamese. Things shifted . . . there's a cultural pulsating that's taken place over decades. So it's not the way it was in my father's time. He came up through the age of Al Capone and all of the different branches of the Mafia in the United States. Many of the neighborhoods here in Philadelphia were supported by those groups during the Depression. And my father, like many others at the time, was involved in liquor, creating gin in the bathtub during Prohibition . . . just to make a living.

Mickey mostly spoke Italian with his friends. In fact, Mom and Dad spoke to each other around the house in Italian. But they never really focused on an invitation for me into that form of communication. I remember, in my very young years, when aunts and uncles would come over to the house and everything was spoken in Italian. And here I am, an only child, sitting there playing with my toys . . . and it's like I'm in another country and don't even understand the language. Lacking the participation in the family in that way, being on the outside, I had to find other interests that would be fulfilling. These were things, I think, that had a great deal to do with my attraction to the music. Maybe because of the lack of that invitation into speaking Italian with them, I moved toward a devotion to another language, not theirs, which I never invited *them* into.

Mickey himself was a guitar player and a singer. As a young man he had a great interest in Bing Crosby and the great jazz guitarist Eddie Lang, who was from the neighborhood and whose real name was Salvatore Massaro. In fact, at some point, Dad actually spent two weeks with Eddie Lang learning how to strum a guitar. That's how he learned how to play the changes when he would serenade my mother. He would sing all these romantic Italian love songs to entice my mother into a smile. It was just beautiful to experience that. So precious. Those were happy moments.

But like the two sides of the coin, there were also tumultuous moments at home. Mom [Genoveffa Orlando] being subject from the 1930s to cancer, having suffered breast cancer at a very early age, and Dad being an extreme alcoholic, their marriage was always on the edge. I observed confrontation after confrontation, and they separated a few times. So there was love but also turmoil. I think that's natural in relationships. But Dad really was so deeply in love with her. That's something that was without a doubt. He was afraid to lose his marriage, but still wanted to have a drink. He used to keep bottles of whiskey hidden all over the house . . . up in the ceiling in the basement, other places. So he was entwined in a really vicious circle, a catch-22 . . . until finally he broke it, he solved it. He finally stopped drinking and stopped smoking, too, just through force of will.

My mother was a Roman Catholic who was so deeply involved in prayer that she was more or less a disciple. A majority of her time was spent meditating and in deep prayer. I remember seeing her often with the rosary in hand. My father was Roman Catholic, as well, but on the fringe of it. I think his connection to the religion was more about the neighborhood . . . being seen in church every Sunday, dressed well, donating to the parish, being involved with the parochial school when I was there. It was never a deep spiritual relationship like Mom's. He was doing what was socially acceptable to fit in with the community, but at the same time he also adhered to all of the ethics and morals that are at the basis for the need for religions. Essentially, he was a good human being. The golden rule was very real for him.

Dad worked in tailor factories as a lapel presser, and on his weekends off he would go to big-band performances and dances in the 1930s. And it would be Cab Calloway, Duke Ellington, or Count Basie playing to crowds of dancers. And he began to really be affected by that.

Mickey kept his guitar under his bed. And when I was maybe three or four years old, I'm told, I was exploring under the bed and reached into the guitar case to strum the strings on his guitar. I cut my fingers on the steel strings and I bled, profusely. And I spread my blood on his bedroom walls like graffiti. From that point forward, he shielded me from the instrument:

"Don't touch! You're not allowed to touch that!" And maybe that was his plan to do so, a bit of reverse psychology on his part.

When I was twelve years old, Dad bought my cousin Joey a guitar, a 1956 Fender Stratocaster, which would be worth a fortune today. And what that did was it caused me to confront him: "Why did you buy Joey a guitar? Why didn't you buy me a guitar?" So it came down to the fact that I then was competing with my older cousin in my relationship with my father . . . with envy. But he finally did buy me a guitar. He took me to a pawn shop and bought me a little guitar, which I still have down in the basement. And he said, "Let me see what you can do with this. If you get serious with it, I'll buy you a serious instrument." And that's what he did.

In a period of four, five weeks, he took me to the Wurlitzer music store here in Philadelphia and bought me a standard model Les Paul goldtop guitar. And I began woodshedding on that instrument. I was enticed by the sound of music. My father would put on the radio, the jazz station, and that's what really got me . . . the sound of these individuals, these instrumentalists. So I would then sit down with the guitar and wonder how it could be done on this instrument. I would try to play and copy what I heard on the radio, and then I began learning solos off of 45 records, mainly rock 'n' roll hits of the day—Bill Haley and the Comets, the Esquire Boys' "Guitar Boogie Shuffle," things like that. Not yet jazz but guitar records.

Every summer since I was a small child, when school was out and my parents had to work, they would drop me off at Al and Jennie Riderelli's house a couple of blocks away on Eleventh and Ritner. They were the parents of Bobby Riderelli, who was two years older than me. Me and Bobby grew up together, playing as kids. By 1956, he became a drummer and I began a guitar player, and we put a band together. The band was called the Emanons, which was the words *no name* backward. Bobby Riderelli would later become the successful rock 'n' roll singer Bobby Rydell [who scored a pop hit in 1960 with "Wild One" and later appeared in the 1963 movie version of *Bye Bye Birdie*]. There was also a trumpet player from the neighborhood named Frankie Avalone, who later gained fame as Frankie Avalon. And Ernie Evans, who used to work on Seventh Street, became Chubby Checker. A lot of people from the neighborhood got swept up in that whole early rock 'n' roll movement.

So I ended up forming the Emanons with Bobby and another guitarist from the neighborhood named Joe Lano. We would play at dances and Italian weddings and parties. Eventually Dad got me a manager, a gentleman named Mike Capuano, who was able to get our band a shot on *Ted Mack's Original Amateur Hour* show, which was a great coup for us.

Bobby Rydell Remembers: We were kids from the neighborhood and we had this little band together. Of course, I knew him as Pat Azzara then. I was a little older than Pat—he was twelve and I was fourteen—but you could tell right away that this kid was so talented. It was ridiculous the way he played "Guitar Boogie Shuffle." I mean, he'd solo like a pro . . . at age twelve! Pat played guitar and I played drums, and we had Joe Lano on guitar and Eddie Lalli on accordion, mostly playing bass lines. Joe Lano has been working in Las Vegas for years, backing up all the big acts out there. Our little band would play around at functions—weddings, bar mitzvahs, dances, parties, and that kind of thing. I really don't know if we had a name for the band, but we would get together and rehearse at Pat's house, my house, Lalli's house, Lano's house. And Pat's father, Mickey—God rest his soul—would say to me, "Bobby, play brushes." And I'd say, "Brushes, Mick? Your son is amplified." And he said, "No, I want brushes." So I'd play brushes. We actually stayed together for about two years. I guess the peak that we hit with that band was when we were on the *Ted Mack Original Amateur Hour.* We had a tenor player by then named Joe Scavetti, and I think we did "Night Train," which is a great honkin' tenor tune.

Pat was a quiet kid and very easygoing; a very different personality from his father, who was more intense and controlling. But Pat was always very cool, very calm. And to this day, he's still the same way. When he talks on the microphone to the audience at his gigs, he sounds very relaxed, very mellow, very cool. I also remember Pat used to practice that guitar all the time. I couldn't believe how much this guy worked out on that instrument. For a kid, he was incredibly focused and serious about playing the guitar.

Those were fun times. Over the years we had stayed in touch. I actually sat in on drums with him and his band last year at Chris' Jazz Café here in Philly. I exchanged some fours with him on a shuffle blues thing, and we had a great time. He's just a dear friend and one helluva musician. And he's come through a helluva lot of adversity, to the point where he thought he could never play guitar again. But he woodshedded and got it together, and he's playing great again. And what's startling now is he looks just like his father. He looks exactly like Mickey.

I continued to play these neighborhood functions with the Emanons for the next couple of years, trading up my guitar for the next model over time, just like how you get a new-model car from time to time. And Mickey bought them all for me. I went from that Les Paul goldtop to a black Les Paul Custom in fairly short order. And I began to progress rapidly on the instrument. Dad and I used to play some duets together, with him strumming the changes and me playing the melodies. I think back sometimes about that and how gracious he was to allow that to take place. As I got more involved with the instrument and continued to evolve and later became technically so far out that it was no longer possible for him to participate in that kind of music, there was an alienation, there was a breakoff in that relationship of playing duets together. But we had those moments that can never be replaced.

My father was an extremely aggressive man. No matter what he focused on, he was very intense about it. So when he saw that I was interested in Wes Montgomery and Johnny Smith, he took me to meet them. I remember one time he went right up to the stage at a place called the Red Hill Inn in New Jersey and went over to Stan Getz and said, "Is Johnny Smith here with you? I want my son to meet him. How do we do this?"

Another of my earliest guitar influences was Les Paul. Dad, always aware of exposing me to these great guitarists, brought me to the Steel Pier in Atlantic City, where Les Paul and Mary Ford were performing. After their performance, we went backstage and Dad introduced me to Les. After we talked, Les handed me his guitar and asked me to play something. He seemed to be impressed with my facility, particularly my ability with the plectrum. [In his liner notes to Pat's 1970 Prestige album *Desperado,* Les wrote:

> Some years ago I was playing an engagement in Atlantic City and a young lad, accompanied by his parents, came backstage to meet me and request my autograph. When the lad said he was learning guitar I handed him mine and asked that he play something. Well, what came out of that guitar was unbelievable. His dexterity and his picking style were absolutely unique. He held his pick as one would hold a demitasse . . . pinky extended, very polite. The politeness disappeared when pick met string, as what happened then was not timid but very definite. I was very impressed and the memory of this lad stuck with me. Although I lost track of him, I figured that sooner or later I was bound to hear him again. Several years later I began hearing reports of a young guitarist playing in the New York area who was really scaring other musicians with his ability and musicianship. I tracked him down to a club in Harlem, and aside from the fact that the reports of his being a great guitarist were not exaggerated, I found that this was the same lad who had visited me in Atlantic City. Now grown up, and with the extra years of practice and experience, he had grown into a musical giant.

Dad wouldn't think twice about going backstage like that or going up to any bandstand and telling the musicians, "I want my son to sit in. Who do I talk to?" I was like his prodigy. He used to bring me around to so many places . . . nightclubs, the neighborhood barbershop . . . and have me play "Moonlight in Vermont" for people just to impress them. He was never intimidated and absolutely knew what he wanted—he wanted for me to experience all the things that he failed to experience in his own youth. He had a dream for me to become the guitarist he never became. And he pushed me into attaining that dream. He encouraged me to be a musician, he encouraged me to be a guitar player, he encouraged me to be a legend . . . yet these had nothing to do with me. He was encouraging me to be something that I didn't include in my identity. I didn't know what I was.

I was always a very reflective, extremely inquisitive child. Not so much in terms of questioning authority . . . more on the basis of questioning their response to myself in terms of being what I am and what I always was. I attended Catholic school, and when a member of the class does not adhere to something that he or she is told to do in a parochial setting, the nun or the priest is liable to turn around and give the child a slap in the face and ask the child to stand with his or her face to the corner for the next ten minutes. Since they had no interest in what was being taught, that was their penance. So that's what I experienced in Catholic school. I was more interested in, "What does this mean?" and sometimes it caused me to get into trouble with the nuns. It also caused me to look closer into, "I wonder who is the sinner in all of this?" since that's what they were teaching at the time.

I was also very small and very thin. The neighborhood where I lived in South Philadelphia in those years and throughout my early days growing up were like certain parts of Brooklyn, where there were gangs. If you were not in a gang, there was something wrong with you. And if you were in a gang, you took your place in terms of status, which was often based on size. And since I was very small and some of the tops in most gangs were very big, I found a solution to that at a very early age by becoming friendly with all the gangs. And I used to go from one neighborhood to another, befriending different gangs and running errands for them for different things, just on the basis of friendship.

I lived at 1130 Garrett Street, and when you went northwest from the house to the end of the block, to your right was a playground. That's where we used to play baseball. And I participated in and really enjoyed playing baseball until I wasn't good enough to keep up with some of the bigger kids. And at that particular time, it wasn't producing stimulation for me. I think with everything that I was doing as a child, there came a time when it no longer produced the stimulation that I needed. By the time I was twelve or thirteen, the guitar did that. And it took me away from my friends. It became a craft, not on the basis of a profession or a career; it became a vehicle for me.

I enjoyed playing with it when nothing was happening with the guys, until finally that started amplifying more and more, to the point where I enjoyed playing it more than hanging out with the guys.

Around that time, my first guitar lessons began to take place at DeLucia's, a small guitar-repair shop around Thirteenth and Wharton Street in South Philadelphia. My teacher was Irv Revell. Irv repaired guitars and gave basic lessons—how to tune the instrument, strumming chords, and so on. Not long after that, it became so fulfilling and playful and addictive that it intruded on my childhood. And it became a serious direction to move in. I developed an active participation in a competitive game. I had developed a situation that would occur again and again and again. And that meant in facets such as other guitar players would then be judgmental critique-wise . . . are you better than them? Are you as fast as them? Can you be faster than them? How much do you practice? Do you practice as much as they practice? That's what the child was going through.

By the time I was fourteen, Dad got me another manager. He was really searching for someone who could help his kid become somebody, and he found a guy named Jerry Blavat, who was a popular local radio disc jockey from South Philly known as "the Geator with the Heator." Jerry had been a mainstay in the dance brigade on Dick Clark's *American Bandstand* in those early years of television, and he later got involved in the music business and became one of the big promoters and producers of early rock 'n' roll in Philadelphia. The first thing Jerry Blavat did as my manager was he brought me to a voice teacher. He was trying to fashion me into another teen star, which meant I had to sing. But I wasn't paying too much attention to my vocal coach at the time. The second thing he did was to give me the name Ricky Tino, which was derived from my first name, Patrick, and my Dad's stage name, Martino. Jerry was a very ambitious manager. He got me gigs at high school dances and stuff, and we actually cut a 45 rpm single, which I still have a copy of somewhere around the house. My single had me playing guitar with a bunch of singers in the background. Jerry brought me to one gig in a helicopter, where I came down a ladder with a guitar on my shoulder, and they were playing my single as I descended. So I was moving in the direction that Bobby Rydell and Frankie Avalon had gone.

For about a year, throughout that period of Jerry Blavat events, I was taking guitar lessons with a wonderful man by the name of John Hall. He taught me how to read simple lead sheets and provided me with basic violin studies containing scales and other common subjects. He would also provide the title of a 45 rpm record for us to purchase at a record store (like "Guitar

Boogie," by the Esquire Boys), and that part of the lesson was for me to copy eight measures of the lead-guitar solo. This continued on a weekly basis for about a year.

What was really profound was what I was introduced to, while none of us (including John) even knew that it was entering my perspectives. I remember how, after avoiding homework (the same reason I dropped out of high school), I would sit through a lesson, somewhat uncomfortable, and afterward, as I was leaving, I'd run the back of my right hand across my forehead (like removing sweat), saying to myself, "You did it! Wow, I'm happy that's over!" Then I would return home and the next stage of the process would begin.

Dad would come home from work, sit on the couch, and read a newspaper while listening to me go through my homework (practice my lesson). I didn't want to practice those scales for violin; I wanted to play something that was more interesting for me. So I did that. I just played, and since my father couldn't read music, I took advantage of that and stood there playing random ideas while pretending that I was reading it from the lesson book. That was the true beginning of improvisation for me, and it invisibly continued to unknowingly evolve.

My dad was a member of an Italian club (located around Broad and Reed) named the Sons of Italy. And they used to have a contest there on Sundays where parents would bring their children to share the talents that Mom and Dad were proud of. I was brought to one of those contests and I came in second place. The winner was an eight-year-old ballerina, and she won $500, while for second place my prize was the ability to select off of a long tabletop, its surface spread out with 33⅓ record albums, any one that I wanted. So I looked and I noticed all of them were similar, and to some degree familiar. There were albums of Frank Sinatra, Perry Como, Connie Francis, Dean Martin, Elvis Presley, and so on. In the midst of all of those, there was the one record that was unique. All of the others had full-color cover art while this one was primarily black and white. The only things in color were the artists' names, the title of the album, and the record-company logo . . . Columbia Records. Plus, there were two serious-looking black men staring at me from the cover. That's the one I selected! I had now gotten my first jazz album—Donald Byrd and Gigi Gryce's *Jazz Lab*. And that really turned me on.

I became transfixed by these heavy players that were speaking the language that I wanted to know more about. That's when Dad sought out Dennis Sandole, a renowned teacher in Philadelphia who had given lessons to such people as John Coltrane, McCoy Tyner, James Moody, Benny Golson,

Paul Chambers, and many others. I already had my ecstasy together on the guitar. I really knew how to get off on that instrument in terms of fun. But suddenly, this was the next step in an amplification of my credibility, career-wise, on behalf of my father . . . to make sure that his son was influenced by this highly advertised individual.

Dennis taught at his own private studio on Watts Street, right off of Pine, which he rented. It was a little room. Symbolically it was very close to an image in your mind of where, say, Van Gogh or Eric Satie might work. It was a little room with another little room, and you'd have to walk up a staircase that would come to the second floor of this incredibly abstract little building that looked like a house maybe in Vienna on this little alley kind of street. It was a very surrealistic kind of place. And all of these great musicians were in and out of there all the time.

Dennis's instruments were his voice and his pen. Guitar was his instrument initially, but he got so far away from it that he really didn't perform at all anymore. He just sat there and wrote and preached and gave ideas and responded in the most abstract ways . . . a very serious individual, an artist of the highest level, a mentor. But in my relationship with Dennis, I was actually more interested in studying the teacher than the lessons themselves, which had a great deal to do with understanding scales and modes. I was more of an apprentice with regard to the aesthetics that surrounded him as an individual, as an artist. I'm always interested in the individual. The outcome of that individual's perspectives says a lot in terms of the nature of what this person finds important to live and share with others . . . and charge them accordingly to do so.

And the essence of what is meaningful in a student-teacher relationship, there's a third place that's invisible to both parties. Here's the student and here's the teacher, and there's a third place that stands between them that is equal . . . they're equal to each other in that place. And if and when both can enter into that phase of contact and interact within that third place, there is no longer a teacher or a student. Both are learning from each other in that place. That's the real thing. As long as they're outside of that inner sphere, it's a game—"It's my way, you're not experienced, I'm older than you, this is what you should do, did you practice?" Keep in mind that the student initially came there and already was involved in the ecstasy, and the only reason that the student came to the teacher was to extend the continuity of that ecstasy.

So here comes the student . . . and in this particular case I can now describe my position in this. I came to Dennis with a problem because I was breaking a lot of strings, and the reality of opposition lay between two

Teacher   Student

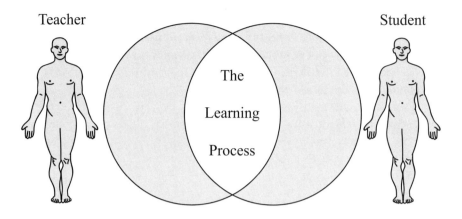

The

Learning

Process

hands—my left hand and my right hand. On the guitar my left hand was extremely intellectual, extremely analytical as to what it was to do and how it was to do it . . . with precision. My left hand was the graduate, the serious student. My right hand was the dropout. It was aggressive and had no control of how it functioned. And I asked it to do nothing but what was natural to do. The one problem that came up from that was breaking strings, because the right hand was so aggressive. And when Dennis Sandole witnessed this, he immediately advised me that I was holding the plectrum wrong and that's why strings were breaking: "You're picking too hard, you need to hold the plectrum like this, don't rest your hands on the strings there. The palm of your hand shouldn't be like that, it needs to be lifted up. And you need to move your hand like this."

Now, I took him seriously because of the admiration and the respect of an elder from an apprentice. I did the best I could for a period of maybe three to four weeks, and it produced what it was meant to produce—it produced frustration and anxiety. And it became an interruptive shield to the very ecstasy that I had already experienced continuously prior to meeting Dennis. It was that comparative position to be in that caused me to come to a conclusion : "Well, maybe it's the strings. So let me try heavier strings." And I kept on looking for heavier and heavier strings. The heavier they got, the less they broke. Until finally I reached the conclusion that I was fine the way I naturally held the pick and the way I performed . . . and that I didn't have to follow this advice. "This is another way—plan B. I'll take plan B."

So switching to heavy-gauge strings allowed my right hand to remain a dropout, with respect. Just as much as the graduate is respected. And hopefully there shall come a time in education itself when the graduate and the dropout can interact and co-relate with insight into totally different dimensions of perspectives. Unfortunately, that isn't the way it is. If you're a dropout, you're a failure. Well, failure is the opposite of success . . . and both function at the same time. That's why there's a mask with a frown on it and a mask with a smile on it. The only thing that is neutral at the moment and not activated socially is the third place . . . the third eye . . . objectivity. To learn these things, to come to these conclusions, to begin to ponder over these values when studying music . . . and the feeling that you get and the experience of the process itself . . . is so profound that the craft is reduced to second nature by comparison to it.

By that time, I had gotten my second Les Paul Custom. I was ready to go to Harlem and immerse myself in the language of jazz. My main concern since conscious childhood was to participate with elders and to be adequate in terms of that participation, for them to understand my opinion. In some ways it seems egotistic, and I guess it is, to some degree. But it was essential for me to do that. And that's what I did by going to Harlem at age fifteen.

3

On the Road

The trigger for me going out from home and experiencing working on the road was Charles Earland. And the story of how I met him is fairly convoluted. It begins with me being expelled from Bishop Newman High School in tenth grade. Something took place between me and one of the priests there . . . if I remember correctly it had something to do with bubblegum. I was chewing bubblegum in class, and this particular priest at the head of the class called me to the front of the class and said, "You're chewing gum. I warned you not to do that." And he held up a piece of tissue and said, "Put that gum here." So I did. I took it out of my mouth and put it on the tissue. And then he took it and he twisted it into my hair.

When I came home, I couldn't get it out of my hair, it had to be cut out. And my father freaked. So the next day Dad went to Bishop Newman and confronted the priest. He wanted to really beat the shit out of him, to tell the truth. Well, the upshot of it was that I was expelled. And I was shifted over to South Philadelphia High School, which still exists, by the way. And that's where I met Charles Earland. He was a tenor player in the high school band, and a good one at that. At some point he got turned on to the great organist Jimmy Smith, who was also from Philadelphia, and we went down to Atlantic City one time to see Jimmy perform at the Jockey Club. We were teenagers, just fifteen years old. Charlie heard Jimmy Smith play the Hammond B-3 that evening and was just floored by the magic. He was just so compelled he thought he was hallucinating it. And that's when Charlie decided he was going to switch from tenor saxophone to Hammond B-3 organ.

Charlie and I then got together and we practiced for two, three weeks, then went to play a gig in Buffalo at a place called the Pine Grill, which still exists. At some point during our set, in came this entourage of musicians who took their place at the bar. It was Lloyd Price's big band. They had finished their concert wherever it was, came to the Pine Grill, and were having a taste. That was the place to go in Buffalo. On the intermission . . . you know how you wander around where you play . . . Lloyd Price called me over and he said, "Listen, if ever you wanna come to New York City, let me know. I like the way you play." So I called Pop and told him, "Pop, I just got this offer to come to New York and join Lloyd Price's band. What should I do?" And without missing a beat, he says, "Take it!" And I did. So I went to New York.

Lloyd Price had an amazing band at the time. There were the Turrentine Brothers—Stanley on tenor sax and Tommy on trumpet—Charli Persip was the drummer, we also had Slide Hampton, Julian Priester, and Curtis Fuller on trombones, Jimmy Heath and Red Holloway on saxophones . . . in fact, Red Holloway was the road manager of the band. He used to take care of all the details. It was an incredible band. I would take a solo and I would try something new and the guys would go, "Whoa!" And that's what really got me . . . seriously enticed me. I was just a kid, sixteen years old, and these elders were all digging what I was playing. It was a dream gig for someone that young and inexperienced. It was an escape.

We toured around a lot in Lloyd's band, traveling to gigs in an old 1948 Greyhound bus with no heat. And it was mostly long drives between gigs, especially through the South. Lloyd would fly to wherever it was, and the band would meet him. Sometimes he would drive. But we were on the bus. And to be honest with you, the instrument was always a comfort on those long trips. It was a solution to all of the problems that would take place. You pick up your ax, man, and you forget about all that stuff. You lose yourself in the eclipse. The problem is at your back and the light shines through the instrument . . . you're in a completely different state of mind. And there you're improvising again . . . lost in the moment. It was just enticing . . . and it always has been. Even now.

Red Holloway Remembers: I went to Pat's house and talked to his mother and father about him joining the band. They consented and asked me to watch out for their son, which I agreed to do. After Pat came onboard, I always tried to keep up with him so he didn't get in no trouble . . . because he was like sixteen. But he was basically a good kid, focused pretty much on the music. So he didn't seem like he'd be much trouble on the road. We had a forty-one-passenger Greyhound bus that Lloyd had purchased. See, at that point

Lloyd was popular. He had hits with "Stagger Lee" and "Personality." Lloyd was making a lot of money then. In fact, we were on salary. When we didn't work, we still got paid. I think it was $175 a week at that time. The days that we didn't work, we would go down to Small's Paradise and we'd rehearse two hours or so during the afternoon. It was a professional outfit all the way.

We went everywhere with that band, mostly playing theaters. We'd go from the Royal in Baltimore to the Howard in Washington, the Regal in Chicago, we'd play the Apollo and we went down the Scott Theater in Indiana. Lot of different places. We'd be gone like six or seven weeks at a time when we'd go out on the road. Pat was so young at the time—in fact, I think we told Lloyd that he was eighteen or nineteen. But there was never no problem with him. And the music? Shoot, he'd just eat that up like he was eating cornflakes. Everybody that heard him really dug him and wanted to use him. I kind of watched out for Pat on that band and just tried to hip him to what's going on.

Being the only white boy on the band and being so young and so skinny, he kind of stood out on the bandstand. But he was already streetwise back then. You couldn't pull nothing over his eyes. But I tried to keep him out of trouble anyway, because he was so young. It was the same way with me when I joined Eugene Wright's big band in 1943 when I was just sixteen and the older fellas pulled my coat and schooled me and told me what was happening and shit like that. So when I first saw Pat come in the band, I just thought of a time when I was young like that . . . and I naturally wanted to give him some of the stuff that was taught to me . . . the stuff you can't learn in conservatories about life on the road. You know, fatherly kind of advice like, "Don't let nobody fuck with you . . . and watch these bitches! They'll fuck you and take your money." But he really wised up real fast. He didn't do a lot of talking, he just listened. And that's how you learn.

In certain ways it was thrilling, but in other ways it was a hard dose of reality. Here you're under the impression that this cat sitting next to you is a bad motherfucker because you've heard him blow on the bandstand, and yet the guy sitting next to him is putting him down for something that has nothing to do with why you respect him. So now you're confronted with real time from people to people and you're no longer allowed to play your dream part in the midst of it. Now you're seeing them as real people rather than icons. Or you go in the men's room and another guy that you worship takes out his false teeth, while he's cursing. The dream is shattered, and you're faced with reality. So it becomes a lesson in definition. There's a lot of things that take place on the road, and you grow up fast.

Lloyd was a strong presence as a bandleader. Actually, he's more like an entrepreneur than a musician. He was an investor. He was always investing in small items that you would find at what used to be called the five-and-dime and now is referred to as a dollar store. And you would find a little item in there that would be fifty cents to buy it, and Lloyd would put out money for these to be made. And he made a lot of money that way. Years later, he bought the original Birdland nightclub on Broadway and Fifty-second Street in New York. He was a smart businessman and a charismatic showman, as well. His appearance onstage was always excellent. He always stuck out.

During my tenure with Lloyd, I remember one engagement at Pep's in Philadelphia when Wilt Chamberlain came down to see the band. Wilt was playing for the old Philadelphia Warriors basketball team at the time, and I'd often see him at Pep's . . . you really couldn't miss Wilt, him standing over seven feet tall. Wilt was a jazz fan and actually was a silent partner in Small's Paradise in Harlem. But this particular evening, I noticed him hanging out at Pep's, checking out the band. And after our set he came over to talk to me. Apparently, he was so taken by the guitar playing that he asked if I could give him a guitar lesson. So after the gig I went up to his hotel room and I brought my guitar. He sat on the edge of the bed, and he was gigantic! I gave him the guitar and said, "Let me see what you can do." And he picked it up and put it in his hands and I immediately said, "It's impossible. Your hands are too large for an instrument like this. You would have to have an instrument custom made, just for you. For the guitar's neck you'd need a telephone pole."

Then there came the issue of when Lloyd's band was not working. And that's when I came to find out about Willis Jackson's band. Somebody in Lloyd's band turned me on to Willis . . . maybe it was Red Holloway. In any case, I came to find out that Willis was looking for a guitar player, so I went down and auditioned and got the gig right away. And from that point, whenever Lloyd wasn't working, I played with Willis. Until finally I got so heavy with Willis that I played with Willis primarily . . . and then whenever Willis wasn't working, if Lloyd had some openings I played with Lloyd from time to time.

> ***Joe Diorio Remembers:*** Pat was a young fella at the time I first met him in Atlantic City. He was working with Lloyd Price's band at that point, and I was with Milt Trenier and Micki Lynn, a boy-girl group based out of Chicago, where I lived at that time. We had a bunch of good Chicago musicians backing them up, including the great tenor saxophonist Von Freeman. And Pat and I were playing, believe it or not, in the same club. It was a Mafia club. I met Pat's mother and father there one time. They came down to this Mafia joint that we

were playing at one night, and they seemed like really nice people. Pat would do his set with Lloyd Price, and then I would do my set with the singers, and we ended up spending a lot of time in the back room in between sets . . . just playing. We also spent a lot of time at his hotel room after the gig.

The gig at this club didn't stop until one o'clock, and so we used to head back to his hotel and play all night. And I remember one night, after playing with Pat for hours, I left the hotel around 4:30 a.m. and told him, "Listen, Pat, I'm gonna go home and get a couple hours' sleep; when I wake up I'm gonna pick you up, we're gonna go for breakfast." Well, he was playing on the side of the bed when I left, and when I came back to pick him up, he was still playing in the same spot. So the thing about it is, people call Pat Martino a genius . . . and he probably is . . . but he worked very hard at it. Very hard. The guy never stopped playing. So that may be his secret—hard work and perseverance. Plus, if you've got the talent to go along with it, then you've got it made.

After I met him in Atlantic City, Pat had traveled with Lloyd Price's band to Chicago about six months later. We got together at his hotel the day after his gig, and I asked him how was the trip out, because they were traveling by car. And Pat said he sat in the back seat of Lloyd's car from Philadelphia to Chicago and practiced all the way . . . and wrote a couple of tunes, too. 'Cause he broke out this tune when we were hanging that afternoon and explained that he wrote it on the way. I thought that was great. Yeah, he never stopped playing in those days. I don't know how he got that mindset. Maybe he got it from Trane or from Dennis Sandole, who he told me he had studied with. Of course, Sandole was famous for being the cat who Trane studied with. Anyway, his work ethic was amazing. Pat never stopped playing . . . just about literally.

We were both interested in Wes Montgomery at that time. Wes had come on the scene, and that was probably when he started to make it big. Everybody was listening to him. And I know that Pat was listening to him quite heavily. We were both trying to find out which way we were trying to go at the time. Pat was also composing at the time. I remember we were talking about harmony and he turned me on to some good books about harmony, so he was clearly well schooled in that.

One of the things that really impressed me about Pat was that as I was leaving to go home after playing with him all afternoon in his hotel room, and it was raining like hell. He actually walked in the street in the rain to call me a cab. I never forgot that. I thought that was a real noble, princely thing to do. Pat's had his struggles, but he's always come through it with that sense of grace and dignity. He was always a very sensitive man, a very kind man.

4

The Kid Branches Out

I started playing in Willis "Gator Tail" Jackson's band in 1962, when I was still seventeen years old. For three or four months during the winter, Willis would work at Small's Paradise in Harlem, and then in the summer he worked at Club Harlem in Atlantic City. These were two big places that were really great rooms. Small's Paradise, which was owned by Wilt Chamberlain, was on 7th Avenue at 135th Street, maybe forty feet from the corner on the southwest side. You would walk into Small's and to your left was a large bar. On the right side of the room was the stage, which was large enough for a Hammond B-3, a set of drums, and the members of the quintet. If you kept walking in the same direction from the entrance, you would then walk into the back room, which was the large room where the show bands would perform. We played with Willis's group on the small stage, prior to entering the back room. There were no tables in the front room, just the bar. The tables were in the back, for the show bands.

Willis was a kind of larger-than-life figure; literally a leader, both on and off the bandstand. In fact, he made sure that he appeared as the leader by providing the group with specific uniforms while he himself wore the finest suits and ties and shirts. He definitely stuck out to the crowd. He appeared with a significant difference from the members of his ensemble, and we played the part as sidemen. We wore tuxedos with satin oval lapels and little thin bowties, and Willis would wear a Botany 500 suit with a custom-made shirt and beautiful silk tie, with diamond-studded cufflinks. That was

Willis Jackson, a total leader in every level of that format, projecting that image. Being onstage was a matter of pride for him. And being on time was a significant demand. He was a very strict bandleader, very serious about taking care of business onstage. But he had his rapport with the audience, which was filled with fans and followers. He was something else.

At that time, I was known by my real name, Pat Azzara. But as I was young and very small in stature and weight, they used to call me "the Kid." People were very amused that a youngster of this capacity would have the nerve to come in and try to put roots there, but I was absorbed into the culture. Racially, there were no problems. In Harlem, jazz was one of the cultural priorities at that time. Therefore, whoever came into that area of activity was accepted immediately.

Every night I would walk with my guitar from the place where I was staying in Harlem and head up 7th Avenue toward 135th Street, where Small's was located. And in that environment, I was surrounded by a different culture, different people with different likes and dislikes than I was accustomed to in Philly. And these things truly affected me, by participating not only in the community, but also even in terms of diet. The food was an enjoyment . . . one of a kind. Sometimes I'd stop in at a friend's house on my way to the gig and have dinner there, and I would deeply enjoy some collard greens and some chitlins or some ribs. This was part of the culture, it was part of the people. And when I would arrive at Small's Paradise, the same thing was in play—it was about the people. And the music that we played was affected by all of these factors—the food we ate, the people we encountered on the street on the way to the gig, and the way they walked and talked, then the people at the club. All of it amounted to a rich cultural experience in Harlem at the time, and it directly affected the music that we played at the gig. The musicians were an extension of that life. They were living it, not studying it.

By contrast, what I often hear today is the lack of authenticity on the basis of serious individuals who are studying jazz and who are studying it with the expectation of reaching a point of absorbing its essence with regard to its authenticity. I don't think that's possible, because the culture that surrounds that has changed. And because of that, authenticity is very elusive. And it's invisible in most cases, because it doesn't exist anymore. You go up to Harlem now, you get to 135th and 7th and you don't see Small's Paradise, you see the International House of Pancakes sprawled out on that same block, in the same architectural structure that used to be a significant mecca for jazz. And Count Basie's at 133rd and 7th is now nothing but a metal screen with a gate on it. That's where Miles and Dizzy and Wes Montgomery played, and now it's an empty lot with weeds growing there. And now you have serious students who are studying the recordings of jazz that took place when it was what it was—a vital form initially in that moment in time. And they're studying it on the basis of scales and modes and harmony and theory—curriculums that have nothing to do with the people and the culture that surrounded it and gave it true significance.

So what you have now is the study of music as a science, as a series of formulas and responsibilities with regard to concrete intellectual awareness, among the players themselves, which is actually a lot closer to a classical-music aesthetic. In fact, I think a lot of the younger generation nowadays has shifted over into classical forms of expression. Whereas then you had Wes Montgomery and you had Grant Green and some of the other players throughout all of the instruments that were at a street level. They were singing the song that would be the outcome of the culture, of the events that took place to a person who lived within it. So that did something to me with regard to the essence of what music truly is when it's alive, and not when it's studied from a book. There is a significant difference. And I think it really comes through in terms of communication, the nature of how aggressive a player can be.

I noticed that even in what we generally refer to as "jazz guitarists," the initial players that I was exposed to as a child, were very different from the players I encountered in Harlem. For example, Johnny Smith, who I extremely admired and respected—why did I respect him? I respected him because of his precision, his perfect pitch, and how accurate he was as a technician. And I noticed there was a difference between that quality—which to me was an extremely intellectual power, gift, blessing—and Wes Montgomery and Grant Green, who had that street-level communication. And I think the difference is very close to what I just described about Harlem itself and the outcome in terms of artists who are the extension of living directly in that culture and not studying it from afar.

I remember a time in 1963—I was still working with Willis Jackson at Small's then—when Wes Montgomery was playing just a couple of blocks south at Count Basie's on 133rd and 7th Avenue. And I made a point of telling Les Paul, whom I knew very well at that point, to come and check him out. Les was always involved in so many darn things as a player and an inventor, as well, and he was always interested in what was going on in the outside world, especially with regard to guitar players on the scene. So this particular night, Les would come out to Small's Paradise, where I was playing with Willis Jackson. And at the end of one of our sets, I took him down the street to meet Wes for the first time. Wes was playing there with Jimmy

Cobb on drums and Melvin Rhyne on organ, and Count Basie's was packed that night, which was appropriate because as we walked in they were playing "Full House." At the end of the set, as we stood at the bar, Wes came over and joined us. After watching them introducing themselves to one another, I heard Wes say to Les, "My two favorite guitarists were Charlie Christian and you. I'm a big fan of yours, and it's really great to finally have a chance to meet you."

I had to return to Small's for the next set or risk getting fired by Willis for being late, but at the end of that night when the playing was done, I came back to Basie's, where I had left Les. And as I crossed 7th Avenue from the west to the east side of the street, I happen to notice that standing outside of Count Basie's were four guitarists—Wes Montgomery, Les Paul, Grant Green, and George Benson. I joined with them to make it five guitar players, just standing on the corner at three in the morning. And the five of us went to a place on 7th Avenue between 132nd and 133rd called Wells Chicken and Waffles and had breakfast and talked about guitar playing until the sun came up.

There's a condition that's more significant than anything about this story. There seems to be something in guitar players, in my opinion, that's latent and more fraternal than any other instrumentalists. Guitarists in general are almost like family members. Maybe it's what the instrument does to us. Maybe there's something about this particular instrument . . . and I do believe this . . . the psychology that is genetic from the instrument to the individuals who dedicate themselves to it. There are certain things that emerge from it in many different ways . . . culturally, as well. It in many ways covers all of the different idioms, unlike some of the other instruments that fail to do so.

And if you look closer at the guitar, it becomes more revealing. Take, for example, the tuning of it—E–A–D–G–B–E. In a circular chromatic scale (with low and high E at the twelve o'clock, in clockwise motion from string to string), it appears as a pentagram. It's literally a circle with a five-pointed star.

So there are some profound facets to the instrument and its identity that make it almost a form of sorcery in what it contains. The idea of six strings being similar to the hexagrams in the *I Ching* from the Far East. The philosophies of the *Book of Changes,* again, contain all of the combinations of the guitar's strings. I think these are incredible facets of that instrument's connotations . . . what it seems to represent in so many different ways. It's almost like a chameleon . . . constantly changing.

The Tuning of the Guitar

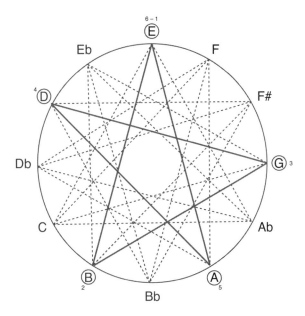

Wes himself was like a shaman with that instrument in his hands, the way he was swinging so organically with it. And if you looked at him performing, the smile on his face and the twinkle in his eyes were separate from the output that was pouring out of the instrument. One is so serious in terms of its connotations, what it represents in terms of its achievement, and the other is so relaxed and second nature to the entire event. That quality of being so burning yet so relaxed has always fascinated me about Wes. And that quality is something than cannot be taught. It is part of his life force. Wes was great, Wes was magic, he was a sorcerer. So were many others in their own way. And it has to be seen for what it is and not to be, in a sense, shattered by a misjudgment of any kind of interruptive abrasiveness on the here and now.

At some point during the time that I was playing with Willis Jackson at Small's, I took up residence at the President Hotel on Forty-eighth Street between Eighth Avenue and Broadway. From that point, I would take the subway up to Harlem for the gig every night at Small's. We played seven days a week, seven sets a night, in the usual forty-minutes-on, twenty-minutes-off format. Can you imagine how sharp your abilities become if you play that much?

Our other base of operations in Willis's band was Club Harlem in Atlantic City, which was on Kentucky Avenue, between Atlantic and Pacific. In the front room at Club Harlem you had two stages for two different groups. Willis Jackson would do forty minutes, and then Chris Columbo's band would do forty minutes. They'd split sets all night long. And in the large back room you had singers like Sammy Davis with an orchestra. That was an incredible place. In fact, Atlantic City itself was an incredible place during those years. You had Frank Sinatra, Dean Martin, and a number of others performing at the 500 Club. And you had Carmen McRae, Ella Fitzgerald, or Sarah Vaughan at the Le Bistro. And of course, you had the Jockey Club, which is where I first heard Jimmy Smith with Charles Earland. Then over at the Steel Pier you had the big acts like the Beatles and Les Paul. AC was a very vibrant, very significant place at that time.

There was no gambling in Atlantic City in those days. This is long before that came along. It was nothing but the arts back then. I'm shocked that these places were not restored, because they're part of the rich history of Atlantic City. That they were just totally broken down and replaced with casinos was one of the most artistically sinful events that ever took place in terms of decision on behalf of the administration that ruled those areas of New Jersey. No support with regard to the history of the arts.

I made my first recordings with Willis Jackson under the name Pat Azzara [*Grease 'n' Gravy* and *The Good Life* were both cut on May 23 and 24, 1963, for Prestige, while *More Gravy* was recorded on October 24 of that year for the label].

It was in summer of 1964, when I was working Willis Jackson in Atlantic City, that I met my first wife, Geri. Her actual name was Audrey Geraldine Sanders, but everyone called her Geri. She was a waitress at a restaurant near Club Harlem. How I met her was, I was standing on Kentucky Avenue by the Kentucky Hotel. That hotel was on the final block before you got to the boardwalk. And down the street was a restaurant where a lot of the working musicians in Atlantic City went to have breakfast after their gigs. She was one of the waitresses there, and I met her on her way to work. From then on, I used to just sit outside the restaurant and watch her walking to work, because I fell in love with her. And we just hit it off. I worked that summer at Club Harlem for two or three months, and during that time my courtship of Geri continued. And pretty quickly, the courtship turned into something serious. We fell in love, and there was no looking back. I'm a man of action . . . no games.

Geri and I moved into a place in Philadelphia on Thirteenth Street. It was like the gay-bar area of Philadelphia. In fact, it still is. Geri had a lot of gay friends in those years. So we lived there, and Bobby Rose used to spend a lot of time with us.

> ***Bobby Rose Remembers:*** In the summer of 1964, I was working in Atlantic City at the club Fort Pit. They should've called it the Snake Pit, because that's what it was. It was just down the street from Club Harlem. And somebody mentioned to me that there was a great group at Club Harlem with a young white guitar player and that I should check him out. So I said, "Good, I'll catch the breakfast show," which was about six o'clock in the morning. So I walked over there and walked into the club, and they were just getting up onstage to play. Well, sure enough, man, he wowed me. I was like in awe. And when I took one look at this guy up onstage I thought, "Jeezus Christ! I remember him from Johnny the barber's in Philly." I used to get my hair cut there, and Mickey used to take Pat over to Johnny the barber's and show him off a little bit. Because he had Johnny Smith down to a T and he was only a little kid at the time. Mickey would bring him in and these guys in the barbershop would say, "Pat, play 'Moonlight in Vermont,'" and he played it like . . . to a T. I stayed through the whole set, and when he took a break he walked outside and I finished my drink and I walked outside, hoping I would catch him. He was smoking a cigarette and just coolin' out, so I came up to him and said, "Pat, you probably don't know me. My name is Bobby Rose. Did you live on Thirteenth and Wharton?" He said, "No, I lived on Garret Street, but my father used to take me over to Johnny the barber's on Thirteenth Street." I said, "Well, Christ! That's where I know you from." So we started laughing and talking, and he said before he had to go back on, "Well, look, the summer's almost over. This is the last week. Why don't we get together in Philly? I'm not sure if I'll be staying with my parents. I might get a hotel or something."
>
> He had met Geri by this time, and they were talking about getting married, and I don't think Mickey was too happy about it, from what I gathered. So anyway he says, "After Labor Day, if you're around Pat's Steaks at two o'clock in the morning, you're sure to catch me there." So that's what happened. After Labor Day, I went around Pat's Steaks and sure enough, there he was eating a steak sandwich. And I walked up to him, we started talking again, and he invited me over to his apartment. We went upstairs . . . he had just got this Spanish guitar and he started playing and talking. We hit it off right away. Anyway, I gave him my number . . . he didn't have a phone yet . . . and I heard from him Thanksgiving Eve. He called me and said, "Hey Bobby, what are you doing for Thanksgiving tomorrow? You're welcome to come over here and have Thanksgiving dinner with us." So I went over to his place and I had dinner with him and Geri. And we all just seemed to click right away. We liked

each other right away, and Geri was great. She was always a gracious host. We ended up talking and playing together all night. And that's what started it off between me and Pat.

By the fall of 1964, I began to work with the great organist Don Patterson. Now, Don had a magical hookup with the great drummer Billy James. When I joined Don and Billy, I was under the impression that this was a greater organ-drums team in terms of the repertoire and in terms of the facility of these two players together as one. And I wanted to be part of that. Working with Don and Billy was something else. Billy James had that beautifully organic swing feel on the kit that you just can't teach. He was authentically an extension of the Hammond B-3—where the two instruments work together as one. And that came from Don and him co-relating to a statement that was theirs alone. That's the same thing that Jack McDuff had with Joe Dukes. It wasn't an organist and a drummer, where another great drummer had to take the place of another great drummer, and took his place and was just as good. It wasn't that at all. The two of them as one created a third instrument which can never be reproduced. That was what Don and Billy had.

I had that rapport with Don and Billy, and I certainly had it with me and Willis Jackson. That's the first thing that I'm looking for . . . the rapport. Don was a complete original. Me and Billy used to call him Duck. You'd see Don sometimes in a long wool coat in winter, all buttoned up. You'd see him silently standing up with something on his mind . . . and for some reason or another, your attention then caught his pocket in the coat. And there in his pocket was a hamburger that was encased in the wrapping that you got when you ordered it . . . and every once in a while he'd reach in his pocket and take it out and take a bite, and he'd put it back in his pocket, and all the grease was coming out and would be absorbed into the coat. There was something about Don that was just so free of even being concerned about what normal people are judgmental about and critical about. Don was Don. And his playing was just overwhelming. What a great player! What a great person . . . but really street level. When I say a great person, I'm not talking about the Dalai Lama, I'm talking about a down-on-the-ground guy that is at a street level of social position. Never really made a lot of money. Just doing as many gigs as he could get. But what a formidable player!

And when I entered that scenario, I learned something else. Don Patterson during those earlier years was addicted to codeine. In fact, the player I replaced in the Willis Jackson group, the left-handed guitarist Bill Jennings, was also addicted to codeine . . . cough syrup, which a number of individuals in music were addicted to in those days. I remember on more than a few occasions before a set would start, me and Billy would be standing around inside the club, waiting for Don to appear. And I'd say, "Hey Billy, we're late to go on. Where's Don?" Then Billy would say, "Hey, come on, let's go see if something's wrong." And we'd go outside and walk down the block and we would find Don in a doorway, overdosed. Now we had to carry Don back into the club and up to the bandstand. We'd sit him down at the B-3 and his head is nodded down close to the keyboard. Then the first tune is counted off and suddenly his playing is incredibly powerful, but his eyes are still closed.

In terms of my facility, my responsibility, look what happened there. What was most important, the music? No. The music was second nature. Either you know how to play or you don't know how to play, and if you can't play, you don't deserve the position to be here. Something else is much more important here than technical ability to be a guitar player. So these are some of things that are meaningful to me that go so far beyond the craft.

Through working with Don Patterson and Billy James, I met the young alto sax player Eric Kloss. Don and Billy and I used to play in Pittsburgh at a place called the Hurricane. Eric's father used to bring him to the Hurricane to hear all the groups . . . he was just sixteen years old at that time we met. And he flipped over us as a trio. He ended up sitting in with us at the Hurricane, and it was an instant connection. And in that moment he decided, "You're the group I'm going to use. I want to record with you." [They subsequently appeared on Kloss's Prestige debut, *Introducing Eric Kloss,* which was recorded on September 1, 1964, and released in early 1965; nearly three months later, the Don Patterson trio with Pat Martino would record the jazzy Christmas album *Holiday Soul* on November 25, 1964].

Eric was maybe three years younger than me, and Don and Billy were both older than I was. But I remember Eric as being so committed and so immersed in the magic of the music. He was always excited about new equations . . . learning new ways, new time signatures, new scalar forms, new compositions. Just a very committed individual. I ended up recording a few sessions with Eric, and I went out to Pittsburgh and did a couple of gigs with him. But I didn't do any gigging with him of any significant length of time.

When George Benson left Jack McDuff's group in 1965, I took his place. Like Willis Jackson, McDuff was the kind of bandleader that preferred band uniforms onstage. But Jack wore the same thing as the band. It was one collective thing . . . and that had something to do with the music, as well. That band really played as a team.

Jack was a very strong individual; his presence was very noticeable . . .

very much like Art Blakey. And after he dyed his hair silver, you'd *really* notice him. That seemed to be a normal form of communication in those years. No matter what you did, it was part of a jazz-in-the-city context. It wasn't global as of yet. None of us were thinking globally, even though in 1965 I went to Copenhagen with McDuff. He still had silver hair then, which the people there regarded as pretty exotic. But that was McDuff. He was a force of nature with a smile. Onstage he was almost like a comedian, projecting humor at everything, but in a very entertaining way.

> ***Red Holloway Remembers:*** When there was an opening for Jack McDuff's group, when George Benson left, I got Pat with McDuff. I had already left Lloyd's group and went with McDuff, so when I heard he needed a guitar player, I recommended Pat. And, of course, he got the gig. I remember one time when we were playing with McDuff's group at this place in Atlantic City called the Wonder Garden. It was right down the street from the Club Harlem. And right past the club was this restaurant. I'd always wake Pat up in the morning and we'd go to eat there. So this particular day . . . we had finished at the Wonder Garden, we went to eat, and I was talkin' to this waitress and Pat wasn't saying nothing. He was just sitting there. When he finished the meal, we were on our way back to the hotel and he says, "Oh, damn! I forgot something. I'll be right back." So he went on back to the restaurant for a hot minute and I waited for when he came back . . . and his room was right across from mine. Anyway, I said, "I'll wake you up for breakfast." He said, "Okay." So that morning I knocked on his door. No answer. "Pat! Wake up, sucker!" No answer. And then I said, "Well, maybe he's really tired." So I strolled down to the restaurant, and who did I see but Pat and this waitress walking hand in hand. I said, "Yeah, you're folks told me to watch out for you. Now I know why." And I said, "You little prick! I'm gonna keep my eyes on your ass from now on!"

By the time I got in Jack McDuff's band, I had taken the name Pat Martino. It's actually in honor of my father, Mickey. In his early years, he loved to sing at any opportunity he could get, so that he could stand up in front of an audience and entertain. So he sat in a lot with different bands, and whenever he did that he used Martino as a stage name, even though it was not a professional situation. It came to pass on one of my father's birthdays, I gave him a guitar—a Gibson flattop. And at the same time, I gave him another gift, which was to change my name. I had already been recording with Willis Jackson as Pat Azzara, my legal name. And I changed my name in respect to Dad as a birthday gift. From that point forward, I used Martino as my name. And he was very taken by that.

So between those two important apprenticeships—Willis Jackson and Jack McDuff—the music that I was playing in Harlem came out of a life experience. And to reduce it to a page in a fake book, to make it an industrial product like that, seems absurd to me. It's almost the same thing that medication is . . . in terms of pharmaceutical products created by chemists.

My mentors were not looking for somebody who could read out of a fake book. That had nothing to do with the real thing. They weren't looking for someone who graduated from Berklee School of Music in Boston. They were looking for someone who was on the street. That's how they found who they were looking for. They found it through word of mouth, from one musician to another. And that's where the competitive line came from. It had nothing to do with graduating from a school. Nowadays, it's about graduation from some conservatory; it's the outcome of who is available and who has done well in school, and who can play well. But to be honest, with regard to some of the younger players today, especially those who are interested in participation in extension of the past, that's a very difficult situation to even participate in as a listener because of its lack of reality. It's not real, it's just a copy. It's like a soap opera. It's like you know that the people are just acting the part. And then when they get done acting the part, they go back to whatever they were living, which has nothing to do with what they are trying to recreate. And that's why it loses its power.

George Benson Remembers: I was playing in Jack McDuff's band when I first saw Pat Martino play in 1962. I had been on the road with Jack for maybe a month and a half before we finally made it to New York, the hub of the music industry on the East Coast. I was still living in Pittsburgh at the time and actually had no real address of my own in New York. But whenever I came to town with Jack, I stayed with my cousin who lived in Spanish Harlem. That was a whole different vibe, man, but it helped me to get to know New York. I did a lot of walking then. I didn't like subways, and I didn't have money for cabs, so I did a lot of walking. I would walk twenty–thirty blocks at a clip. And this particular night I walked over to Small's Paradise in Harlem to see what was happening. When I got there, I noticed on the outside of the club a sign that said: "Tonite! Willis Jackson!" And I remembered that Willis Jackson was the man who gave my boss at the time a job. So I said to myself, "Well, let me see who Willis Jackson is," and I went in there.

Way before I got into the club, I could hear the energy of the band. It was really hot! They were playing something with an uptempo backbeat and I said, "Man, I gotta get in here. This sounds great!" But the place was so packed that you could only see the tops of the heads of the band, until you got right near the stage. And when I finally made my way up closer, I noticed they had this kid onstage, very thin. Nice-looking young fella, but he looked a little bit anemic. And I thought, "Man, I wonder what *this* guy's gonna do. He's just a kid!" They were playing along and he was comping, and he fit in very well with the band. His complementary licks were outstanding, and I thought, "Wow, this guy's good." But then the band went into a two-bar break during the song where the guitarist started to play his solo, and they left him a little space to get started. And boy, did he light that space up! Nobody could believe what came out of that fellow's guitar. And I was shocked more than anybody, because I thought I was the hottest young fella in New York at the time, but when I heard this kid tear up those two bars, and then they went back to the rhythm and he was playing the changes . . . I was flabbergasted, man! He was so outstanding! It was the last thing I expected from a fellow that looked like him. First of all, he was young, and he was on the thin side . . . but what came out of his guitar was just the opposite. Very mature sound . . . sounded like he had been playing guitar for thirty years. And power. Energy. I never heard any energy like that. And it was clean as a whistle, he didn't miss one note. I just couldn't believe what I was hearing. So I had to meet him.

When the set ended, I went over and asked him his name and hung out with him, told him who I was. And I think he had heard about me . . . somebody told him about me. But I found out he was only seventeen. And I thought I was the phenomenon at nineteen! So we were the new thing in New York at that time. There were others who later popped their heads up, but we didn't know about them then. So I said, "Man, you got a few minutes?" He said, "Yeah." We jumped in a car and went to a club on 142nd Street and Broadway called the Staghorn, where I introduced him to Grant Green, who was my favorite guitar player at the time. He had been in Jack McDuff's band before me, and he was a cult hero. And I had been listening to Grant for a couple nights in a row and admired him very much, so I took Pat Martino up there to meet him. And during a break I said, "Grant, you gotta hear this fella play guitar, man." I introduced him, they shook hands, and so Grant gave him his guitar, and Pat took that guitar and started lighting it up, man. He played some incredible stuff. This was not on the bandstand. The amp was turned off, and he was just playing acoustically to us standing right beside him. And Grant Green looked at him for a few minutes while Pat was playing, and then he grabbed the neck of the guitar and he said, "Hold it, man, hold it!" Pat looked up and Grant said, "You gonna burn all the frets off my guitar." And he was right, because Pat was tearing that guitar up, man.

Everybody was aware of Pat after that. He became a cult hero, too, just as Grant Green had been. At that time we both didn't have any works of our own that we could allude to or tell people about, or that people knew about. It was later that we started racking up stacks of albums that people could relate to. And through the years, I would see Pat every now and then . . . our paths would cross. But he stayed on my mind all the time, because I knew that there was another standard out there that all guitar players had to recognize, and he was setting it. He was setting a new pace for all guitar players, especially young guitar players of that time. He showed us that there was much more to the guitar than what we were hearing. We could actually set our own tone . . . we didn't have to be thirty–forty years old to make an impression. You could do it *now*! So that's how I met Pat Martino, and that's how we became friends.

We were friendly rivals on the scene back then. But when people would talk about young guitarists, they would talk about Pat because he was such a genius on the guitar. Whenever you talk about guitar, you're going to end up talking about Pat Martino. Because he had made that kind of impression. And then . . . I knew that if I ever left Jack's band that he was going to be the next guitar player in the band. Because he liked Jack McDuff's music. So when I left the band, it was no surprise to me that Jack called Pat. And it was kind of a sad day for me, because I had been in Jack's band for almost three years, and now I was being replaced by a *better* guitar player. And so it made me believe that my career was going to go downhill. In my mind I was saying, "Well, I guess that's the end of my career. He has THE guitar player, the one Jack should've had all along." I was happy for Pat because I knew he wanted the gig, but sad because my reputation had come up quite a few points by playing with Jack McDuff's band. Now that was all over, I was starting from scratch.

After I left McDuff's band in 1965, I was promised another gig with Don Patterson, the organist from Philadelphia. But he forgot he even hired me. I drove all the way from Pittsburgh to New Jersey, and when I got there for the gig he said, "George, what are you doing here?" And I said, "Man, you don't remember telling me to show up this evening, that you were going to start a gig on this night and that you hired me?" And he said, "Man, I forgot all about it." And instead he had hired Sam Rivers, the great saxophone player. So I didn't contest that. I left it alone. I sent my new wife home, back to Pittsburgh by bus, and she cried, and I told her, "This is fine, because it forces me to do what I know I should do . . . start my own band." And that's what I did.

One last thing . . . I wanna say how proud I am of Pat Martino. I've always been proud of him. Even though we've been rivals of a sort, I've always been proud of him because he set a pace and he showed us what we could do on the instrument. He didn't put any limits on himself, and I think that's so important, man. You gotta have somebody who has that mentality. He's always been a very outspoken and sure-of-himself musician. And that's what it takes to accomplish anything. You gotta believe in yourself. Pat believed in himself, and he had the credentials in terms of his chops, his knowledge of guitar. And boy, I've always been proud of what he could do, what he can do now. And proud to know him as a person, man. He's one of my favorite people I've ever met. And I want to make sure that the public gets that point. I sure love that fellow. I've always appreciated him as a person. And his musicianship has always been impeccable. He's a fellow that I've admired from day one, and I still do.

5

Becoming El Hombre

Nineteen sixty-seven was an extremely busy year with regard to recording projects. It kicked off with an album by the great Philly organist and my dear friend Trudy Pitts [*Introducing the Fabulous Trudy Pitts,* recorded February 15–21 for Prestige with her husband Bill Carney on drums and Abdu Johnson on congas]. Trudy later played on my own debut as a leader for Prestige [*El Hombre,* recorded May 1 of that year]. Sadly, in the course of preparing this book, I learned that Trudy, who had been ill, passed away. She was an institution in Philadelphia, and her loss has been deeply felt by everyone in the Philly jazz community.

El Hombre was essentially an extension of my interest in Wes Montgomery. Regarding album titles, it was the same approach that created *The Incredible Guitar of Wes Montgomery* or Wes's *Boss Guitar,* album titles that were significantly aggressive with regard to marketing. So to me, to offer *El Hombre* was along the same lines and in the same language, and communicating the same terms . . . like a calling card. And I think that was an extension of all the sideman dates that I had been active with for Prestige Records. That's what brought it about. When the time came, they asked me if I would join the family. To me, it was an achievement with regard to notoriety. And it was very successful. [Pat's debut included three personal pieces in "Waltz for Geri" for his wife, "Song for My Mother," and "A Blues for Mickey-O" for his father.]

But in fact, *El Hombre* was not my first recording as a leader. Prior to that project, a full year before, I did a recording which never came out and still hasn't seen the light of day. Essentially, my initial entrance into professionalism as a recording artist was hampered by the recording industry itself and their normal approach to their investments.

I initially signed with Vanguard Records. My first album for that label was produced by Chuck Israels, and on the album were Ron Carter, Tommy Flanagan, and Tony Williams. And as I stated, this was a year before *El Hombre.* But this record never came out, primarily because Vanguard had signed Larry Coryell and they put some money into his recording, production-wise. I was just a young kid up in Harlem who didn't know anything about the business. So in comes Vanguard Records and offers me a contract for $500. To me, I was under the impression that was really up there. But essentially, they got me off the street for a year for a $500 investment. And they effectively eliminated "the competition" in doing so. Then they turned around and put all their promotional money into Larry Coryell. They weren't even aware of what I was into. They only knew that there was this young kid up in Harlem who was getting a lot of buzz and they were determined to "get him off the street," so to speak. And that's what they did . . . they locked me out so I couldn't record, I couldn't put an album out until the following year.

When I did that recording for Vanguard, I had a paper bag with a sandwich, a toothbrush, some toothpaste . . . and what that represented symbolically was telling my mother, who made the sandwich and put it in the bag and made sure I had a toothbrush, that I would be home the following day. Why? Because I was drafted. I had to leave the following morning from the Vanguard studio for an army base in Virginia where I was drafted to. And as I told her, "I don't need a suitcase. I'll get out of it." Which I did. I got a 4-F and got out of the draft. Out of 260 young men, me and another guy were the only ones who got out. So I went all the way down to Virginia with my guitar, a toothbrush, and a sandwich, got my 4-F rating, and came back to Philly the following day.

At the end of my contract with Vanguard, Prestige brought me in and recorded what was technically my second album, *El Hombre.* With regard to that Vanguard session, it got lost in their vault somewhere. I have no idea where those tapes are or who owns them at this point. Eventually it'll come out, unless it was destroyed or damaged. Maybe it was in a flood. We put the word out, more than once, to try and find those original tapes, to no avail.

El Hombre, which as I mentioned featured Trudy Pitts on organ, was my last involvement with Hammond B-3 organ on my albums as a leader, until Joey DeFrancesco in 2000. That's a span of twenty-three years.

Bobby Rose Remembers: Pat was getting ready to play a gig with Don Patterson . . . in Paterson, New Jersey, of all places. And I went with him. Wherever he was playing back then, I would go. One night he surprised me by showing up at my gig with Geri at a little place I was playing just outside of Lancaster, a place called Host Farm. I was playing there four nights a week with an organ trio, and Pat ended up sitting in this night that he showed up. And he really liked the drummer I had in the trio, whose name was Mitch Fine. Pat had just signed with Prestige and was preparing for his first album with the label, so he asked Mitch to be on the album. Pat and Geri ended up staying with me that weekend, and when we went back to Philly I stayed with him and Geri at their place. He was having a hard time then. He wasn't working much, and he and Geri were really struggling. There were times when there was just a bottle of water in the refrigerator. So I would buy some food, and my wife Lucy would bring over some food. Maybe Geri would do a job modeling to bring in some money. We were all just getting by through the skin of our teeth, just barely paying the rent.

Early in 1967 I began working with the great alto saxophonist and composer John Handy. He was always a lovable sweetheart of a gentleman, a very placid personality. And this particular band at that time was really hot. It was with John on alto, Bobby Hutcherson on vibraphone, Albert Stinson on bass, and Doug Sides on drums. John was based in San Francisco, and that was my first entrance into the significant West Coast scene, where the great players were. You would do the gig and then go to a club afterward, and in the club would be Herbie Hancock and Tony Williams and Miles. It was my entrance into a different communal dimension, as opposed to Harlem or the whole East Coast organ-group circuit.

John Handy's band was significantly different than the ones I had been in before, the ones where we had to wear uniforms. John was a different kind of bandleader. He dressed differently. He was living on Haight Street in Frisco, and he was very close with Ravi Shankar. When I first went out on tour with him, I was still very conservative, and I felt out of place. I still had a suit and tie. I was New York at that time. And when I went out to L.A., it was a totally different scene, with people wearing multicolored tops and jeans and beaded apparel. It was the Age of Aquarius, and John dressed the part. And he was a very politically aware, as well, which was reflected in his music. He represented a new school of composer, which is indeed why that record that I played on is called *A New View*. And maybe that had something to do with me moving in directions that resulted in *Baiyina*. Not that I remember doing so for that reason. But I was definitely moving into something else, courting a different muse, so to speak.

I remember we did a monthlong engagement in June with John Handy at the Village Gate in Greenwich Village, and the opening act for us, who used to share the dressing room with us, was Richard Pryor. It was a period of time when comedians were the opening act for jazz groups. And Richard was so nervous before every show that we would have to help talk him down, bring him back down, because he was like a nervous wreck.

> *John Handy Remembers:* I was the old man in that band at thirty-four years old. Next guy in the band age-wise was eight years younger—that was Bobby Hutcherson. Pat was only twenty-two at the time, but he acted much older, like a seasoned old man. He didn't speak very much; he hardly said anything. He was more of a reserved person at twenty-two. I was precocious at twenty-two. But he could play his little ass off, man. Jerry Hahn had been the guitarist in the band, and when he left I replaced him with Sonny Greenwich, a guitarist from Canada. He didn't stay in the band long before returning to Canada, and then I got Pat in the band. This was in May of 1967. He joined us on our steady gig at the Both/And in San Francisco. I think he came on a Wednesday or Thursday and we finished the gig on Saturday. The next week we had a concert at the University of California, and the band played like we had been playing together for fifty years, and Pat was part of that. That was my greatest first impression of him. Playing on the gig at the Both/And was okay, but not as memorable as that concert. From there we went up in Seattle for six days, then we played a concert at the San Jose Festival. I had gigs booked the whole month of June, including a month at the Village Gate and an appearance at the Newport Jazz Festival in Rhode Island. And by then I started to really like the way he played. He was a tiny guy, but he played big music. Pat left the band shortly after that. We were supposed to do a tour of Europe, but he got an offer to play with Ray Charles. I wasn't angry with Pat for leaving my band. He was young and needed to do what he was going to do.

I had just received a call from the people involved with Ray Charles, and I was offered a position. And I was considering it at the time. Then around the same time I got a call from Joe Pass, who was a friend of mine and someone I greatly admired. Joe was a special person. There was always immense respect both of us had for each other. Joe had just left George Shearing and was preparing to join Oscar Peterson's trio, and he called to ask me if I would be interested in taking his place in George Shearing's quintet. I could've gone with Ray Charles, but I chose George Shearing, mainly because of my admiration for Joe. And he needed a sub. So I went with George. It was a good band; Harvey Mason was on drums. So I toured off and on with this group for six months, but we didn't record.

It was a very odd period in my life, with heavy hallucinations and all kinds of stuff going on. I was having seizures, still undiagnosed. I had real long hair at the time, and I was very abstract in my dressing. I remember in George's band, his young manager insisted upon certain facets of appearance. "Get a haircut" didn't work with me, so I put it in a ponytail. And I'd often hear, "What are you wearing? What kind of shoes are those?" And of course, I had very expensive red snake boots on. And I insisted that these were my shoes. Here I was with a ponytail and red snake boots and a tuxedo. Shearing couldn't see anything; he was blind. But his road manager was insistent in terms of the image of the group. He was George's eyes. It was some funny stuff, man!

The last engagement I did with the Shearing band was at the Waldorf-Astoria. In between dates with Shearing, I was preparing my second Prestige album, which was *Strings!* [recorded on October 2, 1967]. This was a departure, because it had no organ. My interest on that project was to be like a horn player with an authentic rhythm section, not a session with Hammond B-3 organ doing the parts and bass lines with a drummer. I got tired of that, and I wanted to move into a completely different setting. So I got Cedar Walton on piano, Ben Tucker on bass, Billy Higgins on drums, and Joe Farrell on tenor sax. [Pat's next Prestige outing, *East!* recorded on January 8, 1968, was a further move away from his organ-group roots, from the depiction of Buddha on the cover to the modal nature of the Trane-inspired title track, written by Philadelphia bassist Tyrone Brown.]

> ***Tyrone Brown Remembers:*** We were booked separately to do a job with a big band at the Wonder Garden in Atlantic City. We exchanged numbers, and Pat contacted me after that and asked me to join his band. I don't recall doing an audition. But we were certainly impressed with each other, and I was extremely flattered. My background is that I had been working on the road with a commercial-oriented group, and then after that I hooked up with singers like Billy Paul and Lou Rawls. So when I got the offer from Pat, I considered that as opening the door to hardcore jazz. And I loved the opportunity, but I properly thought, "I better spruce up my playing." Because going from playing with singers in an accompaniment role to playing with a well-known player, which involves interplay, as well, I knew that I had to move up to a different level. So working with Pat gave me a lot of incentive to do that.

I recall the first recording I did with Pat was *East!* That title track was an original of mine. We had played that tune on a few gigs before doing that record. I remember the producer had an in-house drummer and bassist for that particular recording session, and Pat brought Eddie Green along on piano. And he brought me in just to conduct that piece I wrote. And it turned out that the original bass line was rather tricky, involving some sliding into the notes and so forth, so the studio bass player suggested that I play on that piece because he thought it would be too time-consuming for him to have to practice that. He was used to playing straight-ahead walking, and this required something different. So it was a blessing for me. And I was really pleased that I was able to be at least on that one track on that recording. I did that track on upright bass, but I did three recordings with Pat after that in the early 1970s, all on electric bass.

6

Baiyina and Beyond

Following my initial recordings on the Prestige label [the 1967 debut *El Hombre,* followed by *Strings!* and *East!* in 1968], I engaged in a project that was very different from all the previous ones. It was the first project that dealt with spiritualism, which was an extension of my interest in theosophy and the study of all religions. That particular album was *Baiyina (The Clear Evidence),* the title of which was based on one of the chapters from the Koran.

Baiyina was really quite unlike anything I had done before. Whereas *El Hombre* reflected my love of Wes Montgomery, this project, which prominently featured the use of tabla and tamboura, more reflected my love of Ravi Shankar.

Naturally, some people were confused by this recording. Here I was born and raised as a Roman Catholic, and I'm doing a project based on the Koran. And people asked, "Are you a Muslim?"

At times there seems to be a repetitive result when it comes to the interpretation of an artist's communicative intention. When spiritual impact transcends the shelf it's been politically placed upon, at times it's unfortunately subject to misinterpretation by others, due to being confined to a religion, almost possessed, and protected by it. Of course, it can't be avoided, and an artist who is chosen to move in such a direction must do so with courage.

There was also a psychedelic subtext for *Baiyina,* which reflected the time in which it was recorded. At that time, musicians like Jimi Hendrix and others were experimenting with LSD, as I was myself. Hence the subtitle: *A Psychedelic Excursion into the Mysteries of the Koran.* [*Baiyina* was released five months after Hendrix's *Axis: Bold as Love,* which blended psychedelia with a cover image that borrowed from the Hindu devotional painting known as *Viraat Purushan-Vishnuroopam.*]

Regardless of how perplexed people may have been by *Baiyina* or how they may have perceived it, my intention was very clear on this album—spiritual amplification.

Leonard Feather gave it five stars in *DownBeat.*

> **Bobby Rose Remembers:** I was hanging out at Pat's place in Philly, and we started playing together one night. And I struck a chord . . . I don't remember what chord it was . . . and he says, "Hmmmm, what was that you played?" And I played it again and he says, "Wow, that gives me an idea." So we started jamming on this one chord, sort of a raga kind of thing. We were heavy into Ravi Shankar and Eastern philosophy at that time. We were reading the Koran and the I Ching. We used to just sit around and listen to the evening ragas and the afternoon ragas, and it just inspired us that way. Next thing you know, a song comes out of this one-chord jam we were doing . . . and it's "Israfel." Then he went on and did "Love's a Grownup God" and so forth . . . we wound up putting a whole album on tape. So after weeks of putting all this stuff together, Pat called [producer] Don Schlitten and said he wanted to record another album. And that's how *Baiyina* got off the ground. I don't know how the hell he did it. Of course, the time signatures were so odd . . . time signatures I never played in before, like 10/8 and 7/8 and all that. And we're playing these tight unisons on top of those very difficult time signatures. It was crazy. It must've been magic, man, because it all came together so fast. But the music had such a hold on me that I didn't even think about the time signature at all, I just internalized it and just played. And it worked out. Pat and I were like really, really happy the way that album turned out.
>
> What happened after that was George Shearing calls him for a gig. He did one or two in New York, and then he was supposed to go on the road with him, and that's when Pat sort of went off the deep end a little bit. We were druggin' pretty heavy then—hashish, LSD, mescaline . . . we were out there.

By 1969, I had a couple of different working situations happening. I did recordings with Don Patterson [*Oh, Happy Day!* on Prestige], Charles McPherson [*Horizons* on Prestige] and Eric Kloss [*To Hear Is to See!* on Prestige] and was also co-leading a group with the organist Gene Ludwig that included Randy Gilespie on drums. In fact, that particular trio was the backing band for Sonny Stitt on one album we did together with him in 1969 [*Night Letter* on Prestige]. I remember one engagement with the trio at Lennie's on the Turnpike in Boston where Gene and I got into an argument. In later years, Gene became a very gentle person and close friend, but at that particular time he was extremely competitive and he would really chew off as much as he could get to be upfront. Well, I had reached a point where I had enough, and so I devised a plan. Opening for us at that gig was the comedian Rodney Dangerfield. It was not uncommon in those days to have comedians opening up jazz gigs . . . just as Richard Pryor had opened for us when I was playing with John Handy's quintet at the Village Gate a couple of years earlier. Anyway, on this particular evening at Lennie's on the Turnpike, I asked Rodney to do a favor for me, and the favor was to fire Gene and Randy. And that's how that group came to an end. I had Rodney Dangerfield fire the band.

Buddy Delco Remembers: In 1969, I was playing with Pat at a place in Atlantic City called the Haunted House. It was a large club. In the front room was a bar, and in the back room, where we played, there was jazz. That gig was with Lenny Perna on piano, Al Martin on bass, myself on drums, and Pat was the guitar player. It was billed as the Lenny Perna Trio featuring Pat Martino. I had known Pat for years from around Philadelphia. Everybody knew how good Pat played, and we'd run into each other at little jam sessions. But this gig with Lenny Perna turned into a regular thing. In the summer we'd work for four months at the Haunted House, then in the winter we'd work for three months at a club in Philly called Marco's at Broad and Castle Avenue. These were strictly jazz gigs. We didn't play any dance music, we just played what we felt. And whenever we played in Atlantic City, all these guitar players would come by to check Pat out. I remember the Allman Brothers came into the Haunted House one time. I could see them walk into the club, so I told them, "Come on up and sit in." They looked at Pat and shook their heads and said, "No! No way." Same with Eric Clapton. I saw him walk in one night, check Pat out for a while, and then he walked right out shaking his head. Pat's playing during this period was phenomenal. Everybody would remark how great he played, and he'd say, "I'm still learning, I'm still trying." Very humble. But the fact is, very few people could touch him. I'd play his albums for people and they'd say, "Is this guy real?" There's a guitar player in Philly whom Pat admired named Sonny Troy. Sonny came down to see us play one night and he looked at Pat and said, "Boy, if I could only play like that." There's a lot of great guitar players out there like Sonny and others. And maybe they can play up to Pat, but they can't play past him. And he's sounding stronger than ever now . . . it's amazing considering what he went through.

By the late 1960s, I began leaving my "mark" in a kind of surreptitious way in certain jazz clubs. Let me explain. This was a time when I was very South Philly oriented with regard to graffiti. That's part of this particular culture, part of this city, part of the kids who grow up in South Philadelphia, and part of the kids who grow up in all the metropolitan areas who want an identity and want the world to "look at me, look at me." So they do it on walls, with paint . . . they paint their name on there . . . graffiti . . . I used to do that. Not with paint on walls. But I would sneak around on a gig when no one was looking and I would find a name artist's instrument and I would engrave my initials on the inside of it, or put my full name on the inside. I have my name on the inside of one of Miles Davis's trumpets, which I scratched with a switchblade that I used to carry in my back pocket. I also have my initials under the f-hole of one of Charles Mingus's basses. I was leaving my mark. God knows the karma that it brought. Maybe it had a great deal to do with the outcome that I later experienced. Maybe that was the voice that said, "You don't realize what you're getting into." We don't realize what we're getting into when we're childish about life.

So I did Miles's trumpet at the Jazz Workshop in Boston. I was playing in the front room with Sonny Stitt; Miles was in the back room with his band. And at the end of the night, I spied Miles's black trumpet with a golden rim just sitting on the table in the back room. Miles and all of his band members were in the dressing rooms at this point, and I was on my way to a party when I saw the trumpet there, and I couldn't help myself. So I just picked it up and I put the tip of my switchblade way in the back on the inside of the bowl, and I just scratched "PM" in there. Like Zorro. I did Mingus's bass some years later in St. Louis. It was 1976; Charles was very ill, physically. They used to bring him onstage in a wheelchair at that time. I was at this particular venue with Joyous Lake, and Mingus, of all things, was opening for *me*. That's amazing. Talk about a career! Talk about a historical figure! I was still an apprentice. As incredibly powerful as *Joyous Lake* was as part of a new movement of fusion coming into jazz, still, Mingus is Mingus, man. I often wondered about that, and I said it at the time: How in the world can they have Mingus opening for me? Why aren't we opening for Mingus? I guess we were selling more records at the moment. There's something profound in that—and insulting, as well. Anyway, the same thing that

I did with Miles's trumpet I did with Mingus's bass . . . out of necessity to go back to that particular self that wasn't controllable yet and was still hungry for identification. My "PM" is under the left-side f-hole . . . you can feel it if you run your fingers under there. And I hope it's not seen as an insult or as juvenile crime. But that meant so much to me at that age, at that time. These were like my idols, and I wanted to place a mark, which was really more like an embrace, on their instruments.

7

Consciousness and *Live!*

In 1972, I recorded a live quartet album at Gerdes' Folk City in New York. It was located in Greenwich Village and had been known strictly as a venue for folk music . . . Bob Dylan had apparently played there in the early 1960s. But on this particular night in September that my quartet was recording there, they renamed it Jazz City. For this occasion, Ron Thomas took the place of our regular pianist, Eddie Green, who wasn't available for that date. Ron was strictly a twentieth-century composer and was actually an intermediary for Karlheinz Stockhausen here in Philadelphia. I had gotten to know Ron, and he said to me one time, "I would love to experience jazz in a professional kind of way. I know you're involved as a pro in the business with recording and everything else. I would love, if ever I had the opportunity, to get involved. And in turn, you can have access to all of my connections in contemporary classical music." And he began to expose me to Nonesuch Records, to Elliott Carter, to Stockhausen, to Gyorgy Ligeti and Milton Babbit and that entire school of mind. And in turn, I started to bring Ron into contact with the other part of the musical community . . . the jazz community. So we had a very symbiotic relationship.

Somewhere in there, Ron said to me, "Would you like to meet Elliott Carter?" And I said, "Yeah, I would flip! I'd love to." Ron had already turned me on to my favorite recording of Elliott's, *Variations for Orchestra,* which was recorded by the St. Louis Orchestra. That recording on Columbia Records was one of the finest performances, in my opinion, of Elliott's work. So naturally, I was excited to meet him.

We drove out to Elliott's house outside of New York City, and when we get there we pulled up to a circular structure, which was Elliott's studio, where he did all of his writing. We walked up a spiral staircase to the entrance door, and as we entered, I remember seeing a manuscript laid out on the wall, circling the inside of that particular room. Elliott was writing one of his string quartets, in a circle, on the manuscript itself . . . just moving around the room with his pencil. It seemed to be obvious to me that he had a completely different way of seeing things . . . a totally different perspective. And that changed me a lot. Not in the sense of music with regard to professional or serious commitment to formal training. It was similar to an engineer, an architect, as far as Elliott's equations. If you look at Elliott's scores, they are literally equations in terms of time—odd tempos and odd time signatures. That's not what my interest was. My interest was perspective. How I see and what I think I'm looking at drastically changes.

So it was the beginning of exposure to scores like "Ancient Voices of Children" by George Crumb, which is a circular score, with all the different spatial additions added, including voice. And I was stunned by that. I had never seen music that way, aside from, of course, Stockhausen. Karlheinz is the other end of the extreme when it came to these types of dimensional perspectives. And Ron Thomas was instrumental in exposing me to all of this new music. He was the intermediary who opened that door.

For my next album on Muse, I returned to my regular trio of pianist Eddie Green, drummer Sherman Ferguson and bassist Tyrone Brown . . . the same lineup which had appeared on *Desperado,* my last Prestige album and the one prior to *Live!* Eddie, Sherman, and Tyrone also were very prolific with their own group, which included Philadelphia saxophonist Odean Pope. And that group was named Catalyst. But whenever I had dates that would come through, we had a great time playing together and we always looked forward to doing it. The four of us would join together, and at a moment's notice the magic took place between us. It was just a great, great group. There was a rapport between us that was based on friendship, and we were in tune with each other, onstage and off-. And it was a family. I don't remember other groups that I've had like that, with the exception of the Joyous Lake band. That was similar, in terms of the rapport between us.

On the album that we did together in 1974, *Consciousness,* we played John Coltrane's "Impressions," Benny Golson's "Along Came Betty," and the title track, which was by Eric Kloss. We also did two originals—"Willow" and "On the Stairs." The title for "On the Stairs" came about in the following way. I was performing at Grendel's Lair, a historic jazz club in Philadelphia, sometime in the 1970s. We had already finished the second show, and there was a third, additional one added because of another sudden full house. The dressing room was on the second floor, and I was descending in front of the group down the stairway to begin the third set, the guitar strapped on, when I suddenly halted, turned around, and described the melody of a new theme we could open with. And I titled it "On the Stairs."

I also did two solo guitar pieces on *Consciousness*. One was called "Passata on Guitar," which had a distinct classical influence. And the other was my solo interpretation of a Joni Mitchell tune, "Both Sides Now." I still enjoy playing that tune. There's something about it that's just beautiful.

Now eventually contains the clear sight of dualism—good and bad, right and wrong, birth and death, man and woman, major and minor, tritones, et cetera—to be able to truly see them objectively as one, *Both Sides Now.*

Tyrone Brown Remembers: I had previously been playing only upright bass with Billy Paul and Low Rawls, but getting the job with Pat required me to play electric bass, which I hadn't done on a gig before. But the electric bass, along with the Fender Rhodes, really helped distinguish the sound of the band. That was the popular sound of that time, the early 1970s. When Pat put that group together with Sherman, Eddie Green, and myself, we had a natural chemistry because we played together as a trio and with a popular group at the time called Catalyst. Plus, we didn't live too far from each other, so there was some social contact, as well. So we gelled naturally together . . . and with Pat. The album that was recorded at Folk City in Greenwich Village [*Live!*] was so full of interaction and featured extended solos by everyone. Ron Thomas, who was classically trained, was on that album, which was one of the projects I really enjoyed. It was my first time recording live, and that was quite an experience, too. And the New York crowd made it very interesting. I wasn't one of those guys who felt that I was ready to get exposure in New York, so being in a position to do that with Pat's group was really a thrill for me. And so, working in front of those New York musicians and that New York scene in general was really uplifting for me. And of course, Pat gave me plenty of room to stretch on that *Live!* recording.

Working with singers, you're pretty much in an accompaniment role. And both Lou Rawls and Billy Paul had hits at the time that I worked with them, so you pretty much had to just play the parts. That's how the pop-oriented business is—they're not into musicians being creative, necessarily, and spontaneous on the bandstand. They want to hear in person what they heard on record, and that's what they identify with. But making a transition to Pat's band was a whole different story. He expected you to be creative, he expected you to be a jazz artist and indulge in interplay and bring in your own voice to the music. And that was a challenge for me, coming from that other school.

Actually, Pat did have a hit during the time I played in his band, which was "Sunny." Yeah, that was a very popular piece for us. I remember meeting the composer of that tune at one of our gigs [guitarist-singer-songwriter Bobby Hebb]. He came to a concert, and I remember him complimenting Pat and thanking Pat for recording that tune.

I also remember that I always used to call Pat "Brother Azzara." It was personal to me, because the general public didn't know that was his original family name. In fact, right now I'm working on my third music book with companion CD, and one of the first things that came to my mind was to dedicate a piece to Pat. And I was thinking of titling it "Brother Azzara."

I've stayed in touch with Pat over the years. In fact, Pat reached out to me a few years ago, asking me to do a tour with him. We did Japan, Italy, and Chicago. Then a couple of years after that, we did the Blue Note in New York and Chris' Café in Philly. I did all of those on electric upright, which is what I played in Max Roach's band for nineteen years following those early 1970s years with Pat. And I noticed when I played with Pat again after all those years that he was back on the level that I remembered him being on before he had his health setback. And I was very, very impressed by that. The other thing that impressed me was he had a whole new repertoire of material. We didn't play any of the older stuff, which tells me that Brother Azzara is still moving forward artistically. So he's definitely back on top of his game.

Another thing I'd like to say about Pat is, I've traveled with a lot of well-known artists, but Pat, after all these years, remains one of my all-time favorite bandleaders. And one of the things I learned from people like him, Max Roach, and Grover Washington Jr. is that as a bandleader it is extremely important that you keep morale up on the road. Pat was there, along with the other bandleaders that I just mentioned, in terms of doing that. During my time with Pat, there were never any complaints about the fees . . . he was very giving in that department. There was never any dispute about the salary and never any complaints about the travel conditions or accommodations. Everything was pretty much handled with first class and concern. And I really learned that about keeping the morale up, because when the morale is up, the music is gonna reflect that. And that was a real plus working with Pat.

Ron Thomas Remembers: I got to Philly in 1970. I had actually become a jazz musician in 1965, after having gotten a degree in composition and having some background in classical composition. I got turned on by the jazz of the mid-1960s—Miles Davis's My Funny Valentine and also Bill Evans's Sunday at the Village Vanguard—and couldn't turn away from it. So I essentially became a jazz musician at that point. Having been a classical pianist who became a composer, I had some piano chops and I knew something about playing. So I was determined to become a jazz player and made pretty good progress for about five years. By the time I got to Philly, I made up my mind that I was going to go into the neighborhoods and get myself involved in the urban jazz scene. Previously, I mostly hung around at college jazz venues, and there's some great players there. But I knew I had to do my apprenticeship with the black musicians. So I happily and respectfully went into the neighborhoods and sat in a lot and finally started getting hired. So I made my way through that and did pretty well at getting mentored by a lot of those cats, to the point where I developed a good reputation in Philly among those players.

By the end of 1970, beginning of 1971, I started to get interested in hooking up with someone who was already more established than I was. I had heard about Pat Martino when I was living in New Jersey, before I came to Philly. I knew the *Desperado* album and I knew Eric Kloss's first album, which had Pat on it. And *Desperado* is still one of my favorite albums of Pat's. So I called Pat up and said, "Look, I've got a few gigs up here in West Philly. If you'd like to do them with me, I would really want to learn from you. You call the tunes, you work me over . . . I'd love to start an apprenticeship with you and just really learn what's going on here." Pat just happened to be at a point in his life that was perfect for that, so he happily agreed to do the gigs. So I started working with him and transferred the leadership of the quartet over to him right away.

Along the way in our conversations, Pat found out that I had this rather enormous background in European and American new music. And he was fascinated. Now, he knew a lot about that already. He had quite an impressive record collection. In fact, he turned me on to a few twentieth-century composers I had not even heard about. So at that point we kind of made a gentleman's agreement. We said, "I'll tell you everything I know, and you tell me everything you know." And that's the essential difference between all the other musicians that Pat has worked with over the years and myself, in the sense that we had this mutual body of knowledge that each of us realized was valuable to the other, and we made a deal to kind of trade information. And we did that for the whole time that we were together.

Pat made enormous progress with classical composition. He just needed to know some basic facts about how to set up scores, and what does a string orchestra score look like, and so on and so forth. And I guess the climax of our arrangement was that I turned him on to Elliott Carter's music. I actually had met Elliott Carter in Illinois back in 1965, and I still had his phone number. So I called him, and fortunately it was still soon enough where Elliott remembered me from when he was a guest artist at the University of Illinois and I had taken a kind of token lesson with him, because he was in residence there and he was seeing students at the time, and I was one of them. And he did remember me. So I was able to call him up and say, "Look, I'm working with Pat Martino, and he wants to meet you," and he said, "Fine." So we drove all the way up to upstate New York where he lived, and he met with us for an afternoon.

By the time we recorded *Live!* with Pat in 1972, we did three different six-nighters leading up to that gig at Folk City in September. And of course, I was thrilled. Because in those days it really was a big deal when you were on a record. Nowadays, it's commonplace. But in those days it was really something remarkable. And Pat also got me on Eric Kloss's album *One, Two Free,* which we did in August, before the Folk City gig, with Dave Holland and Ron Krasinski. And then in September we recorded the *Live!* album. So that was a big peak experience for me. It was amazing to me that I was able to make that much progress in just seven years as a player. Of course, I still had a lot to learn at that point and did subsequently increase my experience as a player and went on to make a lot of my own albums and so on.

By the time I recorded with Pat, he had pretty well worked me over in terms of the apprenticeship that I needed from him—about how to really get to the level of playing and playing experience that he had. In terms of the recording that night at Folk City, it was definitely a unique experience, as it would be for anyone who would be confronting that level of celebrity for the first time. And there really were a lot of celebrities in the audience that night. George Benson was there with his father, Ornette Coleman showed up, Richard Davis was there with his whole band. Quite frankly, I was just beside myself with excitement that evening. And Pat had a very well-planned program. And I learned a lot from him about how to go beyond just playing interesting jazz and really learn how to work an audience a little bit, and how to shape your solos and shape your presentation so that you create a climactic aspect of your playing. So by the time Pat would get to the last chorus of his solo, the people were ready to stand up on their feet and start yelling and screaming. There was a whole aspect of being a performer that I really picked up from Pat.

He had me sort of disciplined enough to really be careful about how I played the forms of everything, because I would get excited and I would get all crazy, because I am an avant garde-based kind of musician. And he really had to hammer me a little bit: "You've got to play these forms more carefully, because I'm planning my solos around these forms." And, of course, once I realized what he was doing. then I began to experiment with doing the same thing myself. So by the time we were doing the recording, I was acquainted with that whole phenomenon and was able to apply it. You can even hear on the album; there's a kind of audience response that comes from my solos, and that's entirely because I learned how to do that from Pat. We had an interesting chemistry. There's only three songs on that album, but each one is a little musical journey in itself. And Tyrone Brown was a big part of this. We didn't really have a steady bass player for a lot of these gigs that we did around town prior to this recording. Tyrone had been in Tennessee for some reason, and Pat kept saying, "Wait 'til Tyrone gets back and wait 'til you see what happens to this quartet then." And sure enough, as soon as Tyrone got back in town, we began to rehearse with him and, of course, it was obvious to me what Pat meant. It was just an incredible chemistry that happened between Tyrone on electric bass and Sherman on drums and myself on Fender Rhodes, which I loved playing. I really dug it. I loved the sound of it. All the piano players had one then, because it was the sound of the time. And I was a Fender Rhodes geek, man. I had my tools, and I knew how to cut the tines, and I knew how to tune it up and all of that. I was right into it.

So those qualities that *Live!* had are totally the result of Pat's ingenuity in putting that particular group together. Because we really had a very special chemistry, which is apparent on the record. During our time of playing together, Pat and I had a pretty even exchange, and we've always been just absolutely in love with each other ever since. We had this wonderful relationship that had to do with this exchange that happened between us in terms of the musical expertise and knowledge that we had, and I think both of us walked away with exactly what we were really hoping to get from the relationship. And of course, we were friends. We enjoyed each other's company and we loved playing together, so there was all of that going on there at the same time.

Carmen "Mickey" Azzara in the service, 1940.

Pat, age twelve, with his band the Emanons, featuring Bobby Riderelli (Bobby Rydell) on drums and Joe Magliano (Joe Lano) on second guitar, 1956.

Pat, age thirteen, with the Hurricanes, featuring Nick Delisi on guitar and Eddie Lalli on accordion, 1957.

Pat, age thirteen (with his Les Paul gold top), playing guitar with his father, Mickey, 1957.

Portrait of the artist as a young man, age thirteen, 1957.

Pat Martino and the Hurricanes, 1957: Nick Delisi, guitar; Eddie Lalli, accordion; Pat Martino, guitar.

The Emanons on *The Ted Mack Amateur Hour*, featuring (from left to right) Eddie Lalli, accordion; Pat Azzara (Pat Martino), guitar; Joe Scavetti, tenor sax; Ted Mack, host; and Bobby Riderelli (Bobby Rydell), drums, 1957.

Pat's introduction to hard bop was through the Donald Byrd–Gigi Gryce album *Jazz Lab*, which he won as a second-place prize in a talent contest at "The Sons of Italy" in Philadelphia, 1957.

Pat's father, Carmen "Mickey" Azzara, playing a black Les Paul Custom, 1958.

Pat as "Ricky Tino" playing a high school performance in 1960.

Pat with his father, Mickey, and mother, Jean, at Club Harlem in Atlantic City, 1963.

Pat playing with Jack McDuff's group at Club Big M, 1964 (from left to right): Red Holloway, Jack McDuff, Pat Martino, Al Hibbler, Joe Dukes.

On the road with organist Don Patterson and drummer Billy James, 1965.

Pat in Ventnor City, New Jersey, at Danny Fogel's house, 1965.

Recording of the album *Strings*, 1967.

Photo taken at a jazz club in Asbury Park, New Jersey (in performance with Gene Ludwig and Randy Gillespie), 1967.

8

Starbright and Joyous Lake

There were three albums that took place within a very short span in 1976, all produced by Ed Freeman. The first was *Exit* [recorded February 10], which was a quartet recording with Gil Goldstein on piano, Richard Davis on bass, and Billy Hart on drums. The second was a duet album with Gil Goldstein, *We'll Be Together Again* [recorded February 13 and 17]. And the third, *Starbright*, was my first interaction with Warner Bros. [recorded in July]. That album was so demanding in terms of expectations on behalf of Warner Bros., the label involved in the project, that I think it was that expectation that brought about and triggered *Joyous Lake* as the next move.

There are so many different exits on *Starbright*, one being almost in a sense of an abstract version of rock, one being balladic and lament, another being hard bop, another being fusion, another being this, another being that. These were all exits. And maybe it was because I found it to be so significant to be able to open all the windows in my house, so to speak, with that project. Ultimately, it was unsuccessful due to the fact that it failed to produce a specific target on the basis of marketing. Although they were surprised at the array of colors in *Starbright*, I think at that same time they were confused by it. The immediate response from Warner Bros. was, essentially, "What does this mean? Where are you going? What are you saying here?" And more importantly, "How can we market something like this?" Which I totally understood, although my initial idea (which was never discussed) was to hopefully gain airplay across multiple markets. Eventually it caused me to think, "Oh, you really want something specific? I'm just giving you an idea of all the things that are possible in depth. Yeah, okay, something specific." And that was the result that, in a sense, amplified a recipe for the next move.

Gil Goldstein Remembers: The three records that I made with Pat in 1976—*Exit, Starbright, We'll Be Together Again*—were put together very quickly. These were also the first records that I had done, so it was a great start to my career to be able to play with someone who was a hero of mine. The way that I met Pat was through Jaco Pastorius, sometime in 1975. I had just moved to New York, was staying at my cousin's place and just beginning to find my way. And Jaco, whom I had met in Miami a few years earlier and had also seen play with Pat Metheny in Boston, suddenly showed up at my cousin's pad. He hadn't hooked up with Joe Zawinul yet and was in New York doing his whole outreach program, jamming with everybody he could think of, meeting people, and just hanging out on the scene. Jaco stayed with me at my cousin's pad for about a week, and at some point he said to me, "Hey, man, you want to play with Pat Martino? I just played with him in Philly. Here's his number. Call him." So I immediately went into this other room and called Pat on the phone, but I was kind of sheepish and went, "Uh, Mr. Martino . . . I was thinking that, uh, I would like to play with you." And then Pat said in that deep voice of his, "Are you sure?" And I went, "Yeah, yeah, no . . . I'm sure."

A couple of weeks later, I took the train to Philly and met Pat at his house, and we started playing duets together. That was our fertile period for developing music together. Before I went to Pat's, Jaco had said to me, "Take some very hip tunes that will challenge him." So I wrote a couple tunes for Pat that he ended up really liking—"Open Road," which we ended up recording on *We'll Be Together Again,* and "City Lights," which we later recorded on *Starbright.* Aside from playing duets together at Pat's house, we would just hang out and talk about all kinds of subjects. I remember he would talk about these fourth-dimensional objects . . . the tesseract . . . and he had all these Vasarely prints that he'd show me [Victor Vasarely, leader of Op Art movement and geometric abstract art]. Everything was kind of many-dimensional and philosophical, and at the same time there was a little bit of humor to it, too. And I remember listening to lots of modern classical music during my time with Pat. We did a tour once where we drove cross-country, and I remember twelve-hour stretches of listening to Elliott Carter and Charles Wourinen in the car. And Pat was usually the driver.

We went across the country with a quintet with me on keyboards, Anton Fig on drums, either Ed Schuller or Jeff Berlin on bass, and Bob Hanlon on tenor saxophone. I never quite felt satisfied about the live thing. Sometimes it sounded cluttered onstage, so there were problems hearing each other properly on gigs. So I never felt like I could really engage Pat musically in those loud live settings where his amp was clear across the stage. To me, recording was kind of the payoff. I always think of *We'll Be Together Again* as my first experience as an arranger, because I had to instantly come up with these electric-piano arrangements, like an orchestral pad for him to play over. And it was the most uncluttered format that I ever had to play with him on. I was so tired of being in situations where everything seemed to be getting in his way, which just didn't seem suited for Pat to be able to just let go and play. But in the intimate duo setting, we could really communicate. I remember Jaco said to me after he heard *We'll Be Together Again,* "Man, why didn't you play more lines against Pat?" And I thought, "Well, no . . . Pat was soloing, and I didn't need to go against it." Jaco thought it was a little too supportive, that I should've challenged him more. But I disagreed with Jaco, whose opinion I admired and appreciated. This wasn't bebop, after all.

Also, I thought the decision to have me play Fender Rhodes electric piano on *We'll Be Together Again* was just perfect. When we first started playing duets, and it was piano and guitar, there was such a reference, obviously, to Bill Evans and Jim Hall. It was kind of hard to escape that. In fact, when we started playing a few things together, Pat actually, in a very kind way, said, "You know, I would try to get a little bit away from sounding like Bill." But it was hard for me to do that, because Bill Evans was such a big reference for me of how you play duets with guitar because of those two famous records he did with Jim [1963's *Undercurrent* and 1966's *Intermodulation*]. I didn't know any other way to hear it. And when I discovered that the piano at the studio was so bad—it sounded like a bunch of springs in a box—I didn't want to play it. So I just shifted to the Rhodes. And that instrument also allowed me to be a little bit more orchestral, because you can hold notes a little bit longer than you can hold them on piano. I could get a measure's worth of ring out of a note played on the Rhodes, whereas on the piano it's a little bit hard to project a note for that long and keep it an interesting sound without re-attacking it. So it just fortuitously worked out that the piano was bad and the Rhodes seemed like the obvious choice for that particular session.

For *Starbright,* Pat gave me a lot of responsibility on the record in terms of coaching people and writing music out. I remember writing out some bass parts for Will Lee and kind of getting things together. Pat asked me to write a horn arrangement for one song, which I don't think even made it on the record. But that was the first time I met Mike and Randy Brecker. Pat had hired them to play on that one song. So besides playing on it, I kind of helped produce it in some way. That was a strong album, but there weren't too many gigs after that. And at some point he and his manager found a new band for him. And Pat went off with Kenwood and Delmar into a different phase.

I think *Joyous Lake* was surprising to Warner Bros. in a general context. I don't think that's why they brought me in as an artist to endorse the jazz division. I believe they brought myself and Alice Coltrane in for another reason. We both were signed simultaneously. At the same time they also signed Al Jarreau, George Benson, and number of others. It seemed that their intention was to create a new market. In retrospect, it was the beginning of what eventually became referred to as "smooth jazz," with the power of the corporation investing in production, promotion, and worldwide distribution, and at the same time giving themselves credibility as a serious jazz label. For me, it was totally an embrace by a major label, both financially and artistically—something that is very unlikely to happen now. It was like a window had opened for that brief moment in time, only to close shut soon after. So my intention was to fulfill my responsibilities with regard to participation.

For *Joyous Lake,* Warner Bros. brought in Paul Rothchild, a prominent producer who was still working with Bonnie Raitt and actively involved with Earth, Wind and Fire and had quite a track record in the rock world [the Doors, Janis Joplin, Neil Young, the Lovin' Spoonful]. I found that extremely rewarding as an experience to be exposed to artists in that genre, and I was affected by it. And in turn, the end result was my intentions were changed. I became specifically intended to participate with something moving in directions that were coordinating with opportunities that would really fit what was being displayed to me as an environment. And individuals who functioned within it offered, from my angle, a great deal of respect.

And at that particular moment, my intentions were always governed by accuracy, by precision, by doing the best I could do under any circumstance in any manifestation of any reason. And maybe it's because of that that I always found it difficult to judgmentally, through critique, come to a conclusion as to the value of one thing more or less than anything else. It's like what I briefly said in the liner notes to *We'll Be Together Again:* "It can't be praised, nor can it be judged." When an individual does the best that he or she can do, it no longer is subject to judgment. Because that individual now is fulfilled in terms of their innate intentions, as I was on *Joyous Lake.*

I remember auditioning personnel for that record at a rehearsal studio in Manhattan owned by a gentleman named Bob Crawford. I had the Warner Bros. contract, and I needed a group for the next album and to tour in support of it. So here I'm auditioning players to come in. In fact, one of the keyboard players was Lyle Mays, who eventually went out with Pat Metheny. I had gone through so many players, and it just wasn't working out, and I had two weeks left prior to making the recording. And the way I was holding rehearsals, I had two compositions that I had presented so that I could get an idea of facility, dexterity, in terms of abilities, and then also interpretation—chops and heart. And from that point forward, if anyone could stimulate me in those two different ways, then I would begin to write on the basis of their identities collectively. That's what the framework for the auditions was all about. So in come three exceptional young musicians—Delmar Brown, Kenwood Dennard, and Mark Leonard—and man, they were burning. They were the hot players from Berklee, as well as New England Conservatory, and I didn't even know anything about them. But they came in and just really gassed me. It was an immediate magic between us at that audition. So we hired them as the band, rehearsed for two weeks, and then did a few gigs in preparation for the recording with producer Paul Rothchild, who was a real pro and also a sweetheart. I enjoyed working with Paul.

We went into Criteria Studios in Miami to record *Joyous Lake.* It was us in the small studio and Maurice White and Earth, Wind and Fire in the larger studio. And there we were, partying and hanging out and recording. We had a house on the beach. Warner Bros. was exuberant in terms of budget at that time. It was just a great experience. And while *Joyous Lake* was a very powerful album and successful in terms of sales, I have to confess that I don't really listen that much to the past. If I were to play it right now, it could only be compared to what I am working with at the moment. And it really has nothing to do with reality. That's why I don't really believe in occupying the past as a valid, functional mechanism to come to a conclusion that's precise. More than the music itself, that project triggers the conceptual photograph—where it was taken, when it was taken, the people in the picture—more than it does what a listener might find of value. The listeners might be under the impression that the music itself is tremendous. At the same time, they don't realize that what's really tremendous is the full collection of conditions that it formulated within.

In the case of *Joyous Lake,* all the individuals involved—Delmar, Woody, and Mark—were stellar musicians and very wonderful people. And we forged a very tight personal chemistry together, to the point where it felt like a family, both at the recording sessions and out on the road. And maybe that aspect was heightened by the fact that Delmar's dad had just passed away shortly before the recording and it was a decision on his part to come down and join us at Criteria as opposed to remaining for all of the affairs that were going to take place after the funeral. He flew into Chicago for the funeral and visited briefly, just to embrace the family, then left from there and came right down to Miami in time for the sessions.

Delmar Brown Remembers: A bass player friend named Tim Ingles told me about the Pat auditions in New York, and I told Kenwood about it. We were all in Boston at the time. Tim was working with Alyrio Lima, a percussionist with Weather Report. Alyrio knew Bob Devere, who had been Weather Report's manager and now was managing Pat Martino. So Alyrio found out about the auditions from Bob Devere and then told Tim, who told me. Now, the problem I had at the time was that I was already committed to going to Europe with Hannibal Marvin Peterson. And of course, Hannibal didn't like that too much, but I felt like I needed to go down to this audition. Something inside was telling me, "Look, Hannibal Marvin Peterson is great and you have the gig, but you gotta go down and check out this Pat thing." So Tim and Woody and myself came down for the audition and were hired. It turned out that Tim had another commitment and couldn't do the gig, so Pat ended up hiring Mark Leonard, a bassist from the Minneapolis-St. Paul area who was going to the New England Conservatory at the time.

We started recording at Media Sound on Fifty-seventh Street in New York, but we weren't very happy with the sound. We were spending money, but nothing was really getting recorded. Meanwhile, my father was in the hospital. He had Hodgkin's disease and was in serious condition, so I was kind of like in two modes at that point. I remember one day being in the studio and calling my mother at the hospital, and I spoke to my father a little bit, asked him how he was doing, and the only thing that he said to me was, "I'll see ya later." And my mother said he fell back to sleep after that. So I went back to the studio feeling really strange about that. At that point, Paul Rothchild decided he was going to cancel the session at Media Sound and had already booked Criteria Studios in Miami to finish the album.

That night, I got a call at home from my aunt, telling me my father had passed. So that was a very sad night for me. I didn't really get much sleep, just cried a lot and didn't feel good at all. In the morning I was all confused, feeling completely outside of myself. I called Pat to tell him I had to go to my father's funeral in Chicago. And what happened was, Warner Bros. and Pat flew me out to Chicago to the funeral—they paid for everything. And Pat said, "If you want to stay with your family for a while, that's cool. We're gonna all go down to Miami, we got a house down there. We'll wait for you. Just give me a call after the funeral and tell me what you want to do."

After the funeral, I had a talk with my mother about staying with the family or going down to Miami, and she told me, "You know what you need to do. You should get on the plane and do that record. That's what your father would want you to do. There's nothing for you to sit here and cry and be sad about. The best thing you can do for him, and me, is to get on that plane and go down there and finish that record. And don't worry, he is seeing this. So you have to go." I called Pat and told him I was coming. I got on the plane and flew down to Miami, and when I got there, they were all waiting for me. We stayed at 461 Ocean Boulevard, which was the same house where Eric Clapton stayed when he recorded that album he did back then [*461 Ocean Boulevard*, recorded April–May 1974 at Criteria Studios]. The night me and Woody walked on the beach and I talked about my father. Coming from his funeral, I was in a reflective mood, kind of inside myself, trying to figure out what I was doing with my life. At some point we were looking out over the ocean, and suddenly there was something moving in the sky. At first I thought it was an airplane, but this thing moved and stopped, then moved again and stopped. And in my imagination it was like my dad was waving to me from a spaceship, saying, "Everything is cool, son. Don't worry about it. It's all good." And the whole experience of seeing this thing hovering in the sky kind of brought me out of the numbness.

The next day in the studio, we were on fire! It was like I had been on a drug and just came out of it. All of my energy had turned extremely positive after all I had gone through, and seeing that UFO the night before brought me out of the mode that I was in. And we recorded that fantastic record called *Joyous Lake*. It is truly the greatest musical experience I've had in my lifetime. Pat allowed me to have two songs on the record, and out of the greatness of his heart, he dedicated that record to my father. You look on the back and it says: "To the memory of William F. Brown." I'll never forget Pat for that. For me, that's a lifelong bond between me and Pat for him doing that.

Kenwood Dennard Remembers: The audition with Pat took place in New York sometime in April of 1976 at Josandra Studios on Twenty-sixth Street between Sixth and Seventh Avenues. When we got to the audition, Vinnie Colaiuta was already playing, so I figured, "Oh, man, Pat already invited the greatest players to this audition. What are WE gonna do?" But we just got up on the little soundstage there and started jamming on these tunes. Eventually, Pat showed up. As I recall, he didn't say anything. He just jumped up and joined us with his guitar, and it was feeling good. Then at some point as the music came to a climax, Pat left and we kept playing. And I thought, "Oh, my goodness, what's going on here?" Finally he came back in the room and stopped the band, and I thought, "Oh man, we're in for it now!" And then he said in that very distinctive low voice of his, "Yeah, cats. I spoke to my manager, Bob Devere, and we decided that this is the band." And we were beside ourselves. Here we were, twenty-year-old Berklee grads, playing with the legendary Pat Martino! At Berklee, we had studied Pat's music along with the music of other groups that were popular at the time, like the Mahavishnu Orchestra, Billy Cobham, and Weather Report. But Pat had a special place in all of that. So we went in the space of a forty-minute audition from Berklee grads to Berklee glads.

We took the lion's share of that year and toured around the country—the Agora Ballroom in Cleveland, the Cellar Door in D.C., the Bottom Line in New York, and one memorable gig at a club in Woodstock called Joyous Lake. And I was very excited about and elated by the fact that that name, which is what Pat ended up calling the album we later recorded, was from the *I Ching*. The actual translation of "Joyous Lake" is "perseverance perseveres." Now, if you think about that, this guy has persevered more than anybody. So it seems like a perfect phrase to describe Pat's entire life.

For the recording of *Joyous Lake,* we went to Miami to record at Criteria Studios. And during the time that we were doing the sessions down there, we had a sighting of an unidentified flying object on the beach, which really added a sense of mystique to the recording. It streaked across the sky but stopped dead in its tracks and sort of sat there for a while before taking off again. And in my own exuberant twenty-year-old way, I was scared! So I saw that thing and started running back toward the house with both hands on my ears like that painting *The Scream.* Who knows what it was? But that event kind of anointed the session and made us feel that the record was really something of destiny.

Following the *Joyous Lake* sessions, I toured through 1976 and the early part of 1977 with Kenwood, Delmar, and Mark. It was a dynamic band, and we were creating some very positive momentum on tour. As I said, these young players were energetic and burning. But that was also when I began experiencing severe headaches and, in at least one case, an actual seizure on-stage during performance, which caused me to make some drastic decisions that brought touring with the Joyous Lake group to a halt.

By the summer of 1977 I began doing guitar duets with Bobby Rose, my old friend from Philadelphia who had appeared on *Baiyina* back in 1968. It was a rewarding experience, primarily because of the personal friendship that I had with Bobby as well as the chemistry that we had forged together over time. It was easy playing with Bobby, and we had some memorable performances, including one at the Bottom Line and a performance in Ann Arbor, Michigan, which was actually recorded. The tapes exist, and they may come to light one day.

It's profound how certain events recircle when least expected. I was recently contacted by a gentleman from Toronto, who called to apologize for his participation as a member in a group of hecklers at a concert that Bobby and I performed in 1977, over thirty years ago.

> ***Bobby Rose Remembers:*** After we did *Footprints* in 1972, Pat and I sort of drifted apart. I didn't talk to him for a good five years after that. And then out of the blue he calls me up and says, "Hey, man, I miss you. Why don't you come have a drink?" So we got together at a bar in his neighborhood, hung out and had some drinks. Next thing you know, we're out on the road doing duets. We played mostly Wes tunes, like "Four on Six" and "West Coast Blues," and standards like "One for My Baby and One More for the Road" and, of course, "Sunny." We also did "Israfel" from *Baiyina*, and Pat did a couple of solo pieces during the sets—"Both Sides Now" and "Variations and Song." And Pat's playing during this time was phenomenal, the best I ever heard him. We had one rough gig in Toronto, where they were so rude to us that we stopped in the middle of the set and walked off the stage. They booked us as an opener for Jean-Luc Ponty's fusion group, and the people were there to hear that alone. They didn't give a shit about a guitar duet. So they were quite noisy and rude, and I remember Pat said something over the microphone, sort of told 'em off a little bit, and we walked off. From there we went to Ann Arbor, Michigan, and we were still rolling off that bad experience. Surprisingly, the Ann Arbor concert turned out to be phenomenal.
>
> After Pat's surgery, it was hard for me to get back into the swing of being his friend again, because he didn't remember who his friends were. He was going through an emotional roller coaster at the time. I would get good vibes from him, then I would get bad vibes, then no vibes. It was just crazy.

9

Seizures and Surgery

I was subject to misdiagnoses over many years. But, of course, from what I vaguely remember in terms of the medical conditions, MRI did not become available in this country until sometime in the 1970s, and because of that I had never been diagnosed properly in those earlier years. Until the time that MRI and CAT scans came into regular use, I had been misdiagnosed by psychiatrists and psychologists as having different forms of depression—manic depression, bipolar disorder, and later schizophrenia. I was given psychotropic medication and electroshock treatments and placed in locked wards; I even reached anger to such a degree that I was placed in a straitjacket. To be subject to this kind of abuse was an experience in itself. It taught me a great deal about the futility of anger. Because when I finally came to find out what it was, one of the first things that came to the forefront after the operations was the desire to take them to court and to participate in the details, the paperwork, and the lawyers that are needed when one confronts the system. And then when I began to remain where I was, as opposed to walking through the doorway into another dilemma, I had made a decision as to what the system meant to me. And I no longer was subjected, because it was a decisive move to no longer participate in such things.

So I decided not to sue, and at that point I began to redefine and refine my life. And I began to view all the suffering—the seizures, the misdiagnoses—as a necessity for an ongoing evolution. And now I'm thankful to everything that's happened.

I had three nervous breakdowns. The first was absolutely a horror show, just literally fear at its highest level for me. I was broken into pieces. The second was not as bad. In fact, it wasn't extreme, just kind of heavy. The third was monaural; it had no meaning. The fear was gone. I had become used to it. These three nervous breakdowns happened years apart. And each time it happened, it was a reminder of what was misinterpreted in the prior experience. So that finally, what was being experienced was the entrance of and the interaction with fear itself.

These are some of the things that I see of value, how these things dissipated over periods of time where they began to become more and more defined for completely different reasons than the illusions that they initially projected. Certain experiences in terms of definitive conditions were subject to what brought them about. And once something is brought about, it doesn't make any difference how it was brought about. It's what was eventually activated that really is significant. So the nervous breakdown was no big thing. It's what I learned from it that was a big thing: the nature of fear itself, and how much an important part of life it really can be.

Consider the two sides of the coin: When you see one side of the coin, you must take it for granted that the other side exists, just as provocative as the one that you are currently subject to. And when you see that and you come to see how subject you are to either of the two, it's then questionable as to what either of them really means, in terms of reality, in terms of your definition of what this means. So suddenly you see a mask with a frown, and then when you continue to try to avoid it when it frightens you, you see through awareness that it turns into a mask with a smile. And for a while you feel protected by the warmth and the embrace of that happiness. And then suddenly the smile turns into a frown again when you least expect it, and you begin to fail to trust either of the two. Then you begin to move into a third place, because you're no longer attached to either of the two . . . you don't believe in them anymore. And when you do that, you've finally entered objectivity. And you stand there and watch them in motion from the third place, and that's the triangle. You look at it and you suddenly see the necessity for it, as the process that emphasizes and operates growth as our awareness expands. It's enlightenment. You become more and more enlightened by the process itself, and you respect it and treasure it.

My first seizure came when I was probably ten or eleven years old. It happened, I guess, when I ran away from home. My father came looking for me and found me two and a half blocks away, sitting on a curb at the side of a park. That's as far as I got when the fear set in. It happens when a child is afraid of what's coming next. It's a breakdown . . . of trust, of support. It's a breakdown of all the things that you are taught to believe. And the child makes a decision—to run away from home—and is frightened to death. The child already decided that he or she is safe, that Mom and Dad told me the right things . . . and then suddenly goes to school and discovers that these are not the right things. And then the child sees Mom and Dad fighting, and it all seems wrong. The trust and support are shattered. So the child decides to run away, which is what I did . . . even though I was still in the neighborhood. I was only over at the park a couple of blocks away. And when I sat there, I didn't know what to do next. That's when the fear came. And what to do next came to me: my father appeared. And he grabbed me and took me home and he embraced me with his love.

Each time I had a seizure, there was an immediate interruption in all of my intentions, followed by a period of recovery. I began seeing what was needed to move toward the way I perceive things now. This would not have come to fruition if those confrontations didn't happen.

I know I had seizures during my years in Harlem with Willis Jackson and on the road with Jack McDuff. But they happened so privately, where I would just be withdrawn, that they didn't see it as a physical or psychological manifestation. They just saw it as, "That boy is a little out to lunch sometimes." The only seizure I recall happening onstage was with the Joyous Lake band in 1976. We were performing the Riviera Jazz Festival on a mountaintop just outside of Marseilles in France, and there were about 283,000 people at that festival. This was an outdoor event, like a mini-Woodstock for fusion. Chick Corea's group Return to Forever was there, and so was Weather Report—a major event. And I had a seizure onstage. Right in the midst of a really heavy-duty, burning section, I stopped playing and stood there for about thirty seconds. During these moments of seizure, it feels like you're falling through a black hole; it's like everything just escapes at the moment. Now suddenly you feel a chill within yourself. It's like a change of temperature, and there's a shivering that takes place within you, and the fear is so deep that you feel the presence of fear like it's consciously alive within you, observing the effect it's having, and being inseparable at the same time. You're gripped by it. And it comes with no warning, from out of the blue. Suddenly all the things that you are focused on are disintegrated, and you're left shivering with no floor under you. And you close your eyes and you're hoping that it ends soon, because you don't know what's gonna happen. But then you suddenly come out of it, and you find your place again.

During that period of time, that was a very mystical experience. I was inhibited in many, many ways, constantly interrupted by seizures. There was a period leading up to my situation at GIT, Guitar Institute of Technology in

Hollywood, where I was having all kinds of seizures and hallucinations, even to the point where I felt like I was carrying a crucifix on my shoulder, walking down the street, almost like an LSD hallucination. And these were some of the things my first wife, Geri, was subject to. That's one of the reasons why I never held it against her for a divorce after sixteen years of marriage, under the conditions that caused her to do so. Because those were just some extremely abstract times in our relationship.

In a sense, it's not fair to her, because when I think of her, I think of those seizures. I think of that period of time when it was a nightmare for me, and she became part of that nightmare. That's not fair, because that's not what initially was noticed when I fell in love with her. It had nothing to do with what in time surrounded her in my mind. So because of that, I still respect and continue a lovely friendship with Geri.

Geri Taber (formerly Geri Martino, née Sanders) Remembers: It must've been gradual, but you could be at a point where you overlook something, and maybe I didn't want to see it. I don't know. But I was also modeling, I was doing a lot of work, and Pat was busy. I really don't know. It's something that creeps up on you. And all of a sudden, you know a person who's just the kindest person in the world and they make a statement and you say, "That's not right," because you know this man too well. It's nothing that he would ever say. And it just got worse. And everything was going downhill, just because Pat was not well. And as much as people—strangers, an audience— could love you, they would never understand that you're very ill and just can't go any further. So everything just stopped. **(From Phil Fallo's 1993 documentary** Pat Martino: Open Road**)**

John Mulhern Remembers: Pat was living in New York with Geri on Jane Street, and I would drive up from Jersey to take lessons with him. It was during that period when I was studying with him that I really began to notice that something wasn't right with Pat. This is after Joyous Lake was released [1977]. He'd come off the road and he would get very depressed, or he'd have very severe headaches. I remember going into New York for a lesson one time and Geri telling me, "Pat's not feeling that well today. I don't know if today's a good day." That was the first time I saw the effects either of electroshock treatment or whatever was wrong with him.

Geri Taber: I think that the worst thing I've ever done in my life was to consent to having him receive shock therapy. It still hurts me to talk about it. It was killing; it was brutal to see such an amazing talent and fine person turn

into someone who just couldn't help himself. **(From Ian Knox's 2008 documentary**
Martino Unstrung: A Brain Mystery)

After being misdiagnosed as manic depressive, spending time in a
locked ward, getting electroshock treatments, and then hearing from my
wife that she could no longer live this way and wanted a divorce, I came
back to Philadelphia and stayed at my parents' house. After a period of time
there, I spent a number of months in a Cistercian monastery, where I baked
bread and meditated, walked through the fields, and made recordings on my
Walkman of the herds of cows grazing there . . . and generally reconnected
with life itself.

The following year was the entrance into the eye of the storm, the quiet
before the explosion. And during the quiet is when I stopped playing. That's
when I began to get interested in not being involved in performance. And
that led to my affiliation with Guitar Institute of Technology (GIT). At rest,
it seemed to be like total pleasure. It was indeed the eye of the storm. But it
was there, in Hollywood, that the next event took place. And that's when I
was given two hours to live. That's when the storm really hit—hard!

I remember my intentions at that time: to attempt routing other alternatives. Although participating as part of an impressive faculty at GIT was a rewarding experience, the lack of performing publicly any longer left me empty
and unfulfilled. I finally contacted my cousin Joey in Las Vegas. I made plans
to visit Joey and his wife Karen to discuss a totally different profession, along
with their assistance, which was the idea of working in a casino. As briefly
described in Chapter 2, Joey was a cousin who in the early years was given
a guitar by my father. Somewhere around 1956, he went to Las Vegas with
a band and later decided to give up the music business and remain in Vegas
working in the casinos, which he did as a dealer. He's recently retired after
quite a successful career, eventually becoming involved as an upper part of
management at Las Vegas's International Hilton. Well, for some confused
reason, I thought that it might be a good cover for my procrastination, to lose
myself in such a place. So I went to Vegas, and Joey agreed. He brought me
to where he originally began his career, one of the casinos on the strip. We
went in the doorway, and I stood there in a daze, saying to myself, "Are you
kidding?" At which time Joey looked at me and broke into laughter, followed
by him saying, "Let's get out of here."

John Mulhern Remembers: In 1979, I traveled with Pat to Los Angeles
when he accepted the position at the Guitar Institute of Technology. And I
was excited to go out there, because I was going to be the guy to start the

recording department at GIT. I was staying with Pat, sleeping on the couch at night, then going in to GIT with him in the morning and just helping Pat out in whatever ways I could. And I remember one night we were supposed to go see George Benson at the Baked Potato, but Pat said he really wasn't feeling good and that he was going to stay home, which I found strange. So I went to the Baked Potato alone and talked to George after the set, and he said, "Where's Pat? Tell him I was asking about him." Three days later, I was sleeping outside and Louise, Pat's girlfriend at the time, came out and said, "Something's wrong with Pat! Come on in!" So I run into the house and I see Pat on the bed, and he's just bobbing up and down like a toy, almost. And so Louise grabs his tongue and I hold his arms down. And that was really the first time I had seen a seizure like that, so I didn't realize what was happening. We cooled him out and he slept that night; we didn't rush him to the hospital or anything like that. We went the next day—I dropped him off at Van Nuys Hospital. And that's when he found out that he had an aneurysm.

All of these hallucinations and seizures were manifestations of the AVM (arteriovenous malformation). It was said that I was born with this condition. It's an entanglement of veins and arteries in a certain part of the brain. Like a knot. And in time it grew in size until finally it resulted, at the moment that it was properly diagnosed, that there was a time limit in terms of how much further this could be allowed to expand. It was the size of a pear at this time, and they gave me two hours to live. And the most profound facet of that entire experience was the joy, after decades of misdiagnoses, when they said, "This is what you have." The moment they said that, the hallucinatory hell became concrete. And I had the ability to just put my hand on it and push it aside, with joy. That how I saw it: "I see what you are. And I'm feeling great about it." So when the doctor told me, "You have two hours to live," I felt joy from that diagnosis. Finally it could be trusted, from a machine, from an MRI.

Prior to that diagnosis, having no answer as to what it was, of course I was depressed. I was like, "When is this going to end? When is this going to stop? What's good about life? Is this it? Is this what I'm going to have to deal with the rest of my days?" And they were giving me all these drugs, which were not working. And friends would call me and say, "Hey, I got some good grass. It works much better than your medication." So I tried that, and it didn't help.

Eventually, I gave up smoking everything—cigarettes, pot, hashish, which was very difficult. The effects of that left me with emphysema, and chronic bronchitis—COPD—and I almost suffocated. So I stopped getting

involved with smoking anything. I remember a time when it was very difficult to even consider, being a player, not smoking a joint before the gig. I
used to depend on it. And then suddenly, change had to take place. I couldn't
take a line of coke, because my nose started bleeding—really bad. And it had
to be cauterized. So I've experienced face-to-face confrontations with the
physical apparatus saying, "No more of that, I will not accept that anymore."

"But what will you accept?" I would question.

And the answer would come: "For you to take care of yourself . . . grow
up . . . come of age."

And it wasn't until I saw the entire thing as a challenge, as a legitimate
challenge to accomplish and to feel better about myself in doing so, that it
came to fruition. So when I pick up the instrument now I can sing with it,
and I don't really rely upon anything but the instrument itself and my state
of mind at that moment.

So I look back at all these things, and I do so in a manner unlike the
way it's often propagandized when you hear people talking about the war
on drugs and drug users. I'll admit that I used drugs. And the only reason I
used drugs is that I didn't like the drugs I was being sold by physicians and
by psychiatrists. And I found it more functional and more practical and at
the same time more effective to smoke a joint rather than to do whatever it
was that I was being subjected to by chemists. At the end of that, very much
like I said about misdiagnoses and wanting to bring them to court and then
changing my mind, so, too, did it change in terms of my conclusions as to
whether or not all the years that I did drugs, including hallucinogenics, were
bad to do. The drugs I did in the earlier years were for a reason. They were
my way out from the hallucinations that came from AVM. And in the long
run, that may be the reason that I'm still alive. I'll never know.

When I look back at the entirety of it all, and I do so from where I reside
at this time in life, I see this as the result of all that took place. And I'm
happy. And I'm clear of it. Life's become pure. I've changed my diet, changed
my surroundings . . . I've changed everything.

Pat Hicks (GIT founder) Remembers: Pat made an incredible contribution to the school when he was here. First of all, I was a fan of Pat's from day
one. He's just an amazing guitar player. Our connection began when I went
to hear him perform at the Lighthouse in Hermosa Beach, a famous old jazz
venue down there. I got a front-row seat, and there was Pat on guitar, and
behind him was Jeff Berlin, who was the equivalent of Pat on the bass. And
I was just awestruck at what I heard from those two that night. I went up
afterward to both of them and I said, "Hey, guys, would you consider being

visiting faculty at our school?" This was early on in the school's history, in 1979. And they both said, "Well, who else is involved?" And I when I told them Howard Roberts was on staff, Pat said, "Well, if Howard Roberts is involved, I'll be involved." Both Pat and Jeff eventually signed on as visiting faculty. Pat came out and did a seminar for the students. And the word was out in our catalog and sales letters that I would send out that Pat Martino had decided to join our staff, which again was an amazing thing to have happen—a guy with that level of stature. So the credibility to the school just leaped enormously after that. Sure enough, Pat came out. So we went out and got him an apartment and put him on the payroll. And when we were looking at the apartment, his finger got caught in the elevator. I don't know if it broke it but it damaged it so bad he couldn't play the guitar, which was devastating to him and to me. But that healed after a period of time. When Pat came to the school he was very spiritual, almost mystical in his approach to music and his approach to life. His first seminar he held for the students in front of the whole student body, he got up there and he set a chair down in the middle of the room and he sat down, and he had a man dressed like a waiter with a white towel over his forearm walk up with a serving dish with a Remy Martin on it. It was part of Pat's ultra-cool act. So this guy handed him the Remy Martin, and Pat proceeded to lecture for about an hour. And he never touched his guitar. He just wanted to talk to the students about music and life and so forth, which he felt was more important than giving them a guitar lesson. And I can understand, except you can imagine an eighteen-year-old kid sitting out there saying, "Yeah, yeah, show me them licks." But he never played that day. And I kept looking at my wife Becky and saying, "He needs to play!" Because we're business people, and we're wanting him to blow these kids away and inspire them to want to learn. But Pat had his own agenda. All the time he was at the school, it was Pat Martino's agenda, it wasn't mine or what I wanted him to do or be. That was just who he was and how he was, and I wasn't about to try and change that. The man is who he is.

Pat had an office right down the hall from me, and I left him alone. The students would come and sit with him and either play or learn something or just talk with him. Whatever they wanted, that's what he was there for. And one day this kid walks in—a rock 'n' roll shredder with long hair and cut-off jeans and tie-dyed shirt. And he sits down and plays for Pat and is burning up the neck of the guitar, trying to impress Pat. And when he's done, Pat calmly says, "Have a seat." The kid sits down and Pat says, "Let me see your guitar." So the kid hands his guitar proudly over to Pat, waiting for Pat to say, "You know, you got some real chops there, buddy. You're gonna be something else," or something to that effect. But instead, Pat takes the guitar, reaches into his drawer, pulls out a pair of wire cutters, and cuts the kid's guitar strings, one by one across the neck, then hands him back the guitar and says, "If you're here to learn something, you better listen. And first of all, get rid of these old strings. They're dead and they're flat. And clean your guitar before you come back in here!" And the kid leaves. Outside Pat's office, there was another kid leaning against the wall with his guitar in his hand, waiting for his turn to see Pat. And this shredder walks out with his stringless guitar, turns to the other kid waiting, and says, "I wouldn't go in there if I were you."

During his time at GIT, Pat was a very . . . almost mystical person. He thought deep. My wife and I once took him for a little respite away from the school up to our cabin near Yosemite, just to give him a few days to cool down a little bit. And he sat there with his guitar, and at some point he decided that "Three Blind Mice" needed to be a concerto. So he sat there totally and completely transfixed at that guitar, trying different variations, trying to make something out of that simple melody. And he just pursued it with such single-minded conviction. That's how intense he was about anything that he did. And if Pat was having seizures or anything during the time that he was at GIT, he wasn't sharing any of that. He'd just explain that he had a problem that he was working with. He was not one for complaining. He was very quiet about it. I guess he had been to doctors. And I knew something was wrong, but I didn't know what. And then one day he said, "Pat, I gotta go home. I gotta have surgery. " And then he left.

Just as Pat had to pack up and leave, a group of advanced students came to me. They were devastated and ready to leave the school. They said, "Look, we came here for Pat." They cared about the curriculum, but they cared more about Pat. So when Pat left, these students came to me and said, "We're gonna drop out." Fortunately, I was able to get Larry Carlton to take Pat's place, and that seemed to satisfy the students somewhat. But as I say, at the beginning, I was thrilled beyond words at Pat's presence at the school. And the lasting impact that he had on the students. He, like some of the other greats that were in the school, made a profound impact on their lives. He got them inspired, and their lives were dedicated to music because of Pat and some of the others.

Pat was a mystical person and came from a world of mysticism. He was deep beyond his music . . . to his spiritual connection to the music of the universe. Geniuses like that are messengers from god. They have that gift, that connection with the source of the divine. I believe that about these great ones. They aren't just great by accident. They're tuned in like a radio to say or do or be anything—just a transmitter of invisible airwaves passing through them. I looked at Pat as one of those kind of figures. Music just flowed into him and out through his fingers.

10

Recovery and Return

I was like a zombie for the remainder of 1980, following the surgery. In fact, I was disoriented for years to come. It wasn't until 1999 that a greater purification began to go into function. But through 1980, it gradually began to unfold in terms of so-called recovery, though I can't refer to it as recovery. I think transformation is a better term. Because it's neither greater nor lesser. There's a compression of all the side angles that are within the future and the past—dependence on the past through experience, and hope, and looking for a target for a specific type of future were the original intentions, the original belief. And then after the operation, maybe those two things—dependence on the past and hope in the future—resided in that part of the brain that was dissected and removed. But whatever was left was "Now"; it had no interest in the future or in the past, and that's where transformation began to take place.

After arriving at my parents' home, my father began taking me initially to different facilities for recovery, and they were issuing all kinds of antidepressants. It was the same old syndrome. Once again, the chemists moved in and made a living on it.

I then was put into two different hospitals. The first one was a very expensive hospital, an extension of Pennsylvania Hospital in West Philadelphia. And what it seemed to be was almost like a mansion. When you walked up this stairway, you'd get to this second floor and there would be therapists there on the staff, almost like nurses. And the community was a body of individuals that I was brought in to be included among, the patients. It was like a club of wealthy people, and yet I knew I wasn't wealthy. That seemed clear to me.

I received electroshock therapy at that first place, which was not the first time for me. I had been in a locked ward, receiving electroshock treatments, when my first wife, Geri, decided to divorce me, a couple of years before the inevitable surgeries that robbed me of my memory. I also received shock treatments at the second hospital that I went to. The second place was the opposite of the first—it was poor in every way. It was a city-supported facility for those who couldn't afford something better. It was the Einstein Hospital at Fourth and Reed; that building is now abandoned. The entire structure, an elaborate, extensive, one-square-block building, it's now a haunted house, in a yard covered with weeds and a metal fence surrounding it.

I remember in that second place, that moderate facility, the late Michael Hedges and Phil Fallo came to visit me. Michael brought a guitar with him and played for me, trying to get me to reestablish its significance. But how could you reestablish the significance of something that is just momentarily entertaining but having nothing to do with the reality that surrounded you? So although he was well meaning in his gesture, there was no chance of establishing that. It was enticing to want to leave with them, but not because I had an interest in their music. It was strictly because I wanted to get out of a locked ward. Deep inside I was screaming, "Get me the hell outta here!"

The third place I went to was a place where you went and got refills of medication that you relied on—in other words, that you were addicted to. And that was a place here in South Philadelphia not far from my parents' house. That place no longer exists, either. I think it's now a Cambodian church. Mickey was by no means wealthy. But he had some money. And I had some money, too, which was left over from all the work prior to the operations. So there was a margin of income, too, that was established but I don't think it lasted very long, in terms of the costs of neurosurgery and everything that goes with it.

Meanwhile, Dad was busy trying his best to jog my memory by playing my old records downstairs over and over again. I would lie in my bed upstairs and hear them seep through the walls and the floor, a reminder of something that I had no idea that I was supposed to be anymore, or that I ever was. Finally, the conditions that began to take their toll upon me were so jagged and so negative and so overwhelming that the guitar became a medication once again, a place to reside within and lose myself within, like it had been the first time. But for a different reason now. It manifested in a different way in terms of appearance—just a different mask this time. The first time I picked up guitar was to get closer to my father and also to establish something of value, something of meaning that I could be admired for. Now, what does that really have to do with the nature of humanity, of the human experience, of life, consciousness, enlightenment?

But the more I played it, the more it became alive and functional. The ability to play the guitar was always there but was latent. It came down to wanting to use it, to give it significance. It's like the guitar said to me, "What do you want to do with me?"

I started little by little, just feeling it out with minute explorations. It was a process of sitting there and slowly but surely adding one note at a time to what would happen next after totally absorbing the enjoyment of the simplicity of a couple of notes. Eventually I wanted to extend it and stretch it longer and longer and longer, so I didn't have to go back to the pain of the depressive state of limbo, nothingness, no interest in the outside, no interest in anything that I saw around me . . . no interest in a career, no interest in parents who were slowly dying right before my eyes.

As I continued to work out things on the instrument, flashes of memory and muscle memory would gradually come flooding back to me—shapes on the fingerboard, different stairways to different rooms in the house. There are secret doorways that only you know about in the house, and you go there because it's pleasurable to do so. And that's how you remember how to play; you remember the pleasure of it.

John Valentino Remembers: I drove Pat's parents, Mickey and Gene, to the hospital the day that Pat opened his eyes after his surgery. Pat was in pretty bad shape at that point. He couldn't talk when he opened his eyes. After a surgery like that, nobody comes out talking. He opened his eyes, he shook his head . . . nothing was said. The most he could do at that point was blink his eyes. But you knew he was a fighter. I mean, Pat's had nine lives. Mickey was always very proud of Pat, but during those periods after the surgery he was very frustrated, because he wanted Pat to get out there and play again. He was always pushing him: "Get out there and do your thing! Don't sit home!" Because Pat wasn't playing in public at all then.

John Mulhern Remembers: When I came back to Philly after Pat's surgery, he still had bandages on his head and was a little bald. I didn't know if he didn't want to see me or he didn't recognize me . . . I mean, he forgot a lot of stuff. But I got a call from Mickey and he said, "Why don't you come over and get together and play a little bit for Pat, 'cause he won't play his guitar. He just walks by it and won't even look at it. Maybe you can come over and play him some of the stuff and just hang out like you used to." Of course, Mickey was very concerned that Pat would never play guitar again. He said, "He looks at it, but he doesn't play it. He doesn't do anything!"

I had been in Atlantic City and had gotten a job as house guitar player in the orchestra at the Golden Nugget, so I was busy playing like six nights a week. But I drove to Philly on my day off and went over to Mickey's house to see Pat. I brought along this book of guitar exercises that I used to practice with Pat when we were out in Los Angeles together. And I remember he would get pissed at me because I would do these things as a major seventh instead of a minor ninth. He would say, "Why don't you do it the way I taught you how to play it?" And I'd say, "Because I don't hear that way. I hear major, you hear minor. I hear happy, you hear sad."

So now I'm over at Pat's house and I'm going through this book of exercises, and when I played that major-seventh chord, it triggered something for Pat. He looked at me and said, "Move over!" And he picked up his guitar and started playing again. And it was amazing. And as soon as Mickey heard the music, he came upstairs and saw Pat playing again and then shouted downstairs to Pat's mom, "You better put on some pasta! It looks like they are going to be a while." I spent the next couple of days transcribing and working with Pat. He'd play, and I'd write. And since I write slower than Pat, once he really got in a groove he would play *and* write. The relentless Martino drive was back! It was like I had the key for him to start playing again and I turned the ignition. Playing that major-seventh chord just opened up a door for him that had been closed. I was the apprentice who helped the master at the time he needed help.

One of the first songs that I wrote during this period was on a C-major scale, which is something that I never did. I never played like that. And it sounded like Bach. The piece was unusually bright-sounding, and that's what I was looking for at the time—some brightness to shine on the sheer gloom of my existence. Of course, what I was beginning to play on the guitar then had nothing to do with jazz. And that was the next confrontation. Suddenly, from all the things that were giving me a saving grace, the question always came back again and again: "When are you going to put a group together?" And in silence within me, I was yelling, "What does that have to do with this? Why do I have to stop doing this to do that, to be something like they tell me I used to be?" And that was painful, very painful.

Rik Jonna Remembers: While he was recovering after his surgery, Pat found solace in working with Letraset graphics and Mac computers and writing in his journals. Many of his activities countered the debilitating effects of depression. He invested a great deal of time in the art of calligraphy. It was then that his beautiful penmanship evolved and the distinct and graceful Pat Martino signature was developed. Pat made me copies of many graphics he had created on his Mac, including, to name a few, "Tritone Inversions," "Modes," "Organization of Strings," "Numerical Junction," "12 Keys to Heaven," the Azzara logo, and "Alphabetical Junction," which his Coltrane-inspired composition "Think Tank" was based on. There were also several journals beautifully written and filled with his own personal thoughts. Pat experienced therapeutic benefits from writing. As I understood it, he could take control with a pen, overcoming the sense of powerlessness that he was experiencing from his illness in the recovering stages. And he wrote about what was important to him at the time—mortality, faith, relationships, and other deep topics. I also recall that for Mickey, Pat's illness and recovering periods were extremely difficult to deal with. We spoke regularly, and he often wondered what to do in an effort to reignite Pat's interest in the guitar.

Chas Marcarelli Remembers: I met Pat in Philadelphia in the early 1970s, and we became really good friends. Then in 1974, I moved to L.A., was playing drums out there and living in Venice Beach, but Pat and I stayed in touch. He actually came out there with a group he had at the time with Anton Fig on drums, Jeff Berlin on bass, Bob Hanlon on saxophone, and Gil Goldstein on keyboards. They played at the Lighthouse in Hermosa Beach, and after the gig Pat and I ended up hanging out together. When I moved back to Philly in 1980, I called his house and spoke to his dad. And Mickey said, "Pat's had surgery. He had to get rushed back here, and he's in Pennsylvania Hospital." So I went down there to visit him in the hospital, and then when he got out I'd go visit him at his parents' home. As Pat began recuperating, I would go for walks with him. I would get him out of the house, because I know that the best thing to get out of depression is to be active, and Pat would get depressed at times. Eventually we began working on music together, with me on percussion and him on guitar, just getting him active.

In the spring of 1981, I was at Pat's place when I received a call from Jeff Rhodes, who wanted me for a gig at a jazz club out in some town called Media, Pennsylvania. He was also looking for a guitarist, and I was thinking about recommending Ed McFadden, whom I had played with years earlier. But I asked Pat if he wanted to do the gig. I told him, "Ah, you don't want to do this, Pat. You'd have to read out of a Real Book or fake book. Do you think you could accept that challenge?" That's all you have to do is put a challenge in front of Pat. So he thought about it for a moment and then he said, "I think I might have eyes for that." So we went out to this club about a half hour outside of Philly and played. Pat read the gig down from a Real Book, and he was smokin'!—just playing his butt off. And that gig went so well it made him start wanting to play again. Later on I got a call from Jeff Rhodes about another gig, this time backing a vocalist named Mary Kay Duffy, who had a gig in Cape May at a place called the Shire. So we started working there during the summer of 1982, playing standards behind Mary Kay. The band was me, Pat, and Jeff Rhodes, and the bass player was either Gerald Veasley or Chico Huff. Pat went under the name Azzara, but that lasted just a weekend, because word got out and people started coming from all over the East Coast to see him play; from New York down to the Carolinas. The place was packed at that point, and the singer was getting a little bit ticked off because it was really her gig. But she understood that it was a treat for a lot of people because they had not seen Pat in that kind of an intimate situation in years. He had not been playing around hardly at all.

We had some gigs after that at Grendel's Lair in Philly and a couple of other places. Shortly after, we hooked up with a bassist named John Hart and a trumpeter named Al Moretti. Pat especially liked the way Al played, and he also liked how the trumpet and flugelhorn blended with guitar. We started rehearsing Pat's original material and putting some different feels on it—more contemporary-sounding material. And that's what we ended up playing when we went back to play at the Shire during the summers of 1983 and 1984. Then we played at the Bottom Line in New York City in October of 1984. It was a big event. We opened for Stanley Clark's band, and I remember seeing Al Di Meola and Jaco Pastorius out there in the audience that night. That was actually supposed to be a live album, but Pat's manager at the time, Bob Devere, couldn't come to terms on that with Joe Fields at Muse. Eventually we changed the name of the group to Pat Martino and Friends.

We were supposed to play at the Shire in Cape May again the summer of 1985, but there was some kind of problem with Pat. We came down to the club and set up all our equipment, and Marc Dicozzio, for whatever reason, did not bring his Yamaha keyboard. He brought something else, and it pissed Pat off. So he just left, and we played the gig without him. Pat looked under duress, big-time. I think he was going through some stressful things at that time with his second wife, Tina. There was definitely some hassle going on there.

What I now remember . . . at that time, first and foremost, I still owed Joe Fields [head of Muse Records] two albums. And I believe that Joe constantly contacted my father to see how I was doing while recuperating at my parents' house. Of course, I would have never believed that Joe even cared about how I was doing. Joe just wanted to get these two albums from me. And then Steve Getz came into my life with an interest. He was running Fat Tuesday's nightclub on Third Avenue and Seventeenth Street. It's where Les Paul played every Monday night prior to his longstanding engagement at the Iridium. So my plan was to quickly record a live album at Fat Tuesday's, strictly a bebop album, and deliver it to Joe Fields at Muse Records. The Bottom Line engagement I had done in October 1984 was something else. I think my intentions there were to go in the direction of Joyous Lake again, but first I had to get those two albums done to be able to do that. Mom and Dad were still alive then. But it was a very confusing period of time. Maybe it was an escape, in a way, from the responsibility to put everything down and take care of them in their final years, which I actually did later. But in early 1987, I was focused on preparing the material that would eventually come out on the Muse album *The Return*.

When I did the Fat Tuesday's engagement with Joey Baron on drums and Steve LaSpina on bass, my father came down one night and got together with a gentleman who used to be his best friend. But they'd had a falling-out and hadn't spoken to each other for decades. And this gentleman, Mike Capuano, was my first manager when I was a little boy at the age of twelve. It was a reunion for them . . . very surrealistic for me. It brought me back to stages of childhood. I don't remember much about that Fat Tuesday's gig. I don't remember how long the engagement was or how many days we recorded. The record came out, and I haven't listened to it since.

Joey Baron Remembers: I believe at the time that we did *The Return*, Pat had contractual obligations to fulfill with Muse Records. I remember Pat telling us that he was interested in closing that chapter, as he put it. So there wasn't a whole lot of planning for that recording. I think for him it was an opportunity to rid himself of this thing. And to my understanding, that's why the record came when it did. I had actually met and played with Pat some years before that, in 1979. I was living in Los Angeles at the time, and he was teaching at the Guitar Institute of Technology in Hollywood. I remember we got together one afternoon in the school auditorium with Carl Schroeder on piano and Bob Magnusson on bass, me on drums, and we recorded some music that he wanted to do at the time. And it was a thrill for me. Growing up in Richmond, Virginia, I would listen to those records he did with Willis "Gator Tail" Jackson. I just wore the grooves off of *Live Action*. Those were some of the first records that really inspired me, just from a sheer directness of feeling that Pat generated, that the whole Willis Jackson band generated. Anyway, at some point when we were playing Pat's music in that auditorium, Schroeder started playing that riff from "Rock Candy," and Pat jumped on that shit like white on rice. It was one of those moments when you just have to smile. That was my introduction to Pat.

I ended up moving to New York shortly after that and didn't see him again until he called me to do some gigs around the time of that live recording we did at Fat Tuesday's. As far as Pat's playing during that week at Fat Tuesday's, I think he was getting used to playing out again at that point. We would play his songs and maybe the A section would happen once, maybe more than once . . . maybe the memory thing was still not completely together for him. But for me it was like, "Wow, okay! It's a surprise every time!" It added an element into the playing that actually made it a lot of fun. You had to really listen on that gig with Pat. I do anyhow, but you really had to be on your toes that week at Fat Tuesday's.

The week after that Fat Tuesday's gig, we played at an engagement at Ethel's Place in Baltimore with Harvie S. on bass. And I remember one night Pat had a nosebleed. He was wearing a white suit, and we were playing . . . and suddenly I see him leaning his head back and I'm thinking, "Wow, he's in the zone!" And then I realized he had a serious nosebleed, so we took a break. It turned out he couldn't really play the second set, so he got up there on the stage and said, "I want to talk about life and what a privilege it is to have one, because I almost lost mine." And then he went into this incredibly amazing talk. The club owner, of course, was fucking horrified. But it was an amazing evening.

To be honest, I wasn't that crazy about *The Return*. I'm not sure that anybody was. I mean, it was a nice thing to see a documentation of, "Yeah, Pat's alive and well and he's playing." But I don't think it really represented him that well. But in terms of the big picture, I think it was great that it came out, because it kept his name out there at that period. And maybe it helped provide a launching pad for his resurgence. He's just inspired so many people since then.

Some months after we recorded *The Return*, I was invited through Mark Koch, an earlier student of mine, to participate in a symposium at Duquesne University in Pittsburgh. And a very close friend of mine, Geno White, was with me as an intermediary to carry heavy equipment and help me get to the destination, because I still was not fit or able, and still on medication, as well. The symposium was scheduled to be with myself, saxophonist Eric Kloss, and guitarist Emily Remler. And the night before, I was staying at the house of Bill and Lynn Purse. Bill was the head of the guitar department of Duquesne University. Geno was sleeping downstairs on the couch; I was upstairs in the guest room in bed. Suddenly, I noticed something as I was lying down. I felt fluid in my throat while I was breathing. So I got up out of bed, went to the bathroom sniffling, looked in the mirror, and saw blood coming down my face. I wiped it off and got some tissue paper, placed it in my nostril to try to dry it. I took the paper out and it was soaked with my blood, and I couldn't stop it. I tried everything to stop it, so much so that again I reached this state of mind that was like, "Holy shit, here we go again!" No matter what I tried, it didn't work. I wound up giving up and lay down in bed, resigned to die that evening.

At some point I put my leg over the side of the bed while lying on my back—maybe it was the part of me that wanted to survive—and with my bare foot I weakly tapped on the floor. Geno heard it downstairs. He awoke and came upstairs. I was covered in blood. And I said, "Geno, call an ambulance. I don't think I can make it." So he called an ambulance, and two cops came upstairs along with the paramedics. They stood at the side of the bed, and this one older cop said to me, "Do you want us to take you to the hospital? The paramedics can't do anything until you tell them they can." I said nothing. And the older man said again, "Hey, look, let me tell you something, man. We don't have time to waste with your problems here. Either you wanna go, or you don't. What the fuck do you wanna do?" And I said weakly, "Take me."

They took me to this hospital . . . it was on the weekend, a Saturday. And there were no specialists in the hospital, only interns were there. And they began to try to cauterize the vessel that was bleeding. Actually, by the time I got to the hospital, the blood that was inside of me was almost the size of a grapefruit in a big clot that eventually came out. And I sat in this chair while they were trying to cauterize, inefficiently—yet I didn't feel the pain, because of having gone through so much of it that by that time I was numb. It's hard to compete with that level of confrontation in crisis mode. Many things have taken place that have led me to this state. I have no idea what the events that are yet to come shall be. But at the same time, my only reality is now. That's why I don't succumb to any difficulties or uncomfortable reminders of these descriptions, because they don't exist.

Geno White Remembers: I heard this tapping sound on the ceiling that woke me up at three or four in the morning. So I ran up to Pat's room, and he was just lying there hemorrhaging out of his nose. The whole scene was just incredibly intense. I was never in the war or anything, but it was like being in Vietnam or something, one guy helping a wounded soldier on the battlefield. Because Pat was in such bad shape. Eventually, the ambulance came, and we actually went to three different hospitals that night before they would take Pat. At the third hospital, where they took him, they didn't have room, so we got pulled into a utility room, basically a big closet. Pat was sitting there, and off the light in the ceiling they hung an IV thing. I was left alone with Pat for an hour, holding one of those kidney-shaped cups under his nose. All this blood's coming out, and I'm emptying it and he's filling it up again. Finally, the doctors came in and they wheeled him out. And when they cauterized his nose, it smelled like a slaughterhouse. So we got the hell out of there the next day.

Between 1987 and 1998, I worked on something I did privately here at home called *Seven Sketches*. It was an orchestral work performed on a Roland GR-707 guitar synthesizer in MIDI with a Korg keyboard and using a sequence system called Vision. This is what I was doing during my period of recovery, and it represents one of the abstract directions I was moving in compositionally. Of course, at that time the backlash was, "When are you going to play something like you used to play, that you can go out and perform? You can't do anything like this live." And yet it was one of the most creative and productive periods I can remember, compositionally. So this was a period of dilemma. Nevertheless, it was a very significant period of time in my experience.

This happened after *The Return* [recorded live at Fat Tuesday's in February 1987], but of course this music had absolutely nothing to do with the music heard on *The Return*. It was strictly personal music and was a direct result of exposure to the music of Elliott Carter as well as a manifestation of the turmoil that I was experiencing in my life at the time. *The Return* had come about as another opportunity to move into an act of career once again—to ignite it. And when you do that, it's impossible to take into consideration all the things you are committed to. I had been committed to privacy, above all. I was still in recluse mode. And it was part of the demand that came from *The Return* to prove to the public that I could still play the guitar when I was in the midst of an orchestral work. My mind was elsewhere. There were just many, many things involved in that period of time that remained outside of my career. In fact, they were just so abstract comparatively that they were static on that career and on those directions.

The material that I threw together quickly under the pressure of getting involved with Joe Fields again to record *The Return* for Muse Records brought me into a situation that was so demanding that it immediately phased out all of the ecstatic creative, productive, positive, stimulating experiences that were the fuel that was carrying me through these suffering stages of that recovery. Suddenly, now I was involved with responsibility, to come up with something that was going to fit that particular industrial machine, Muse Records. And that's what brought about *The Return*. It was Steve Getz at Fat Tuesday's who presented the opportunity, and it was Joel Chriss, whom I was subjectively being assisted by for bookings, who ignited that opportunity, which was an excellent thing.

When I was done with that project, my mother was still alive. But my main support was, in a sense, beginning to crumble to pieces, because she was dying. She was in her last stages of strength. She was bedridden. When Mom passed away in 1989, that interrupted my career. At that point, my responsibility was to assist Dad. That became my top priority. I no longer had the time to follow up on what was a necessity for promoting and performing on a regular basis. And my dad was so sad that she was gone, I don't think he wanted to live anymore. What I was trying to do at that point was to be there for him. I started investing in a wardrobe for him under the impression that we would go out together and he would come out of the fog that he was in. He was so deeply depressed.

During the period of time that I was working on *Seven Sketches*, Pop passed away. It was then my responsibility to handle all of the loose ends regarding the possessions, the deathbed wills, along with other facets of the so-called estate. I was stuck with lawyers and all of the certificates and documents, city hall, the taxes, and everything else that goes with how cities make money on death. Of course, whenever I did something like *Seven Sketches*, there was always someone, on the basis of friendship, who took it as a warning that it was a deviation into directions that would prove to be negative in terms of my ongoing continuity as a jazz guitarist. So there was always that red flag or that stop sign that remained, in a sense. So while *Seven Sketches* was seen as a deterrent by some, this music was fulfilling another side of what wasn't expressed anywhere else. It was honest expression, no more than that.

Naturally, no record company was interested in releasing it. In fact, everyone just said things like, "You're not going put *that* out. That's not even jazz. You can't make any money with *that*." Or I also heard, "Don't you play guitar anymore?" These were many of the things that were being discussed by people with regard to my career. But I was in a state of here and now, which could care less about recordings or upcoming engagements.

The most profound aspect of it all, definitively during this period, was the peeling off of my parents as a shield, comfortably blocking responsibilities on my behalf. I'd had the opportunity to reside with them, and they honestly took care of me while I was there to recover. And then that recovery became an addiction, to some degree. It became an easy way to say, "I don't have to do that anymore—I don't have to learn how to play guitar again." But then my parents started dying; it was almost over. There was no longer any more time to recover. Now it was, "What are you going to do with *this*? How can you handle *this*? Why are you here? They need you. Are you here for them to help you recover? What about them?"

I couldn't take that. I couldn't accept that. So I began to put down my own recovery as an excuse—put it aside and begin to see it as an interruption in what was really of top importance to me, which was my love for both of them. So now it was time for me to take that clothing off and put the outer armor back on. I began to get socially active and do everything I possibly could to make this happen in a way that wouldn't be too hard for them. Eventually, after Dad's departure, to take care of his funeral, to take care of the interaction of the surrounding family—these were things that gave me no opportunity to recover anymore. Recovery was done. Actually, in my opinion, it was done long before then.

While I was in the midst of all the loose ends with regard to the estate and all of his belongings, I would go out at night and get a glass of wine, sit at the bar at different places, and just think, just relax after the day of legalities and getting together with the accountant and people about the will and everything else that went with it. One night I went to a place in Philadelphia and there was a local group playing, and Jim Ridl was in this group. It was a terrible-sounding piano, but terrible piano or not, Jim was exceptional! And there I was, sitting at the bar wanting to play, because that's what happens when you hear the real thing. Even if the group is not *it*, but somebody in the group is *it*, you're still affected by it. It's a power that is not based on the group, it's based on itself. It's a power in itself. It's a presence of itself no matter whom it's using to facilitate its intentions.

Well, its intentions were successful on this night. It made me want to play with this guy. So I took his number that night, and when the time came, I called him and said, "Listen, I'd like to get together and rehearse some material. I'm going to record." And that's when we did *Interchange*. We had Marc Johnson on bass, and for drums I got my old friend Sherman Ferguson, who had played on *Desperado, Live!* and *Consciousness*. It was a great group, and it was especially rewarding to play with Jim Ridl, who is quite a significant player. There's something about him that immediately activates respect from other players. You've got to seriously play if you want to play with Jim. It's an excellent challenge.

Jim Ridl Remembers: I was playing this little jazz club in Philly in September 1992 when Pat happened to come in. After our set, I had a nice conversation with him; he liked my playing, and we exchanged numbers. Within one or two months, I went over to his home in South Philly and we started playing together. I don't think he was doing any playing out at the time. We got together to play through this music, just as duets, and the connection felt really strong. Yeah, definitely a chemistry was there from the beginning. And then I recorded with him in March of 1994. That was Interchange.

I continued to play with Pat off and on for ten years, from 1994 to 2004. I played quartets with him, and then there was a good chunk of it that was duets. Pat always played at such a high level, but over the course of ten years it seemed like his playing became more focused. Things in his personal life were getting better, and he was stepping out into the public and getting recognized by people—critics and the industry—getting signed by Blue Note, things like that. I think that had a very positive effect on him. And meeting Ayako had a huge effect on him, I think, just in terms of him feeling better. When I first met him, he was kind of on his own; he wasn't in a relationship with anybody. He was very nice to me, but he was also a little bit of a darker persona. But when Pat met Ayako, all of a sudden he fell in love again and it was just like a light bulb turned on inside of him and you saw some light emanating from him. So I feel like during the ten years that I played with Pat, his playing got on a much stronger path and more of his personality flowed through his instrument. Of course, one of his trademarks has always been his tempo playing—these constant lines of his. But his ballad playing, I think, deepened. I've always been so greatly moved by his ballad playing. There's more space, but there's a thing that he gets to where he's like a really old soul when he's playing. I think he's probably had that from an early age. I always got that sense from playing with him. He goes to a deeper place on ballads.

Though I was back performing regularly, I was still somewhat plagued by memory loss. I remember playing at the Blue Note in New York City to a packed house, and at the end of the performance I went upstairs to the dressing room. I went into the restroom and took a dry towel to wipe the perspiration off and just refresh myself. And when I came out of the restroom and into the dressing room there were two gentlemen standing there—Joe Pesci and Tommy DeVito, Joe's personal manager. They had been standing there waiting for me to come out, and when I came out, Pesci gave me a few compliments about the show. Then there was a pause and he said, "You don't remember me, do you? You don't know who I am." And I said, "Of course I know who you are. I've enjoyed quite a number of your films—*My Cousin Vinny, Goodfellas, Raging Bull.*" And he stopped me and said, "No, it has nothing to do with that. You don't remember ME, do you?"

I was bewildered by this and told him, "I don't understand what you're referring to." And he said, "I'm going to tell you what you used to drink back in 1963 at Small's Paradise." And he mentioned the cordial that I used to drink when I was at Small's with Willis Jackson up in Harlem, when I was a teenager. And the moment he described the drink, a series of images appeared in my mind. I flashed back to Small's Paradise; I remembered the bartender and the stage and the position of the instruments that remained on the bandstand in between sets. I remembered walking over to the bar and ordering that drink. And then I remembered Joe Pesci, who at that time was a vocalist/guitarist singing at a lounge on Route 46 in northern Jersey right outside New York City. And after their sets finished, they would come into New York to hang out at Small's and similar places, because we used to play there until four a.m. Joe and I had actually become close friends way back then, but I had forgotten all about that—until he used that word, the name of the drink, which was the trigger for me to reclaim those memories.

11

Rebounding on Blue Note

By the end of 1995, the invitation came to me from Bruce Lundvall, the president of Blue Note Records, to sign with the label and join their roster. Naturally, the opportunity to record on a label that had an entourage of countless historical individuals was exciting. Blue Note, to me personally, had been a target for quite some time, just like all the record labels were targets—career-oriented, professional targets. To me, it was a significant achievement to have the opportunity to work with Blue Note at the highest level of ethics and professional interaction. It was almost a notch on the handle of your gun, so to speak. That's what it meant to me. And I think that feeling was a leftover since childhood.

At the time that I joined Blue Note, of course, the essence of what that originally meant kind of evaporated due to a reorganization of perspectives. Definition changed after the operations. And although it didn't have the same meaning to me in terms of true value, it still resided within that part of me that was hungry for it. So I proceeded accordingly.

My first interaction with the label, in terms of recording projects, was *All Sides Now*. It was explained to me by the producers of that particular project [Bill Milkowski and Matt Resnicoff] that it would be a kind of "tribute recording" and would involve the necessity of doing tracks with different artists in different cities throughout the country, and that the whole process would take several months to complete. This was in conflict with my own intentions at the time. It was secondary to what I had planned for Blue Note, and it was a really time-consuming event or series of events.

Prior to this project, my choice of personnel and engagements to perform was selective in a very intense way. Suddenly having to adapt to situations that I was not prone to feel comfortable in was very painful. And in the end, that's what came about. And to be honest, it reminded me of the operations. It produced itself like a surrealistic extension of the same dilemma—something that the victim can never get out of. It just manifests in different masks again and again, like a catch-22. So in many ways it was an impossible situation, but it was a challenge. And there's something inside me that on a moment's notice when something comes up, I'll say, "Yeah, I'll accept that challenge." Again, the fire . . . the temperance. The flame and the sword placed in the flame. There's something that forms callous from that experience, and then the pain is not as excruciating in the future. So it's a necessity for the elongation to be able to confront this again and again and again with less complaint.

So I made the adjustment, gathered up the courage to take it as it was and to have faith in any situation that I found myself in . . . to trust and to go through that and then on the other side of it to feel stronger by doing the best I could under the very trying circumstances. I did enjoy some of the personal interactions with the individuals who participated in that *All Sides Now* project. And most of all, I continued to learn more about my "self."

Those are always some of the most significant things in these recording experiences. The records themselves, they're like photographs in a catalog. To me, personally, they have no value. But interacting with people like Mike Stern, Michael Hedges, and Les Paul was very rewarding to me. Les, of course, I had a longstanding history with, going back to 1956 when my father took me to see him and Mary Ford perform at the Steel Pier in Atlantic City when I was twelve years old and I played his guitar for him. And Michael Hedges had come with Phil Fallo to see me in the hospital shortly after my brain surgery in 1980, and he played his guitar for me then in the hospital. So that was something in itself, to see that relationship culminate in his participation in this project.

Musically, there were some very satisfying moments to come out of this project. The track with Les ["I'm Confessin' (That I Love You)"] is a classic. And the duet with Cassandra Wilson [on Joni Mitchell's "Both Sides Now"] was a precious moment. The interactions and intentions of all the players involved on that project were very genuine. Nonetheless, I was very eager to move in a completely different direction. And I did precisely that shortly after completing *All Sides Now* by accepting an invitation to go San Francisco and record with some musicians for what was described to me as a world-music session. The album was called *Fire Dance*. The project itself was initiated when I received a phone call from the flutist Peter Bloch, inviting me to partake in this particular session. He sent me some material he had just finished recording that reminded me of Oregon. It was world music, but also fusion at the same time. Due to my lack of courage at that time, I gave him a big price, hoping he would turn down the offer, but he said, "No sweat. It's all yours."

So then I had to go out to San Francisco and get involved in this session with the tabla master Zakir Hussain and other players of that caliber. The violinist on the session, Illya Rayman, was from Moscow, and there was also Habib Khan on sitar. So my wife Aya and I went out there. And we were at a difficult period of time when we were still adjusting to the demands of our relationship . . . her coming from the Far East and me coming from South Philadelphia, our differing cultures, and the significance of our perspectives and how we view and determine and define everything. We were at a stage in our relationship that was very new and very demanding as opposed to now, where we're both so in balance with each other.

At the session, I immediately found rapport with Zakir. We really hit it off from the get-go. It was just violin, guitar, tablas, sitar, and alto flute, and we were interacting on these motifs based on northern Indian music. Then at some point I said to Peter Bloch, "What about me laying down some second guitar tracks so I have something with changes to play against?" And the moment I did that, suddenly the entire structure of the project changed. All the music took a new direction and began to form in quite a different way. It's a very significant record, a beautiful session. And it very much reminds me of *Baiyina,* which I had recorded back in 1968. So I see them as almost a cyclic orbit in a very long time spiral . . . they come around years and years later. And between *Baiyina* in 1968 and *Fire Dance* in 1997, it took nearly thirty years for that cycle to come back around. By then, I was ready to undertake my next Blue Note recording.

> ***Kirk Yano Remembers:*** Pat's manager Joe Donofrio and I began working with Pat in 1997, sometime after *All Sides Now* had come out. Originally Joe and I went to Philly to talk to Pat about the next record he was going to do on Blue Note. He was talking about getting Ron Carter and some other musicians and just doing a record of standards, but I said to him, "Pat, you really should tie in more with the younger people that you brought in back when you were on Warner Bros. You should go find the guys from *Joyous Lake*." And three days later he calls to tell us that he found Delmar Brown and Kenwood Dennard. And then he was thinking of bringing in a young sax player he liked, Eric Alexander. He asked me about bass players, and I suggested

James Genus. And that's how the lineup for that *Stone Blue* record came about.

Joe Donofrio Remembers: In 1977, Pat was in need of artist management, and my friend John Mulhern, who was also very close with Pat, thought I might be able to help him. This was right after *All Sides Now*, so John arranged for us to get together and talk. We met at the Brigantine Diner near Atlantic City. Pat told me the whole story about what had happened with *All Sides Now*. He seemed very agitated, and I could tell that there was some turmoil going on in his life. But listening to him was captivating. After about an hour of hearing his stories, I said to him, "Pat, if you want, I'll try to help you. I can't promise you anything. I don't know if I can help you or not. But if you want to try this, I'll put one year in. No obligation but the one year. We'll just see where it goes, and then anything within that year, if either one of us wants to go in another direction, let's just talk about it. No problem. But I would have to have you sign something for one year."

Pat didn't really have a manager all during that *All Sides Now* fiasco, though it was clear that he probably needed one. At the time we met, he wasn't working, he wasn't earning, so I guess he needed a booking agent as much as a manager. Anyway, Pat agreed to my proposal, and that began our working relationship. I spent the rest of 1997 trying to put all the puzzle pieces together, trying to learn all about him. I had him send me all his guestbook entries from his website, and I kept reading them over and over again, and he revealed himself in the guestbook, which helped me to better understand him as a person. At that point I also began keeping a daily diary of all my Pat-related work, which I kept up for two years. Then I went to check the band out at Catalina's in Los Angeles, just to familiarize myself with his whole presentation. Finally we signed a contract in January of 1998.

My next move was to meet with Bruce Lundvall. I wanted everyone at Blue Note to feel comfortable with him. Whatever acrimony may have come up during the *All Sides Now* project, I wanted to assure them, "It's changed. Pat has someone representing him now." When I went into Blue Note for my first meeting with Lundvall, he told me Michael Cuscuna was going to produce it. And I said, "No problem, but I'd like to have our own engineer," because I wanted to have someone in our own corner, so to speak. And I told him I wanted Kirk Yano, whom I knew from Cleveland. Kirk had moved to New York and was working around town. Bruce asked for his bio and credits, and about a week later he called to say, "You know, I like this guy. You can use him." And that's when we began to work on the *Stone Blue* project.

[The following is from Pat Martino's liner notes to 1998's *Stone Blue*]: For me, it has always been important to connect with the past, the present and the future in terms of my own creative intake as well as output—to be forced into a cohesive form of intelligible evolution. In the initial preparations for this album, other ideas were in play. Had they been put into effect, a totally different album would have resulted. *Stone Blue* would not have come about. What did bring it about was the important reunion of a number of powerfully gifted people with whom I've shared experiences in the past, as well as others in the present, who were just as necessary to the realization of this project. And we started recording on a very special date—Valentine's Day! The music itself came about in a way similar to the original beginnings of *Joyous Lake*, except this time with much more experience under our collective belts. Each of *Stone Blue*'s songs holds a personal meaning, a touch of importance, a time to remember—fantastic days with Jack McDuff, unforgettable moments with the late Michael Hedges [who died in a car accident at the end of 1997]; memories as well as continuance shared and enjoyed with Delmar Brown, Kenwood Dennard, and particularly Michael Cuscuna; and connecting with Eric Alexander and James Genus, two great players I first played with on this project.

*Michael Cuscuna (Produer of **Stone Blue**) Remembers:* The sessions themselves [February 14 and 15, 1998] were long and productive. There were logistical problems and stressful moments, but the whole thing seemed like a party at Pat's house on Sunday afternoon. Visitors at a record date can be a serious distraction, but not in this case. People that Pat had known from various decades and far-flung cities showed up with love, encouragement, and respect. It was a lovely series of reunions and subplots that never interfered with the work at hand. And Delmar, who sees solutions where others see problems, was an amazing presence. And the music has its connections. Jack McDuff's signature three-part harmonies on "Mac Tough," Wes Montgomery's octave sound on "With All the People," Monk's twists and Miles's turns on "13 to Go," and Pat Martino's relentless invention as a composer and guitarist throughout. "Joyous Lake" is a rare instance where Pat has gone back to rerecord a tune. It is a tribute to what he, Delmar, and Kenwood shared once and what they are now. It's glancing back and moving forward. (From Cuscuna's liner notes to *Stone Blue*)

At first I had a completely different session in mind for the next Blue Note recording after *All Sides Now*. I had envisioned completely different personnel, but at the last minute I changed my mind and contacted Delmar

Brown and Kenwood Dennard. My intention was to again activate the Joyous Lake band, primarily because there was nothing like it. And twenty-one years later, it was like having your favorite food again after not having it for a long time. The whole concept came about in a period of maybe three weeks, and I wrote all the music at a moment's notice. And the resulting album, *Stone Blue*, remains one of my favorite recordings.

Woody and Delmar, of course, were magical on the sessions. And I really enjoyed stretching together with Eric. I like the sound of Eric and myself in dead unison, hearing the tenor sax and guitar together as one. On the recording was James Genus on bass. He did some gigs with us, but on the majority of the tour, Chulo Gatewood was our bassist. He's just an excellent player. And personality-wise, he was very much like Woody. Between Woody and Chulo and Delmar and Aya, we just partied the whole time on that tour. We really enjoyed each other, like a family, just like it had been back in the 1970s when we initially did *Joyous Lake*.

It was in March of 1999, while touring with the Joyous Lake band on behalf of *Stone Blue,* that I contracted pneumonia while in France. I flew home from Paris, and by the time we reached Philadelphia, I was very ill. The group was due to open at Birdland in New York City in five days, so I immediately went to bed under the impression that I might recover after some rest. Things quickly began to escalate to a degree that caused me to have Aya call an ambulance. I was taken two blocks from my house to the Methodist Hospital. In fact, when the ambulance arrived, they began taking me to another hospital, the Jefferson Hospital at Eleventh and Chestnut. When the paramedics looked at their meters and saw the condition I was in, they said, "No, he's not going to make it there. Let's take him to Methodist, the closest place." It was two blocks instead of twelve blocks or more.

I was in Methodist Hospital for one week, at which time both my arms were black because of the incisions done by personnel there that were clearly incompetent. Then it was decided, "Let's get him out of here," and finally I was taken to Jefferson Hospital. By that time my weight had gone down to seventy-six pounds and I was placed in a plastic encasement for oxygen. They came to the conclusion that they needed to transplant both my lungs and my heart, at which time Aya, for the first time, stepped forward and refused. She and a very close friend, Marian Garfinkel, who at the time was involved in research on carpal tunnel syndrome at Pennsylvania University and was also a formidable yoga instructor, carried me out of Jefferson Hospital and got me back home.

At the time I arrived home, I couldn't even climb the staircase to go to the bathroom on the second floor or go down the stairs to the basement

Cover photo from the album *The Visit* by Manfred Prost, 1972.

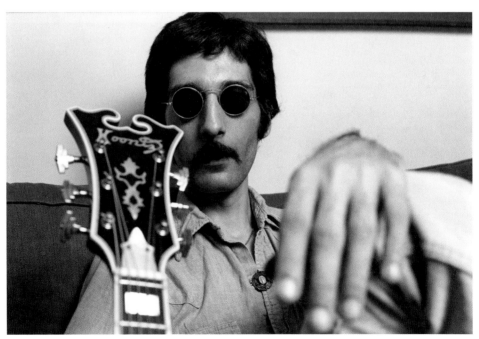

Pat in Powelton Village on Hamilton Street in University City, Philadelphia, circa 1973, with his Sam Koontz guitar.

On stage at George Wein's "Guitar Summit" in Central Park, 1973, with George Benson and Pat Martino.

Warner Bros. contract meeting in 1975, Pat flanked by WB executives Joe Smith (left) and Bob Krasnow (right).

Top: Back cover of *Joyous Lake* album with Delmar Brown (electric keyboards), Mark Leonard (electric bass), and Kenwood Dennard (drums), 1976.

Left: With the Joyous Lake band at "Riviera '76" in France, 1976.

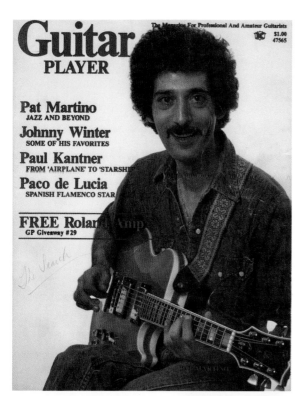

Pat on the cover of *Guitar Player* magazine, 1977.

Pat in 1979 with a student from Corinth, Greece (Vassillis), just prior to the brain operation, holding a double-neck guitar designed by Ovation/Adamas (top neck: E, B, G, D, A, E; bottom neck: E, A, D, G, B, E).

Touring Japan in 1995, when Pat met his wife Ayako Asahi in Tokyo at On Air East.

At a jazz festival in Ravenna, Italy, 1995, with Geno White (center) and unnamed Italian promoter.

In the studio with Les Paul for the *All Sides Now* sessions, circa 1996–97.

With Les Paul on the cover of *DownBeat* magazine, 1997.

In the studio with Joe Pesci. (Pat appeared as a guest artist on Pesci's 1998 recording *Vincent LaGuardia Gambini Sings Just for You.*)

Teaching a master class at the University of the Arts in Philadelphia with his Abe Rivera guitar, 1999.

Pat and Ayako Martino performing together at Chris' Jazz Cafe in Philadelphia, 2009.

Performing on his signature Benedetto guitar at Birdland in New York City, 2010.

bathroom. The only way I could go to the bathroom was in empty gallon water bottles. I was in bad condition, and that came from years of smoking, and at the same time from being subject all my life to the environment where jazz took place. I had been functioning in a cloud of smoke in every nightclub for over thirty years. Along with smoking three packs of cigarettes a day and also smoking grass and hashish, I was being inundated with secondhand smoke to the max in all the nightclubs where I performed. Of course, the upshot of this was that my lungs were destroyed.

Again, this was the condition created. There were times throughout my career in earlier years, like with Jack McDuff and with Don Patterson and Billy James and a number of others, when cocaine was abundant, in terms of use, along with grass and hashish. I never involved myself with needles—heroin or things of that nature. But I did get involved with taking a blow of cocaine before the performance. And it was a rush. And, of course, my dexterity, my technical ability, was magnified with exponentials of aggression because of the intake. Well, that did something to the arteries in my nostrils, and my health in general declined, as well.

But finally, due to my wife's advice, we altered my diet. Aya was very aware of the physical structure, because her father was a doctor. So she was exposed to it in depth when she was growing up in Japan. And as a dietician, she advised me about what foods I should be eating. With her help, I eliminated meat and fish from my diet. It became strictly raw vegetables, fruit, nuts, fiber, at that time as much water as possible, just to cleanse the structure. Meanwhile, Marian taught me some basic, simple techniques of yoga that would expand and stretch my respiratory system. Suddenly, I no longer had to use an inhaler whenever I couldn't breathe, which had been prescribed. Essentially, I had been allowing these chemicals into my body for years. And over the course of four or five months, with the help of both Aya and Marian, I went from 76 pounds to 140 pounds and returned to a much healthier condition. It was definitely a wake-up call.

Joe Donofrio Remembers: For our second project together, and Pat's third on Blue Note, he decided to return to his roots and do an organ-trio recording. Everybody I had ever talked since I started working with Pat seemed to be waiting for this one. I remember running into John Scofield one time at the Blue Note, and the first thing out of his mouth was, "When is Pat going to do an organ record?" So that was what we decided to do after *Stone Blue.* Around that time, Pat participated in a Charles Earland tribute recording at Rudy Van Gelder's studio in Englewood Cliffs, New Jersey. Charles was the organ player Pat started out with, and he had just passed away in December of

1999. This record was for Joe Fields's label HighNote. And while Pat was no fan of Joe Fields at that point, he called me up and said, "I want to do this because I really love Charles. He's the one who got me on the road, and there's a lot of good feelings from that era, so I feel like I want to do it." So I went with Pat and Aya out to Rudy Van Gelder's, and we walked into the studio, and there was Joey DeFrancesco on organ. And Eric Alexander was there, too. Eric had played in Charles Earland's band for a while, and Joey was a musical colleague of Charles's going back many years. So Pat took out his guitar, and right away he connected with Joey musically. They just hit it off on the spot at that session. On the way home, Pat turned to me and said, "Let's make this organ CD with Joey DeFrancesco."

So we got Joey, and we also got Billy Hart on drums. And I thought, instead of rehearse them, let's put them on tour. I had them tour across the country, ending up in Yoshi's in Oakland. And by that time they were really meshing. We recorded six shows in three days there [December 15–17, 2000]. The chemistry between Pat and Joey . . . I was getting goose bumps just standing there watching them work together. And the crowds were crazy that whole week. We had one set where there was like ten to twelve minutes of applause after they finished. And that CD, I think, really helped Pat. *Stone Blue* was good because it kind of got Pat noticed and got him out on the road with a touring band again, but I knew it wasn't going to sell a lot. But *Live at Yoshi's,* man, we got a lot of noise with that. That one sold a gang of records.

The *Live at Yoshi's* record was very memorable for a number of reasons. It received accolades and sold well, but what was more personally rewarding for me was the camaraderie I had with Joey DeFrancesco and Billy Hart. I had played with Billy before, back on the *Exit* sessions with Richard Davis and Gil Goldstein in 1976—again, another cycle had come back around. I had an especially good rapport with Joey on that tour, which is evident from the recording. How could I not? He's such an exceptional artist. As a player, he's just ferocious, in that tradition of Jimmy Smith and all the great Philly organists. Joey is the one, just an incredible player and a lovable person. You wanna put your arms around him . . . which is hard to do. But he's adorable, just great, great people. The same with Billy Hart. That's another thing that is considerably effective with regard to the rapport that takes place on a recording project. There are those professional commitments that get you involved in—projects where there is no rapport, there is no love. It's so commercial, and the attitude is just get in, knock it out, make your money, and run. That's one thing that has always repelled me, and I have tried to avoid having to participate in that kind of situation. But on projects like *Stone Blue* and *Live at Yoshi's,* it was all about love and sharing, respect and rapport.

> **Joe Donofrio Remembers:** Following the success of *Live at Yoshi's,* Bruce Lundvall suggested using some of the artists on the Blue Note roster for Pat's next recording. So we got Joe Lovano and Gonzalo Rubalcaba, and we put them with Christian McBride on bass and Lewis Nash on drums. We went from that very popular organ thing to something that was more esoteric, which was *Think Tank.* I thought the record was good, but I don't think we got as much use out of it as we should have, because you couldn't tour that band. That's a problem. If you can't tour a band, it's really rough. We toured all over with Joey D and Billy Hart, and that's what helped make *Live at Yoshi's* so successful.
>
> Sometime after *Think Tank* had come out, I got a call from Peter Williams from Yoshi's in Oakland. Peter is a big fan of Pat's, and he said, "I have an idea for Pat to do a tribute to Wes Montgomery." So essentially, it was his idea. And Pat just loved the idea. That was a no-brainer. So for that recording we got David Kikoski on piano; John Patitucci on bass; Pat's regular drummer at the time, Scott Allan Robinson; and percussionist Danny Sadownick, and we recorded *Remember: A Tribute to Wes Montgomery.* That was the most-played CD on radio in 2006. So that was a big record for Pat. Unfortunately, around that time, Blue Note was going through its own internal problems—corporate restructuring by the parent company, EMI. And Bruce Lundvall told me, "Look, for right now, we're going to have to let it go. But we can do one-offs. Bring me a project. But for right now they're making me cut my roster."

I've always been excited by change. There'll always be a meaning to be found in the midst of it. So that was the initial ignition for *Think Tank.* And I thought it would be great to market this opportunity, to go closer into a collective multiplication by including the successes of Joe Lovano and Gonzalo Rubalcaba into the formula. The idea was, "Let's put all of us together and start from there." That became a project in itself, in terms of coordinating itineraries and everything that went with it, which was very difficult. Then I began to think about the music itself, and the title tune, "Think Tank," was the first thing that came about. In thinking about this piece, I was reminded of a student who was interested in John Coltrane's "Giant Steps." And more than anything, his interest came because of what it brought to him regarding facility—to be able to move through this series of chord changes quickly. That was the complex, but I wanted the simple, as well. If you ask for the complex, I will give you the complex, but I also will give you the simple, primarily because the totality of it has to be seen holistically, otherwise you only have half the coin.

So I took the alphabet from A to Z, and I took the Aeolian mode, A–B–C–D–E–F–G, in the C-major scale. I took those notes and spanned them from A to Z so that the entire alphabet now became the A-minor scale. And then I took the words C-O-L-T-R-A-N-E and T-E-N-O-R, assigning the proper note to each letter. And there was "Think Tank." It was derived from the alphabet and was an interface of two systems that transcended musicianship.

The *Think Tank* sessions [January 8–10, 2003], with Joe and Gonzalo and the other players involved, had nowhere near the social connection that we had with Delmar and Woody on *Stone Blue*. There was a real family feeling with that. The session for *Think Tank* was a professional gathering of top pros, which was a political production on behalf of Blue Note. So there always seemed to be a professional barrier in that. In spite of how great these players are, they were only there for the day. Everybody's got their own space and responsibilities with their own bands and projects, so there's no time to develop anything on the road like a real band would.

There was some of that aspect, as well, with *Remember,* which was done out of deepest respect for Wes Montgomery, one of my early guitar inspirations. My father had taken me to see Wes when I was fourteen, and while I was completely overwhelmed by his dexterity, I was moved more than anything by his warmth as a person. And that opened up a completely different motive in upcoming definitions of what's important in life.

On that tribute-to-Wes session, I had a very strong rapport with David Kikoski, who is a tremendous player. And I also very much enjoyed playing with John Patitucci, who provided a definite focus for the band on those sessions. Again, this was not a band that was going to be touring and developing and growing on the road. But it's a very honest tribute, done with a pool of respect for a great artist. We focused primarily on those hardcore swinging tunes that Wes did on the Riverside label prior to his marketing success on Verve. And we were striving for a motif of authenticity on that project. Something that I think is important to share is what my private intentions really were with regard to that project. In my record library still remain quite a number of albums that go back to the very beginning of my interests, and quite a few of those are the early recordings of Wes Montgomery. At the age of fourteen, I was startled by his magic, and even more curious with regard to how he brought it about. I've often reminisced by looking at the backs of many of those album covers, where as a child I wrote scribbled inserts with a ballpoint pen, above the liner notes. Like on the song "Full House," the ballpoint question was "3/4 or 6/8?" Or on a ballad like "'Round Midnight," I wrote, "I wonder how he got that feeling?" These were the penned-in questions that were answered in years to come through experience. So the album wasn't solely recorded as a tribute to Wes; it was based more on the answers to those questions finally coming to fruition. The realization of a child's dream coming true.

Thinking of Wes reminds me of a story that Joe Carola, an old friend from Pittsburgh who recently passed away, told me in a letter he sent to me. In it he wrote:

> Before I met you, my friend Harold Bailey used to call to tell me who was coming to play at the Hurricane. He told me Wes Montgomery was coming to town and asked me if I wanted to go see him, and I said yes. On his break, Wes came over and sat down with us because he knew Harold. Wes asked me if I had heard about a new "white boy" from the East who had "fast, fast fingers." I told Wes I had not heard about him yet. Wes told me he would have to sharpen up his thumb to keep up with that white boy. A few months later, Harold called me up and told me, "I think that white boy is coming to town. His name is Pat Martino." So naturally, we went down the Hurricane to hear you play. And that, Pat, is the story of how I first met you. And it has been a love affair with your style of playing ever since that day.

12

Ayako

My connection with Aya is the biggest change in my life there ever was. I could talk for a whole day about her. It was almost like certain facets of our relationship over time were almost like sorcery. And indeed there were times when I thought that she was a witch. Maybe that had to do with our different cultures and our different perspectives and how we define things.

Essentially, she saved my life. I have experienced throughout my life many people who have tried extremely hard to be of assistance for me. And I'm sure they were successful, otherwise I wouldn't be here at this time. Although their success was not as pure as hers.

Her name is Ayako Asahi. And together we seem to be much closer in terms of the inner self than what you see from the outside. We are husband and wife, but it's more than that. It's spiritual . . . it's a very similar relationship on the basis of definition to what life truly is all about. I guess you could say I've found my soulmate.

I was doing a tour with my quartet in Japan when we met in early 1996. We had already played in a number of cities throughout Japan, and Tokyo was the last. We were scheduled to perform three nights at a place called On Air East. And we had great turnouts all three nights. At the end of the last show—like we had done every other night—the promoter, Ms. Kyoko Murata, requested that I go to the front entrance of the concert hall and sit behind a long table and sign autographs for the people that remained for that. And I did so. There was a long line of people, and I signed autograph after autograph—on programs, on guitars, or whatever they brought up to the table. And then finally there was the last couple in the line, and it was a young fella and the lady with him. He asked me if I would sign his guitar. And I magnetically was caught by her eyes. I was stunned by her. It was literally love at first sight. And later I said to the guys in the band, "Wow! I just saw this woman—this girl—she really took my attention. I'll probably never see her again, but she was a knockout."

The next day I had an endorsement get-together at the biggest store in the Ginza area of Tokyo for musical instruments. And I was endorsing Ken Parker's guitar called the Fly at that time and was giving a clinic in collaboration with the endorsement. In comes the same girl I had seen the night before. It turns out she was working in the Ginza area at that particular time. So she came into the clinic and brought me a bouquet of flowers, and a letter containing contact information. When I returned to the States, I began writing to her. We started corresponding, sometimes up to five letters a week. At that time, Aya wasn't speaking English. By the time we started communicating by telephone, it began costing us up to $1,700–$1,800 a month. When August arrived, I gave myself a birthday present, a vacation for ten days in Tokyo, and planned to propose to Aya.

Prior to this trip, I paid a visit to Michael Del Viscio, a very good friend who was a professional jeweler, and I gave him a picture of a guitar that the luthier Abe Rivera had made for me. I'd given the guitar a name—Scepter. Michael made a copy of that guitar in the form of a pendant, then divided it into two separate halves. Then I sent Aya a gift, which was one half of this guitar. I possessed the other half. My intentions were clear to me from the beginning. I figured, "If we ever got together, I'll give her the other half, and join them as one," which finally I did. And she still wears it to this very day. Also, prior to going on that vacation, I had my jeweler make a diamond ring.

So I went to Japan with the intention of proposing to her. I also went there to meet her family. I wanted to experience her life, so I went to her home in Todashi. In fact, her parents have an Italian restaurant there. Susumo, her father, is an excellent cook. And her mom, Yukiko, is, too.

After that ten-day vacation in Japan, I returned to the States. In that winter we were married in a ceremony just outside of Philadelphia on February 7, 1997. Bobby Rose and his wife, Lucy, were our best man and bridesmaid.

When I had met Aya, I was still in descent, which was the aftermath of all of the medication I endured, the aftermath of years of my misuse of drugs and improper diet. My life was immersed in objects and products that were directly purchased from chemists, such as certain brands of toothpaste, hairspray, cologne, shampoo, soap, even the inhaler that I used . . . just about everything that we here in the West are subject to. All the products of chemists. And she taught me the practicality of taking a moment and sitting down and giving a thought to what I truly needed in my life. So if I wanted to eat a filet mignon, she would take the time out to say to me, "Let's talk about it. Do you know what was done to the animal prior to its preparation for the product that you've purchased and now want to consume? Do you think it was embraced with love? It was murdered. How would you feel if you were going to be murdered and were being prepared for that? Do you think that the animal is not conscious of that? So what do you think you're eating? Why do you think you're unhappy? Do you think the animal was happy? Why are you eating unhappiness?" Even guitar cleaners became organic.

Medications that were prescribed and I had been taking throughout those years had quite a number of negative side effects which began finally to diminish through the use of wheatgrass and other raw juices. In terms of diet, she got me into eating fresh fruits and raw vegetables, sprouts, grain, and soy milk . . . no dairy products. It has improved my health significantly. I now feel more energetic, focused, and balanced. I think the prior years of my own experiences dulled my senses to some degree compared to what she's guided me into.

Also, one of the most significant friendships born over the last few years was with a woman by the name of Marian Garfinkel, a master of yoga. Marian took the time out to also give me guidance, and some of the basic procedures and positions for the expansion of the respiratory system are something I've used as much as possible. Placing a yoga block under my back at a certain position between the shoulders and the waist is part of her procedure. I'll lie down with that under my back and it pushes up, and I'll spread my arms on the floor, and that really opens up the respiratory system. I'll be there for fifteen to twenty minutes, and that provides what's needed. That's canceled my need for an inhaler.

So many things have changed since I began my relationship with Aya. And it went far beyond what is seen as a love affair solely for the relation as man and woman. In fact, we're so spiritually connected that the farthest thing that we have between us is the way we look—our shells, our apparel, what we appear as.

Joe Donofrio Remembers: Managing someone's career, in a weird way, is like a marriage. There are highs and lows that represent a complex array of emotions. Ayako and Pat have my utmost respect for how they prevailed where others would have failed. Theirs is a love story that movies are made out of—a lesson in love and understanding.

Geno White Remembers: I was there the day Pat met Aya in Japan. It was March 9, 1996, at a guitar clinic/demonstration at a big music store in Tokyo. I was working then as Pat's roadie and personal assistant, helping him with his gear at gigs and those types of situations. Aya was a guitar fan who attended the clinic. She met Pat afterward and had him sign a guitar. It was a typical crowd, a long line of fans wanting autographs and merchandise. But somehow they exchanged numbers. A few months later, Pat explained how he had met someone in Tokyo and was thinking of going back over to be with her. And sure enough, he did. When he did go back over, I didn't go with him. That was strictly his own personal trip. I think he stayed for ten days and he met the family and stuff. And he mentioned before he left to go back to Tokyo that he was going to get her a ring. So I guess he went back over to propose, to get permission from the father and the whole deal. And she ended up coming back with him. And it's interesting, because I remember a few years before this, when we were hanging out at the Melrose diner, Pat telling me, just out of the blue, "You know what? I think my next wife would be an Oriental woman." That must've been some kind of premonition, because it came true.

I don't remember Aya speaking much English when she came over to the States the first time, but there was clearly quite a romance there, and she seemed totally dedicated to Pat. In the beginning of their relationship, Pat would expose her to his American customs, like eating roast beef sandwiches at Nick's, where we used to hang out a lot. Now, I've been a vegetarian since the 1970s. I basically stopped eating red meat in 1976. As a matter of fact, the first time that we were in Japan together, Pat called me a traitor as a joke because I was going full Japanese the whole way—nato beans and brown rice and all that stuff. But Pat was always big on those roast beef sandwiches at Nick's. And very gradually, Aya began introducing healthier alternatives for Pat. And as things began morphing over into a healthier lifestyle, Pat's health began to improve.

They began juicing a lot, and Aya would make her own sushi and all these great organic foods for him, and it just started rolling out. All of the bad stuff that Pat would regularly eat, mostly all the red meat, all of the fish, was slowly eliminated from his diet, and he was getting better and better physically. Aya even got him into yoga and got him off of his inhaler, which he was using constantly for his emphysema. I remember that first time in Japan, they would have to get cabs even for just a two-block jaunt, because Pat was having a hard time walking. But Aya got him into all kinds of great stuff over the years, and Pat is healthier and more alert now than I've ever known him to be. And he owes that to Aya. She has been his personal doctor, nurse, caretaker, voodoo charmer, everything. The best thing that has happened to Pat is Aya.

Ayako

Ayako Asahi Remembers: When I first met Pat, I guess I was already in love with guitar. My mother played folk guitar, and I thought it was an instrument for adults, so I had a special respect for guitar. As a child, I was given piano lessons and I felt obligated to play that instrument; piano was an expensive responsibility for my parents. So I couldn't ask my parents for more than that, but I secretly wanted to have a guitar. In later years, when I said to Mom that I had really wanted to play guitar, she said, "Why didn't you tell me? Guitar would've been much cheaper."

I first saw Pat play with his band in Tokyo in March 1996. They had three nights of concerts, and I went all three nights. That first night was the first time I had ever heard of Pat Martino. I didn't know who he was. My friend took me to the concert. The following day I saw a poster for Pat's clinic at Yamano Music in Ginza. Since I had just seen him the night before, I decided to go see his clinic that afternoon, just out of curiosity. And I went. And there he was.

It's strange, but later on when he showed an interest and began calling me from the United States, I wasn't surprised. I guess you can call it destiny. Then on my birthday, June 16 of that year, I was surprised when he sent me a diary and, along with it, his mother's rosary. And my first entry in that diary that Pat sent to me was: "I'm going to heal this person." Which I didn't remember writing until I read that page again for the first time in fifteen years. That was before he asked me to be closer to him. But I got the message. At first I thought, "What is this—this is so heavy!" But I accepted the intuition I was feeling, because I was not afraid, just curious. I was on the ship already.

In that package, he also sent me an advance sketch of the song "Ayako" which was on his Blue Note album [*All Sides Now*] later that year. That was amazing that he wrote such a beautiful song for me. By August, as a birthday present to himself, Pat came to visit me in Tokyo. And he met my parents during that trip. Then I came to the United States on November 23, which is Pat's father's birthday. Some people might say it was courageous of me or maybe strange to leave my home and go off like that. But I took a chance with my intuition. You can say it was lucky, but I say, I know what I'm doing. Trusting intuition for everybody is the most important thing, I believe. So I came to the United States and went to Pat's home in Philadelphia. And we married the next year on February 7, 1997. And I knew at the time that a jazz musician's life is not easy at all, but that didn't bother me.

As far as me instantly changing Pat's lifestyle and diet and everything, it's not actually like that. I wasn't a vegetarian at the time. Japanese people eat meat and fish. But very gradually, I began making changes in my own diet and lifestyle. I realized I had to start living up to what I was saying about healthy choices by first doing it myself. Pat started recognizing the advance in my change, and he followed. I wanted to introduce him to the idea of a "natural high." In his past, Pat did drugs, so he knows about the state of being "high." When I gave him a shot of wheatgrass in between sets at a club in New York for the first time, he said it reminded him of "speed," because of the rush. And when he played after that natural high, he made magic happen. So first I learned myself, and then I wanted to share that high with him. And he recognized that high was greater than the one he knew.

So Pat's life-changing recovery was depending on my own growth—spiritual growth, as well. And until I grew up, until I recognized that part of me, I didn't have power to guide him in any kind of lifestyle changes. That was the greatest lesson for me, that somehow destiny gave me the chance to grow up. We have been together now for fifteen years. And at times it is hard. Sometimes it's difficult because I do have a short temper—I'm emotional. I just cannot hide something that I feel honestly. I don't mind if people are upset, but that's my honesty. I have hurt some people in the past, but I'm growing by making mistakes. I enjoy darkness so I can see the light brighter, too.

I find the relationship with Pat is more spiritual now, and I'm very interested in unity, the idea of two as one. And along the way I discovered that a smile on us is gold. If we can smile, there is nothing more I want to have in this world. I need Pat's smile.

Still, now, my concern is for Pat to be a guitar player. That's my major issue. Pat not being a guitar player is not a style that I can accept. He's a guitar player. I've been learning guitar myself, and we play together every day. Harmony's my interest. Sometimes our opinions go against each other's, but music always turns them back to harmony. We've played live in several places. The first time was at the Iridium in New York on my birthday, just a brief appearance together onstage, but in Connecticut we recently played in duet for ninety minutes. That was the longest one. We've also done some clinics together. Being able to play together has added another layer of depth to our relationship, and it's something that comes out naturally. That's my heart. Without me loving guitar, I don't think this relationship would have lasted this long or have gotten this deep. I'm so crazy about guitar, and being able to play along with Pat is like getting a new hug from him.

13

Here and Now

When it comes down to the definition of love and what it is, I think that many of us are under the impression that love is something separate from us and that we should live up to, and participate in—we should be more like this, and give this to others, do for others. In that way we're still looking for relationships with others, and we're still looking for the *use of* love to embellish upon those relationships. We expect others to give to us through their *love of us* what's needed to live a more comfortable and more fulfilling life. In that process, we've failed to have a relationship with love itself, by itself. Not the use of it, being in love with someone, but more with its sacred presence. Every time we try to use it for a purpose we fall short, and it disappears.

To live for the sake of love itself is as pure as one can be.

All the mistakes I've made are the reason why I'm where I'm at. Well, of course—that's what I've done, that's what I am, that's what my life is . . . the result of. It's obvious that unless there's a continuous reevaluation, a decision to use experience to one's benefit will fail to take place. If one stops there and asks, "What did I learn about myself, about my own faults?" then shares, that's something that I think an autobiography should touch upon. The value is in the process that's been described and where it leads us.

We're back to the analogy of the guitar and the calluses. To acquire calluses, in the process of learning the instrument, it's impossible to avoid the pain. If you want to be steel, you can't avoid the fire. You'll be placed in the fire, for temperance as well as other virtues. That's what I've shared with students at master classes—"Eighty-seven percent of the time spent on tour has nothing to do with the thirteen percent of performance—or does it?"

We spend time in airports, waiting for a flight's departure—along with feeling the disappointment if it doesn't take off—spend time in taxis and on countless other things unrelated to music. These are things we have no control over. The music, and its performance, is the remaining thirteen percent. Begin to see the definition of consciousness. The music, and its instrument, is what got us there. It's our ticket in, and once we're in, that's when the temperance comes, and that's where virtues take place. And if we don't take that as the issue, we'll fall short and lose value. When reduced to a craft, it becomes a profession. Music, and all that it thrusts one through, should lead to a devotion of life itself: in Coltrane's words, "A Love Supreme!"

So what's the instrument there for? It's an important part of the human experience. It expands sensitivities, abilities, and our perspectives of what's meaningful in our existence. My instrument is the moment. It includes all the things that emerge from itself, in every situation I'm in. It would be foolish for me to give more credit to any one of them, for it would take my attention off of here and now . . . reality. It has to be that way.

The first time I picked up the guitar was to participate, to compete, to be the best, and to escape oblivion. At this point, at this very moment, I'm in a different place. I'm in a place observing all these things at once. And observing life itself. That's what interests me, that's my intention—to gain more insight into what I am, and why I am.

The idea of students sitting down and transcribing famous bebop solos by Charlie Parker or Clifford Brown is half-sided. Of course, there's a mechanical gain that comes from familiarity with musical terms, but I don't think you can analyze a section of time without participating in the culture that brought it about.

I had a bassist student who transcribed a Paul Chambers solo. I found it important to bring to his attention a session that I did with Richard "Groove" Holmes and Paul Chambers. Paul had just come in from Russia, directly from LaGuardia airport to the session at Rudy Van Gelder's studio in Englewood Cliffs, New Jersey. His contrabass was in a cloth case within a heavier anvil case. Upon opening the case, he discovered that the difference in room temperature was so drastic that the instrument snapped. There was a bass of lesser quality in the corner that Paul was forced to use. The instrument was totally alien to Paul, but he adjusted to it like water takes the shape of what it's poured into. A true artist has the ability to adapt at any given moment.

Responsibility is a funny word; it exists only when one thinks of pleasing others. When one continuously does the best one can do under any circumstances, it resolves responsibility. So I think these are values that embrace everyday living, and I see it all as nothing more than a prelude to what I am experiencing.

After the operations, during a period of recovery and therapy, I found it necessary to rejoin the parish where I was recovering. I found it rewarding to go to church. In fact, in a brief period of time I joined a charismatic group. Eventually I departed from that group when it ceased to provide stimulation. It was merely another change, like C7 to C7$\sharp$9.

Similarly, in a clinic, invariably a student would ask, "This particular chord . . . what do you play against this chord? I want to learn how to be quicker in thinking about such things." I bring to his or her attention that thinking has nothing to do with it. In fact, thought is a distraction to the process. It comes through intuition, not through thought, not from the mind. That's improvisation. Experience is always the culmination of trial and error. It's from our mistakes that we decide what's valuable, what's profound.

Change . . . will happen at a moment's notice!

One of the most astounding things is to have faith, and that comes down to fear and its presence. When fear enters, it reminds one of the importance of having faith.

I used to think that fear was something to be avoided. At this point in my life, I've come to the conclusion that it's a necessity. Courage is created by fear. It's when a person experiences fear and not only faces it, but decides what has to be done to overcome it. So without fear, there would be no courage.

You're sitting in a dressing room when suddenly the door opens, a fan enters, and he asks, "Would you autograph my guitar?" I've enjoyed calligraphy for a number of years, but at times I've felt apprehensive to commit myself to that style of signature, worried that it might not come out as flowing and poetic that it sometimes does. I signed it intuitively and was amazed at its accuracy.

Conclusion, you don't really have to think about it, you just do it. That's how I feel about playing the guitar: Becoming one with the object the moment you focus attention on it.

There's a very mysterious relationship that exists within Sacred Geometry and music. Actually, the tuning of the guitar is a pentagram, E–A–D–G–B–E seen as a five-pointed star inside a chromatic circle. Even the dollar bill with a pyramid inside the circle has been defined by some as Masonic. There are even social warnings from certain sects that warn us of mysticism—"Do not touch . . . it's sinful for you to go there."

All the questions I've had are the result of my pursuit in such directions. Extremely intriguing, warnings by those who forbade such inquisitions.

At a very early age I thought that having dexterity, being powerful as a player, was what it was all about: precision. Through the years I've come to the conclusion that adaptation is what is truly of value; the playing became second nature. What will artistry at this level bring you? What are your intentions?

In a conversation with a taxi driver, he announced he was an unemployed physicist, driving to support his family.

In life we need to consciously remove the blinders and, like a chameleon, naturally shift through each responsibility with grace, with precision—a parent, a neighbor, a physicist, a taxi driver . . . most of all an artist. It's how we use our blessings.

Teaching music as a craft can be insulting to its true value, its mystique, its spiritualism. How can one reduce "A Love Supreme" or "Giant Steps" to nothing but a challenge for a technician?

The music business itself sometimes seems deterrent. Moving in directions that have nothing to do with a greater purpose—enlightenment. We're happy when we're accepted, we're sad if we're not, and repetitively subject to duality.

When we objectively step outside of these opposites and trust our cognitive intuition, it allows our artistry to truly become creative.

I've never considered creating music to be work, or having a job; it's been my career, what I thought I'd set out to do in life. Professionally I'm considered a jazz guitarist, although that's merely what appears at the surface. That particular instrument has proven successful as a valid tool for survival, but it's also been my scepter.

When a student comes to interact, I attempt to truly present a spotlight on the moment, what's being obtrusively limited due to the individual's intentions. One's intentions are the aftermath of training, and a major problem of education is how it confines any individual to its purpose. "So let's begin. Why are you here?"

From a very early age, I've always had a personal need to consider multiple meanings. When I see a sign, when I see a logo or any symbol, it has so many different connotations that it forces me to keep an open mind. It doesn't mean only what it was designed to function as. I see everything in that way, the repositioning of definition in itself.

The activation of certain ailments, certain functional problems–psychological problems—these are the early grades of development for an artist in the process of gaining experience. And whether they are going to be overcome or not doesn't affect the art itself, nor the creative productivity. A good example was Van Gogh cutting off his ear.

Trying to get a break in the music business is a disease in itself. To expect to be capable of presenting yourself to others in the light of your intentions is not about what's marketable. It's about what's pure.

Appendix I

Guitar Players' Testimony
Everybody Loves Pat Martino

Carlos Santana

I first became aware of Pat's music around 1971–1972, when I started getting my first royalties, so I could go to Tower Records and actually buy records that I could afford. And I started buying organ trios—Jack McDuff. That's when I started seeing George Benson, Pat Martino, Grant Green. I didn't know Pat was so young, because for me coming from John Lee Hooker and Jimmy Reed and Lightnin' Hopkins, I thought the music of jazz, and specifically organ trios, was more older people, in their thirties and forties. And me being in my early twenties, I just thought it was older people's music, because it was so advanced also, in the vocabulary. So it really made an impression on me, the extent of Pat's vocabulary and especially him being so young. Because that's exactly what you have to have to hang out in Harlem with those guys—a different vocabulary than just one-chord blues.

He was really blessed to be growing up playing in clubs, although I understand he was also doing tours with some bands when he was still a teenager. But musically, Pat had his own calling and I had my own calling. Ultimately, the destination is the same—it's how you touch people's hearts. That's what we have in common. I love Pat's tone. That's the first thing that I listen to in musicians—the tone, the fingerprint, the identity, the individuality. And of course, I love his choice of notes, and his sense of romance, which is something else we have in common.

Later I heard about Pat becoming ill. He and my brother Quincy Jones both have survived brain aneurysms. They're actually miracles walking. And I couldn't imagine to start all over again like that, to be so gifted and then to begin to start from pointblank how to articulate your fingers again. Because your fingers become your tongue, you know. And so it's a wonderful miracle that Pat is able to start all over again and take music from his vision and his heart into a whole level of expression that is still mindboggling to most musicians like myself. Pat is really, really cool, but he has this knowledge and vocabulary like Wayne Shorter and Coltrane. He can go there. It's serious; it's not cute and clever. Miles Davis didn't like cute and clever, and neither does Pat Martino. They're deadly serious, like Bruce Lee. They're very disciplined and focused on the music. Yet I hear humor in Pat's playing.

I celebrate his spirit, because I do have a lot of the CDs that people send me all the time from different parts of the world, and I'm always in awe and appreciation of the brilliance of his spirit. Because I don't listen to his mind, I listen to his heart. Certain musicians like Pat and Wayne Shorter and myself, we're coming from another point of perception—that music puts wings in your heart and allows you to go beyond your ego. And I have deep, deep respect and admiration and gratitude for Pat Martino for his laser-like concentration and devotion to utilizing music to inspire people into a higher form of consciousness.

(From Ian Knox's 2008 documentary *Martino Unstrung: A Brain Mystery*)

John Abercrombie

I remember seeing Pat play live when I was still going to Berklee, around 1964 or so. He had been recording at that time under the name Pat Azzara, and the couple of records that he had been on with Willis "Gator Tail" Jackson were floating around among all the guitar students at Berklee. We were all listening to them and being completely blown away by them. The first time I heard him live was with Jack McDuff's organ group sometime in the mid-1960s. I had heard the group about six months prior to that with George Benson on guitar and was completely just floored by that. We had never heard anybody play like George Benson, so we went back to hear the band, a bunch of us, but this time it was Pat Martino playing guitar. I had heard his name but didn't know anything about him. It took me a minute to understand that Pat Martino and Pat Azzara were one and the same. So there we were at this small jazz club in the Roxbury section of Boston called Connolley's, on Tremont Street. I had heard Art Farmer with Jim Hall there, I heard McDuff with Benson there, I heard several bands there. It was a very comfortable little club, and all the guitar students hung out there regularly.

That night, Pat came on the bandstand, and in those days he was playing a black Les Paul Custom guitar. We knew the guitar was like carrying a Buick on the stage—it was so heavy. And Pat was such a frail little guy. So when we saw this young, very thin little guy walking up to the bandstand with this heavy guitar, I think our first reaction was, "Oh, man, this can't be the guitar player! Who is this? Where's Benson?" He was like a little kid, you know? So we were all chuckling. And then, of course, he started to play and then we ceased chuckling. Because he just floored everybody in the club. I never heard anything like that. I remember they did McDuff's "Rock Candy," and it burned so hard. And when that band played, it was like the whole club was moving because the band had such a powerful drive and rhythmic feel. It swung so hard, it was infectious. It almost made you wanna dance. It was that kind of thing where the music was really inventive but it could also be danced to, because it was swinging so hard. That was that other element that seems to have disappeared from music. But that original stuff, boy, it was stomping!

During the break, one of my friends introduced himself to Pat and he came over and sat with us. Then the next day—he was in town for that whole week—he came to an apartment where we were all hanging out and he played with everybody, heard us play and played us live tapes . . . he had a reel-to-reel tape recorder and was taping a lot of the gigs at that time, maybe just for study or whatever. And we were just completely floored by everything he played us. He was probably the first professional guitar player on the jazz scene that I met that I actually talked to, who was willing to talk to us and share information and demonstrate things. The thing about it, which made it inspiring and also terrifying, was the fact that Pat was our age. I mean, we were used to hearing somebody like Wes Montgomery or Kenny Burrell or Jim Hall, you know, an elder statesman playing. And of course, we were just in awe of that, but these guys were maybe fifteen to twenty years older than us. But now you're hearing somebody who was seventeen or eighteen years old, which is how old I was. When you hear somebody from your own age group, when you're that young, playing that well, it does a couple of things to you. One, it makes you want to throw the guitar completely away and say, "I could never play like that." The other side of the coin is it kind of inspires you to think, "Well, if he did it, maybe there's some hope for me. Maybe I can do something."

Seeing Pat in the club that night, I remember really liking his tone. He had this warm, velvety kind of sound, very warm and fat, and it just projected off the stage. Everything was very clear, but it was also very warm. There was no harshness to the sound at all. And he played, to me, from where I was sitting, he played so very smooth, and of course it was the constant stream of eighth notes and his amazing time, his feeling that was so perfect. I think that made a big impression on me. It made me realize how important it was to play with really good time, because I think a lot of people dismiss that when they're first studying. They think, "Oh, I have to know all the scales, all the chords." But then they forget about playing in time. And if you're playing that kind of music, it has to swing and it has to have a certain something. And Pat had it. And of course I think everyone would say it's the complete evenness of his playing, it was very kind of flawless, even at that age he had that kind of thing happening. It was completely smooth and swinging and a beautiful sound.

Compared to Benson, whom I had already seen at Connolley's, what Pat was doing on the instrument seemed more controlled, like he thought about what he was going to play. Whereas Benson seemed kind of wild and off-the-cuff. George just seemed to "go for it," so there was more of an element of surprise in his playing. I think with George it was more like, "How's he doing that? Where's this coming from?" It just seemed amazing, but a little wild. But with Pat I felt this very focused quality. I guess another word for it would be *mature.* There seemed to be a purpose in what he played. And yet there was a similarity between him and Benson that I could hear, a certain thing that I guess you could refer to as the way guys played in organ groups. These two guys really just raised the level of that kind of playing to the highest it could go. I just thought Pat was a little more controlled, smoother, more focused in that context. I liked him better at that time, because I could hear it better. It was much clearer. But Benson was astonishing.

Years later I heard Pat's *Joyous Lake.* And there was an acoustic piece that he did on that album that was just a solo guitar piece. It was really beautiful . . . very different from the stuff when I first heard him play with McDuff in that club in Roxbury. It was a little more classical-sounding. And that's when I realized this guy was always developing and trying to find new things.

John Scofield

I was in high school, and when I was about sixteen I decided I wanted to learn about jazz and play jazz. So I set myself on the course of study, checking out all the great jazz guitar players. And when I found Pat, it blew me away. The guys who were really getting popular then where John McLaughlin, who had just come on the scene, and Larry Coryell. And those guys, they were kind of jazz but also rock. And then, of course, there were the older guys—Wes Montgomery, Jim Hall, Barney Kessel, and Tal Farlow. Pat fit in this niche that was like the older players but even slicker. He really sounded like jazz to me; his lines sounded just so thoroughly jazz, compared to Coryell and McLaughlin, who had that sort of rock edge. And I loved it. I just wore his records out. First it was his *El Hombre* and *Strings!,* his first recordings on

Prestige. They were really some of the first jazz guitar I had. He and George Benson were in this niche of sounding like complete jazz musicians to me, where I no longer thought of them as guitar players but held them in the same esteem as the great horn players. And with Pat, I got obsessed with his playing and tried to learn his lines, which was really frustrating, because I could never get them.

Then I went to Berklee, and every few weeks I'd put on one of his records, and I'd be stuck there, listening to it over and over again, just so in love with his playing, just a complete mastery of the instrument in a way that is so special to him. His sound, his chops, his execution, and the evenness of his lines were all so personal. It was a new energy, but he really did sound like such a swinger, the way his eighth-note lines could just burn. I just loved it. I got all of his albums and also got into the records where he was a sideman during that period. There was an Eric Kloss record that I really loved his playing on. There was one by Don Patterson that I loved. I had other stuff, too, but the Eric Kloss stuff, especially, made a big impression on me. I had a Groove Holmes record that he was on that I really loved. By the time I went to Berklee, I think it was around 1974, I went to his house in Philly and took a lesson with him. It was just fantastic. I had no other encounters with Pat until 2002, nearly thirty years later, when we played together at the Umbria Jazz Festival. We played "Sunny" and a few other tunes, and Pat just tore it up! He plays the guitar so beautifully. It's such a hard-driving, fantastic thing to witness, especially being so close to him right onstage.

I think every time I hear him or play with him, it makes me rethink the guitar. And I think good players will do that to each other. Also, it turns out, Pat is a wonderful, generous soul. I just love hearing his stories about playing on the chitlin' circuit when he was a teenager and then playing at Small's Paradise back in the day. I mean, what a background, man. To come from Philly at that time . . . such a fertile scene. He 's a phenomenal jazz player and a great storyteller.

Mike Stern

I heard Pat on record when I was still in high school, before I enrolled at Berklee. I was living in Washington, D.C., where I grew up, and I was more into blues and rock, just kind of getting into jazz. And this record knocked me out. I think it was *The Visit!*—just a smokin' record. At the time I didn't know what he was doing, but what I heard was just a soulful motherfucker. That's the thing that jumped out the most, and still does. And that's the kind of players I love. That soulful thing is what gets to me first about music, and everything else is just icing on the cake. And there's a lot of icing on Pat's cake, because he's got a lot of knowledge and a lot of stuff that he's worked out. He's really got an amazing vocabulary and interesting ways of looking at the instrument, but then he swings really hard and he's definitely funky. And I love that about him. I love that balance between the cerebral and the street. My favorite players have that. He's an incredibly intelligent player, but he's also rooted in the blues . . . there's so much blues in his playing, which is what I initially related to when I first heard him on record back in high school

Pat is just an exceptional guy, and I had so much fun playing with him on that record we did together [*All Sides Now*]. That was such a treat for me. He came over to my place to run down some stuff, and we were talking a lot. I had known about him from Gil Goldstein, whom I've been tight with for years. Gil told me the whole story about Pat and his aneurysm and all that stuff, so I knew that he had gone through a fuck of a lot and yet was still playing his ass off and his spirit was really strong. On a personal level, having to go through all the physical stuff that he did, and come out on top . . . it's very inspiring to see someone just keep going. He didn't stop for a second. And I know there were really tricky times there after the surgery with his memory. One time I saw him at the Bottom Line and he had music in front of him of tunes that he wrote. And he told me later that he forgets it sometimes. So he was struggling. But it's pretty remarkable that he's made it through, and he's always playing beautifully now . . . just such a soulful cat. And the other thing I find inspiring about Pat is that he's not stopping. He knows that you don't even get close to learning all the possibilities on any instrument . . . or getting even remotely close to learning all the possibilities of music in general. It's just a journey that never ends. And he's into that. He's always learning stuff, and he always seems that he's open to it . . . and kind of a beginner, as great as he is. He's got that mentality of just always wanting to learn more. It's very cool. I love that.

Larry Coryell

I was first aware of him as Pat Azzara. I might've been in Seattle at the time. And I was immediately impressed by what I heard. It really caught me. It might've been with Willis "Gator Tail" Jackson, but it just had all the hallmarks of great playing—a great sense of timing, impeccable way of expressing his ideas, articulation that was just second to none. And, of course, you could hear from his playing that he loved Wes. And so did I. So we had that in common. I remember hearing "Sunny" on the radio all the time back then. Back then, between the last half of the 1960s and even into the first half of the 1970s, there were actual jazz hits on the jukebox—"Song for My Father," "Sidewinder," "The In Crowd," and "Sunny" by Pat Martino. And when he extrapolated on "Flight of the Bumblebee" in his solo on that tune, that made a big impression on me. Even today, whenever I'm in trouble, I pull that one out of the files. That was just incredible.

We played together one afternoon at Lennie's on the Turnpike just outside of Boston. It was a Sunday-afternoon thing, and I remember George Mraz had just come to town, and he was so good. The reviewer of that concert opened his review with "Martino continues to grow and grow"—I loved that. We played several tunes together, including "I Can't Get Started," which I haven't played since. And then years later we worked opposite each other at the Blue Note. I believe I had the Count's Jam Band with Steve Smith and Steve Marcus, and Pat had Joey DeFrancesco in his band. He and Joey together, man . . . really nice! And I listened to every set they played. I loved the way he played "You Don't Know What Love Is." He did a different thing with it every night , very bluesy. Pat's a very intelligent guy, and he's a reflection of the times in which he evolved, no less than Abraham Lincoln or Mark Zuckerberg or Van Gogh. He is unbelievably perceptive. If he deigns to have a conversation with another musician, the other musician should definitely pay attention to what his views are—the way he sees things and what his feelings about events are. Because he's very much right on the money. He's a very intuitive person.

Aside from Wes, that's who Emily Remler worshipped and practiced. It was Wes and Pat the whole time. She put on those records every morning when we were doing our little duet gig together, and she'd play along with those recordings. So I heard a lot of Pat Martino in the mornings during that time period. I also think *Joyous Lake* needs to be reissued. That was the biggest fusion sleeper of that whole era. You play that record today and people would freak out—their jaws would drop. Younger listeners would probably say, "I didn't know that was possible to mix jazz with that kind of sound," a lot like Miles when he started immersing his own personal style in unfamiliar surroundings to the listener. That's what Pat did. His playing stayed the same, it just worked real good in that context, especially with Woody on drums. That was such a great record. That should've won awards. Pat should've won a Grammy with that one.

Bill Frisell

When I was in high school, I heard Wes Montgomery and a door opened into a fantastic, beautiful world. I went in, took a few steps down this path, and soon found Pat Martino. The first album I bought of his was *The Visit! (Inspired by and Dedicated to Wes Montgomery)*. Look at the cover! Who was this guy? Where was he coming from? The music was so solid in the whole history, but it was already into the future. Philadelphia. History-mystery. Billy Higgins and Richard Davis. Wow! Around this time I heard Pat play live at the Jazz Workshop in Boston with Bobby Rose, duo. Man alive! A few years later came *Joyous Lake*. Atmosphere. Delmar Brown and Kenwood Dennard. I LOVE this album. Over the years I've gotten to hear Pat quite a few times, and I always come away inspired. The lines, the rhythmic power. More recently, I've had the chance to meet him. What a beautiful person. I wasn't surprised. To play music like that, he would have to be. Humility. He talked about playing music based on the constellations. Wow. The stars. Form, logic. Incredible. Never predictable. Nature. His music continues to grow. I've heard he has written music for orchestra. I want to hear that! A beautiful big, strong old tree. Coral reef. Music. No one has ever made music like Pat Martino . . . before or since. Thank you, Pat!

Russell Malone

The first jazz guitarist I heard that made me want to play this music was George Benson. And whenever I'd read articles on George, the name Pat Martino would come up. So there was a gentleman in my hometown [Albany, Georgia] who was a huge jazz guitar buff, and he gave me a couple of records. He turned me on to Wes Montgomery's *Smokin' at the Half Note* and also Pat Martino's *Consciousness*. And the thing that struck me about Pat's playing was the articulation. Every note was so clean you could hear everything. And he was swinging so hard! He had the technique, had great time, and he had the feeling. And that big, beautiful sound, man—it was just so amazing to hear that. I would sit next to the record player and try to cop some of those lines, but his lines were a little more difficult to cop than some of the other things that I heard by other guitar players. So after a while I just gave up and said, "What's the point?" And eventually I just said, "Well, I can't get those lines, but I will at least try to play on that level," doing what I do, but trying to play with the same kind of conviction I heard in Pat's playing.

Years later I got to meet Pat Martino. He's such a generous and giving individual, one of the nicest guys that I've ever met. And he's very passionate about the music. I got a chance to go out on the road with Pat a couple of years ago—me and him, Mark Whitfield, and Chuck Loeb. We did a couple of gigs together over in Europe, and I have to say, it's very scary standing next to Pat Martino onstage. Imagine seeing a lion in a cage. You get one perspective on the lion when you're on one side of the bars and the lion's on the other. Imagine yourself inside the cage, standing next to the lion. You can hear it breathing, and it looks a lot bigger when you're inside the cage next to him . . . a lot bigger, a lot stronger, a lot more powerful. That's the way it was standing onstage next to Pat Martino.

Kevin Eubanks

I don't really remember exactly when I first heard Pat or where I was at in terms of my own development at the time. I just always have the memory of knowing Pat's sound whenever I heard it. I always knew it was Pat Martino. And hearing him play, you always felt like you were getting something bigger than just hearing somebody play guitar. You could hear and feel that somebody had a deeper knowledge of things. So you felt the emotion, and you felt the symmetry of it. You felt the science behind it, but you also felt the emotion behind it. He gave you more of an artistic view of the thing. It just kind of was imparted to you by the way that he played. Wes Montgomery was like that for me, Oscar Peterson, too. When you hear them play you get a bigger sense that there's a huge understanding there, almost like there's a sense of physics behind it, a connecting-the-dots thing that makes it music and art, not just a formula. So Pat kind of broke that down, and when you hear him play, that's all in there—the intellect, the emotion, the physics of it, there's all that. Which brings it all together and to me creates art.

I remember seeing Pat at Fat Tuesday's in New York, just after the time he had had his operation. I heard he had a brain aneurysm, but I wasn't exactly sure what that was at the time. So I went to check him out, and I was really pulling for him in the audience, you know? "Kick some ass, Pat! You can do it!" Because he's kind of like the guitar hero for me in that bigger sense. And seeing him play makes you feel like you're part of the club, part of this guitar fraternity, where everybody is happy for the next person and learning from the next person at the same time. And as long as he's out there, then it brings it to a high level for all of us. Historically, if you look at jazz, we guitar players don't have such a big voice. I mean, we get run over by all these piano players and tenor players. But when I see Pat out there, it makes me feel like, "Yeah, yeah, yeah . . . we bad! We got Pat!" We wanna give him the ball, you know?

We haven't played onstage together, but I did get a chance to play with Pat on his Blue Note album *All Sides Now*. And I'm talking with my record company [Mack Avenue Records] now about doing a project with Pat. The idea is to just get in, get it done, have a great time, and keep it nice, keep it cool—just the way Pat likes it. As a footnote, I went up to Pat some years ago and asked him, "Who makes your guitars?" And he said, "A guy by the name of Abe Rivera." And Abe Rivera has made every one of my guitars since then.

Chuck Loeb

I first heard Pat Martino when I was sixteen years old, and I still haven't fully recovered. I am fifty-five now. Being lucky enough to grow up around New York City, I went to hear Pat live in 1972 at a Greenwich Village club called Folk City. The night I saw him, they changed the name of the club to "Jazz City." Anyone familiar with Pat's recordings will know that that engagement resulted in his *Live!* recording, featuring his classic version of "Sunny," along with "The Great Stream" and "Special Door." After that night, which is indelibly etched in my mind as a classic jazz-guitar performance, I immediately began buying every record I could find, transcribing Pat's solos, and researching where he studied.

That led to me signing up for lessons with his former teacher Dennis Sandole in Philadelphia. Ultimately, a few years later, I made the trek to Pat's place in South Philly and took one lesson from him directly. So to say that he had an impact on my musical development as a jazz guitarist would be a great understatement. Since starting my own career, I have been very fortunate to perform and become friends with the man himself. We have done several multi-guitar concerts together, and he has participated in my "String Training" guitar clinics. He is a warm, generous, funny, and bright soul, and it is always a pleasure to collaborate with him in any setting. So now every time I hear Pat play, whether it's on the radio, on CD, or live in concert, it is another chance to bask in the light of a rare talent and see what happens when the "great streams" of talent, dedication, perseverance, and the joy of jazz guitar align. Play on, Mr. Martino!

David Gilmore

I was first introduced to Pat's artistry maybe a year or two after I started playing the guitar back in high school. I don't remember how I heard about him, but I remember that it was *The Visit* album on Muse that I heard first. Growing up on a heavy dose of R&B, funk, and some rock, and just beginning to get into jazz at the time, I think what I was drawn to in Pat's playing was the rhythmic propulsion behind virtually every note he played. In addition to these incredibly rich melodic lines was a rhythmic execution that had this sense of weightlessness, floating over the top of the music, but still deeply rooted in the rhythmic tradition of masters like Sonny Rollins, Bird, and Bud Powell. If I have one complaint of the so-called jazz-guitar idiom, it's that a strong sense of rhythm is often sorely lacking, in even some of the more well-known players. Wes started to change that, borrowing from the Charlie Christian legacy, and George Benson added to that. The other major force of this era was Pat, who in addition brought more melodic and harmonic sophistication to the instrument, yet retained the groove factor in every single note. As I was a funkster starting to discover the world of jazz at the time, this strongly resonated with me, and I started to look for as many Pat Martino records as I could find and began to cop a lot of his phrases and solos. When I discovered *Joyous Lake* and *Starbright,* I knew I found my new guitar hero. I can definitely trace some elements of what I play today back to some of those early Pat lines.

I first saw Pat play in New York around 1985–86, shortly after I moved to the city, and around the time he was making a comeback from his near-fatal operation. I caught one of the earliest gigs after he recorded *The Return,* at Fat Tuesday's, on Third Avenue. Seeing him in person for the first time, I couldn't believe how such a big sound came from such a frail-looking figure! I saw several appearances of him there, as well as at the Bottom Line, but never got the chance to meet him in person until years later (around 1994–1995) when I was on tour with the Indian percussionist Trilok Gurtu. We were in a small town in Italy, and in the audience was Pat. We met after the show, and he told me how much he enjoyed my playing, as well, and he said it with such genuine and warm affection that I knew he wasn't just bullshitting me. Several years went by, and I caught him again at the Blue Note in New York in a reunion of the *Joyous Lake* band, with original members Delmar Brown and Kenwood Dennard, along with Chulo Gatewood on bass. I met up with Pat after the show, convinced that he wouldn't remember me at all, but to my surprise he not only remembered me by name, but he recalled the name of the town in Italy where we had met—and the year! Every time I've met him since then, he has been more warm and gracious then the previous time.

In 2004, I wrote and recorded a song for my *Unified Presence* CD, and after composing it I realized it contained some compositional elements which reminded me of Pat's stuff. The title "Vertical Path" came to mind, alluding to his approach to improvisation and composition. The title also refers to the concept of advancing spiritually on what mystics refer to as the Vertical Path.

Pat is clearly one of those spirits on this planet who is firmly on that path and shining the way for all of us to follow.

Fareed Haque

To say that I was influenced by Pat is an understatement. If anything, you might say that I'm a disciple of his approach. And it's a big part of everything that I do. I spent a lot of time studying his music, going from fan to aficionado to almost scientist on Pat's music. What make's Pat's approach so distinctive? There's a lot of obvious things—his approach to articulation, his control over lines. But more than anything else, he can connect a modern approach to the blues tradition. I think I first encountered Pat's music through *Joyous Lake*, which to me is some of the most technically challenging and sophisticated guitar improvisations ever. By far. Then I went back to the earlier stuff like *The Visit* and *Desperado*; hearing him playing Sonny Rollins's "Oleo" on twelve-string guitar blew my head off. Also *We'll Be Together Again* was big for me. Nobody was touching what he was doing back then. The lines that he's playing on the records are so sophisticated—traditional and modern. He had his little licks, but he used them in a very creative way. And of course he had a feel like nobody got, where it's like driving 4/4 and swinging but laid-back all at the same time.

To me, Pat is the only modern jazz guitarist, period. Everybody else is a rock guitarist who plays jazz, or a fusion guitarist who plays jazz, or a modal guitarist. You have a lot of really great roots-oriented guitarists— Grant Green, Kenny Burrell, George Benson—but none of them were really modern. George didn't have a clue what to do behind Miles, because he just doesn't have that harmonic vocabulary. And Pat was a guy who could take a traditional guitar sound, feel, and vocabulary and bring it into the twenty-first fucking century. He's the only guy to play Wayne Shorter tunes. And I'm talking about someone who's playing jazz guitar, not kicking on distortion and playing jazzy lines on a Telecaster. There's nothing wrong with that; it's still great music. But don't call it jazz guitar. It's not really jazz guitar. It's rock guitar. Frank Zappa played sophisticated lines on a rock guitar; we don't have to call that jazz. And he played in odd meters and rhythms with all kinds of complicated harmony, but we don't call that jazz. Just because you can play jazz doesn't make you a jazz guitarist. But Pat Martino is a jazz guitarist. And no matter how modern Pat got in his playing, it still had the playing of Harlem in it. Even when you listened to something like *Consciousness,* it comes down to all the modern stuff being channeled through the chitlin' circuit. And yet the way Pat plays a melody, so very intensely melodic and vocal in his phrasing, in that sense he is the most classical of the jazz guitarists, which is strange, considering that he's so *street.* But me being a classical guitarist, his clarity and articulations and use of tone color in playing melodies are a huge connect for me because of my experience with classical guitar. And it's further demonstrated by all those classically sounding pieces he wrote, like "Passata on Guitar." So on so many levels, Pat means a lot to me.

Paul Bollenback

If you play jazz guitar, it's tough to escape the influence of certain players. Pat Martino is definitely one of those players. I made my initial discovery of Pat sometime in the early 1980s. I couldn't even say which recording it was, although it may have been *Consciousness,* the one with "Along Came Betty" on it. That is still one of my favorites. What Pat was playing on that was very similar to the ideal sound I had in my head at the time, so it just knocked me out and made me say—yeah, that's it, that's what I'm looking for , so smooth yet expressive, warm yet relentless. Hearing that recording was inspiring, but it also made me want to burn my guitar at first. Years later, I got to know Pat through working with Joey DeFrancesco. I asked Philly organist Trudy Pitts for an introduction and soon after was thrilled to be talking to Pat on the phone about taking some lessons. When I showed up, of course, I was a nervous wreck, even though I'd been recording and touring for a number of years already. But Pat was so relaxed: "Hey, man you want a sandwich—how about a beer?" He totally set me at ease. We did the lesson, and what he showed me in those two hours changed the way I play, even to this day.

What Pat showed me in that lesson wasn't so much some specific lines, where I would be trying to copy him, but more a way of looking at the neck that was very illuminating. He asked me at the outset, "Do you look at the neck in pieces, or as a whole?" Years later, I realized it was a typical Pat "zen" trick question, because what he showed me was how to look at the neck BOTH ways, in pieces and as a whole. So if I'd said, "as a whole," he would have said, "Let me show you how to look at it in pieces," and vice versa. Fortunately, the answer I gave was along the lines of, "Duh, I don't really know," so he showed me both facets. I still use his technique today and teach it to my own students. So Pat's influence has been profound but in a subtle way—not a direct copy, but more a way of looking at things. It's always very interesting to talk to Pat, as he has a very analytical mind, a probing curiosity about a lot of topics, and he's very articulate, too. The last conversation we had, he was talking about taking religious symbols and translating them into musical concepts . . . and here we get to the rub. I think for Pat, as for so many other great artists, the instrument is just a vehicle for expression. I think he would "paint" no matter what the medium, whether it was a guitar or a set of spoons. I did have the great pleasure of playing with Pat once onstage as part of a big Joey DeFrancesco organ bash, and of course it was a thrill, and I learned a lot. And the best part is that he is still out there doing it—searching, exploring, and knocking the rest of us out.

Vic Juris

Pat is a true genius. And guitar playing is only a small part of his genius. He is equally versed in mathematics, mechanical drawing, calligraphy, you name it. But his guitar playing, of course, is something special and very personal. You can try to transcribe his solos all you want, but the notes are his alone, and it's impossible to really get a grasp on what he is doing. At this point in my life, I sit back and enjoy his shows and just get blown away by every set and every note he plays. And he is playing better now as a senior citizen than when he was in his thirties. I met Pat in 1976. I was playing a little duo gig with bassist Steve LaSpina at a little bar in Greenwich Village, a noisy place, as I remember. Somewhere in the middle of the set, Steve tapped me on the shoulder and gave me the heads-up that Pat was sitting at the bar. What the hell would Pat be doing in this dive? Anyway, on the break we ran over and introduced ourselves and learned that Pat had just moved to New York earlier that afternoon. We hit it off immediately, and he invited me over to his apartment on Jane Street the following day. We were unpacking boxes and things. I was in a daze. Pat was my idol, and here I was hanging out with him. I was in my early twenties, subletting a place a few blocks away and going over to Pat's constantly. Pat was working on music from morning till night during that period. His work ethic was and is astounding. After Pat's surgery, he got a computer. He was the first person I knew to own a computer. And he had the whole thing sussed out in about a week, even after brain surgery. Pat has been a true friend, and he has made my life a better one. I love this man dearly.

Glenn Alexander

I first heard Pat Martino in 1976. A drummer friend in college, in the middle of Kansas, turned me on to him. I believe the first thing I heard was "Sunny" from Pat's *Live!* I was really into Joe Pass, Tal Farlow, George Benson, and Wes Montgomery at the time, but hearing Pat just blew my mind. I had never heard such powerful playing from a jazz guitarist before. The complex, fluid, and harmonically rich melodic lines were absolutely captivating, and the accents in the lines, from ghost notes to those powerful accents that gave incredible shape to even simple pentatonic lines, just blew my mind. I was immediately attracted to his sound and aura and went out and bought *Exit*. The side with "Days of Wine and Roses," "Blue Bossa," and "I Remember Clifford" just knocked me out. I had already played these songs many times, and I remember how everyone would frown when "Blue Bossa" was called on a jam session or gig. Then I heard Pat's recording of that tune, and it was a revelation to me. I thought, "This is the way it should sound!" It was unbelievable and undeniable. I transcribed his first chorus on "Days of Wine and Roses" and a whole world opened up for me. The beautiful, powerful complexity of even the opening solo break just sucked me right in. I tried so hard to emulate Pat's playing on that tune—the accents, the placement and shape of the lines. It became a standard that I strived to reach for many years, always falling short, of course.

The duo record *We'll Be Together Again* killed me with the interpretation of those beautiful ballads. Gil Goldstein is just stating the chords, no one is really playing the time, yet it was so strong in Pat's lines. I instantly fell in love with "Dreamsville," "Send in the Clowns," "We'll Be Together Again," "Willow Weep for Me," and "You Don't Know What Love Is." To this day, the clarity and beauty of Pat's improvisations and interpretation of the melodies on this recording just knock me out. In 1977, Pat was pictured on the front cover of *Guitar Player* magazine with his Gibson Custom L5S, and that was immediately on the wall of my practice room for inspiration. I was devastated when the aneurysm took him down in 1980. In 1983, I took some lessons with Pat, as I had moved to the New York area, was gigging with Chico Hamilton, and a friend gave me Pat's number in Philly. At that time I had transcribed many lines and solos, so I was really interested in his writing, what he was thinking about in music. He was deep, his awareness was incredible, his presence inviting yet intimidating. At that time, he was writing music eighteen hours a day. His discipline and dedication were so inspiring. He had just finished his third symphony, had composed over a hundred solo guitar works and I believe somewhere around three hundred string quartets, as well as several theory manuals. His brilliance was obvious. Our first lesson began with him writing middle C on the staff and starting into his "Semantic Expansion of Sonic Linguistics" theory. Six pages later, I was lost (this after having studied music theory for four years in college on a very high level, or so I thought).

I ran into Pat many times after that in airports and what have you, and he was always gracious, polite, humble. He's one of the kindest, sweetest human beings I have ever known. Pat is a genius and an extraordinary human being. He ranks among the greatest, most influential guitarists of all time, without question.

Adam Rogers

I first heard Pat's playing during the first summer that I studied jazz theory, before I really knew what was what in terms of harmonic vocabulary, substitutions, modes, anything like that. I used to listen to a jazz radio station out in L.A. when I would visit my dad in the summer, I think it was KCRW. And I had one of those radios with the tape in it where you could record things off the radio—a little boom box. So I would listen to the jazz station, and if I heard something I liked, I would just press record. I didn't really know anything about jazz at the time, but I was pressing the record button a lot. And through all that taping I eventually made what became my Rosetta Stone, if you will, of really seminal influences. And there were two things with Pat—his version of "Impressions" from *Consciousness* and him playing "I Remember Clifford" (from *Exit*). So I heard those two tunes a lot from listening to this tape I made over and over again. And funnily enough, the guy that I was taking lessons with that summer at the Guitar Institute of Technology was this really great player and dedicated teacher named Tony Baruso, who was a real disciple of Pat's. So early on, Pat Martino was just somebody that I heard on this tape of mine and somebody that my teacher was into. And over time, I came to know who he was. So his influence, along with other great jazz musicians', was really important and really seminal for me.

When I was younger, I had a sort of tunnel vision when it came to guitar. When I first started playing, someone played me Hendrix and I said, "Okay, that's the only music that exists." And then I spent about two or three years just trying to play like Hendrix. Then I had the tape I made from the radio, which included those two Pat Martino tunes, along with Joe Henderson's "Inner Urge" and Woody Shaw's "Moontrane" from Larry Young's *Unity*. And I thought, "Okay, I guess this is what jazz is." Fortunately, it was a nice collection of things to start out with. In terms of Pat's playing, I was just riveted by his sound and articulation. His instrumental mastery and ability to just so clearly articulate ideas just knocked me out. It was just some badass guitar playing, and it just wiped me out. At that same time I was trying to figure out what it was about the way jazz musicians played that sounded so much more sort of open and extended than rock-influenced or blues playing. Pat plays in such a clear way that it sort of illustrated everything that was new and interesting about jazz music to me. It almost sounded like anything superfluous was just removed from his playing until it was just this incredibly clear articulation that sounded like the locus, the meat of the thing. Like anything unimportant was removed. Even though he plays a lot of notes, it was just like this pure, incredibly swinging, rhythmically articulated jazz-guitar thing that just blew me away. And coming from where I was coming from, having listened to a lot of Hendrix, it was really sort of shocking to me, in a way.

I remember reading around this time a *Guitar Player* interview with Pat where he talked about chord voicings on guitar like they were these miraculous spiritual hieroglyphs or something. The way he expressed it was like some Hopi Indian ritual or something. I would reread this interview over and over again, and at the time I really didn't understand music theory and I didn't know what voice leading meant, but I was just fascinated by this. Later on, my primary influences became saxophonists—Trane, Joe Henderson, and Sonny Rollins. And there was something in their playing that had gotten in as influence in a foundational way really early on from my exposure to Wes and Pat. That was like a whole universe there for me.

Dean Brown

My first exposure to Pat Martino was in Boston, circa 1975. I was studying at Berklee, and a trombone player friend of mine was playing a transcription of a solo with all these really unique phrases. I asked him whose solo it was, and he said it was a Pat Martino solo. I told him I never heard a trombone play stuff like that before, and my friend explained that Pat is a guitar player! Well, that was it. I set out to find Pat's music on record. The first one I got was *The Visit*, which was dedicated to Wes Montgomery. That dark tone with all that attack and precision was intoxicating and addicting for me. His uses of thematic development and reharmonization were totally new, bold concepts for jazz guitar. It should be mentioned that the unsung hero on this disc is the accompanying guitarist, Bobby Rose, who provides a beautiful canvas for Pat to paint on.

After that, Pat's music evolved into a much more polyrhythmic and polytonal approach. I loved the fact that no matter how challenging his directions became, he always played so fluidly and soulfully. I was fortunate to see Pat many times at the Jazz Workshop and Pall's Mall (two erstwhile iconic jazz rooms on the Boston Common). He later made a record called *Joyous Lake* that featured two of my Berklee classmates, Kenwood "Woody" Dennard and Delmar Brown. Both of these guys were innovators on their instruments before they ever played with Pat, and the music that ensued was jazz/rock/fusion at its finest. I was struck by the fact that Pat's style worked so easily in a more rock/funk environment. It is a rare thing when an artist's style works on almost any kind of music. Wayne Shorter and Joni Mitchell come to mind. In any case, I think it's a relatively short list. His style is so compelling that I had to stop listening to him for a while, in order to find myself.

Fast-forward to 1981: I had just gotten my dream gig with Billy Cobham. That band included Tim Landers on bass and Gil Goldstein on keys. Gil had played a lot with Pat in the past, and he and Pat were good friends. Our second gig of the tour was in Philly, and Gil comes into the dressing room and tells us that Pat is coming to the show. Now, you've got to understand that I practically idolized this guy, and I'm playing the most challenging music that I had ever played to date for just the second time, so I'm nervous. I ask Gil if the Pat he is referring to is Pat Paulson, or maybe Pat Nixon. No such luck. It's Pat Martino, and he's now sitting in the front row, right in front of me! Fortunately, music has a way of becoming more important than the people playing it, so I got through the performance without crashing and burning, in spite of my nerves. After the show, Pat came backstage and invited Gil and myself to go out and experience a "real" Philly cheese steak. The next day he invited us to dinner at his place, and Pat showed me a seven-thousand-page, hand-illustrated manuscript on music he called "De Nexus." He also turned me on to his double-neck guitar. One of the necks had the strings upside down. Pat said he would play on the regular neck, then play the same fingering on the upside-down one to see if there was some inspiration there, just using it to "break out of the box." It was great hanging with Pat that day. And while he no longer remembers me—because of his near-fatal brain aneurysm and subsequent surgery—I will never forget him and what his music means to me.

Sheryl Bailey

Pat Martino transcends the moniker of great guitarist. He goes beyond instrumental virtuosity because he is a great artist in the sense that he encompasses a wide and expanding vision as an instrumentalist, composer, educator, and spiritual being. He blends them all together to create something unique and expresses his soul's voice. He has something deep to say, and he uses all avenues to speak his truth, and that is a gift that goes beyond virtuosity on an instrument. It is that vision and voice that reaches out and touches his audience. Being one of the greatest guitarists of all time is just an aspect of the total package. I was fortunate enough to have studied with Mark Koch, a dedicated disciple of Pat's, when I was a teenager in Pittsburgh. Mark was so generous as to make copies of his notes from his intensive studies with Pat, and that really shook my world. Pat's ideas were beyond just technical studies, they were about the cosmos and mathematics and the beauty of how all of those concepts intersect. Later on I wore out my recordings of *We'll Be Together Again, Live!,* and *Consciousness.* These became the theme music to all aspects of my life and the work that I set out to imitate on my guitar. But his work as a composer should not be dismissed. I feel that his compositions have influenced my writing more than most. Open-ended, harmonically hip, rhythmically rich, they are fun vehicles for improvisation. Again, a complete package of technique, artistry, and inspiration.

Prasanna

Pat Martino stands in a unique place in the pantheon of jazz greats. He has redefined the possibilities of jazz-guitar playing. My first introduction to Pat was his records *Exit* and *Consciousness,* and after that I heard his intriguing record *Baiyina.* Pat's incessant rhythmic drive, propelling a forward motion, and his sophisticated harmonic language come through strongly in all his playing. I have studied a few of Pat's solos and have gone over a couple of his books. Not only is he a great player, but he is a great teacher who has a unique improvisational concept that unlocks a lot of the mysteries of playing over chord changes. His courage, dedication, and extraordinary comeback from serious illness to make music at a consistently high level are all tremendously inspiring factors for me. I am truly honored to say a few words about a legend who has had a profound influence on me at many levels.

Lee Ritenour

I was a fan of Pat's ever since I was a teenager. He's older than me, but not that much older. But he's been successful since he was sixteen. I was hearing about him when I was still a teenager. His first records came out when he was probably in his early twenties. I was sixteen or seventeen, checking out this machine-gun-picking bebop player with the scary figures, just going, "Oh, my God." So I've admired Pat practically all my life and finally got a chance to play with him last year on my *Six String Theory* album. I ended up writing a piece called "L.P." on the record, and it features Pat and me playing with organ great Joey DeFrancesco. And I dedicated it to Les Paul, though I really did write it with Pat in mind. So the letters in the song title could stand for either Les Paul or for Lee and Pat, I guess. And it definitely was one of the highlights on the album, for me to play with Pat. He is such an amazing player.

Scott Denett

Knowing Pat for over twenty-five years has given me a sea of personal experiences that I am truly blessed to have. Let me share just one. In my first year of taking lessons with Pat, I would take the bus from Washington, D.C., to Philly to study with him. About fifteen minutes or so into a typical Pat lesson, my desire to learn was so strong. It was a flood of questions, compliments, and awe. One day he put the guitar down and for the first time looked a little sad, maybe concerned. He then wanted to know why I was there, and if he didn't feel like playing guitar did I feel there would be any value for me in being there today. Without hesitation, I told him that all I cared about was to be given the opportunity to spend time with him, and if he didn't feel like playing, that was totally fine with me. I explained to him I was there to be present with him and that if the guitar was in the way of that, please put it down. We had a good laugh, and Pat kept me there for a couple of days showing me the workings of what would become *Seven Sketches* on his O1/WFD Korg Workstation. I learned more about myself and music with a capital M that weekend than I ever will again. Not only had Pat unlocked my mind by showing me that expectation itself was a distraction, he had unlocked my humanity by showing me, in real terms, what life is about, here and now.

Rez Abbasi

When I was eighteen, my teacher, Paul La Rose, gave me the monumental task of learning two very dissimilar solos on similar chord changes. One was Miles Davis's "So What," and the other was Pat Martino's recording of John Coltrane's "Impressions" (from *Consciousness*). As a young guitarist, I was thoroughly amazed by Pat's ability to carry the rhythm section with his clean, fluid eighth notes and strong, accented phrases. This sort of playing was something I'd gotten used to hearing from horn and piano players only. However, facility was not the only standout attribute of his playing. His warm, round tone; feel; and modern, linear expression have also made an indelible mark on the history of jazz guitar. That same year, I came across an unreleased tape of Pat playing solo. It captured an entirely different side of his playing that was less linear, more harmonic, and all played on nylon string guitar. He played original material, as well as a piece from the great modern Cuban composer Leo Brouwer. For me, this shed more light on Pat's creative scope and further cemented the notion that modern jazz guitar has found a profound voice.

Peter Bernstein

Pat Martino is one of the greatest ever to play the guitar. He is instantly recognizable, as everything he plays is completely "him." Like all iconic players, his playing seems to come so naturally from the instrument, yet no one else ever thought to do it that way. His harmonic and linear mastery, as well as his articulation and attack, are what set him apart—he showed you could phrase with the intensity of the horn players that came out of the 1960s. Pat's musical persona is a beautiful and unique blend of ferocity and finesse. He is also one of the great conceptualists of the instrument: infinitely curious about how physics and mathematics can explain its mysteries. Thank you, Pat Martino, for the infinite inspiration!

Pete McCann

I first heard Pat when I was in high school. My guitar teacher was Mike Irish, and he had a number of Martino recordings. The first one I checked out was the *Live!* LP, and the tune that impressed me was "Sunny," which still floors me to this day. My iPod is full of Pat's music, my favorite albums of his being *Live!, Footprints, Joyous Lake,* and *Desperado.* I will never be able to play like him, but I have always enjoyed his incredible sound, masterful chops, and compositions. I have never had the chance to play with Pat, but I did play *for* him once when I was subbing for Ben Monder in the Maria Schneider Orchestra. He came down to hear the band (probably to check out Ben), and he heard me comp for an entire set. After the set, I went to talk with him and told him I wished I could have played a solo for him, but he said that he enjoyed my comping! Laughs all around. Pat will always have a place in the Guitar Greats category in anyone's "all-time" list. He has influenced so many of us, and continues to do so.

Jeff Berlin

In 1975 I was asked to replace the bass player that was playing in Pat's band at the time. I had just left music school, and Pat was the first professional jazz musician to hire me. His playing blew me away right from the start! I had already played with Pat Metheny and John Scofield when we were all kids, but I had never played with anyone with Martino's charging eighth-note bebop flair. His time was impeccable to the point of being ridiculous. He just never veered from the quarter or eighth note. For a kid just out of music school, Pat's guitar playing was riveting. I had a pretty easy gig to play, because the time was always there, mostly due to Pat's unfailing ability to swing like a son of a gun. The first thing that I noticed about Pat's tonality was that he spelled out the chords that he played over without a single extraneous note. He resolved every phrase that he played, and he never made a mistake doing it. I never knew that such perfection was obtainable, not until I heard Pat. This perfect playing ability inspired me for years afterward to try to make clear every note that I soloed on as a bass player. One time, I got hold of a cassette of a gig that we played in Seattle, Washington, and I wrote out his solo. I played through the solo and saw the academic flawlessness of his musical ideas. Pat swung, bopped, and nailed the time like no one that I had played with before. I learned a lot that summer and ever afterward from Pat's influence, and I never forgot the lessons and the fun of playing night after night in that terrific band of his.

Bobby Broom

I first heard Pat when I was around fourteen or fifteen years old. I'll never forget that night lying in my bed in excruciating pain and scared to death about the emergency appendectomy that I had to have the next day. I could barely move, it hurt so bad. Then this guitar player came on the jazz station playing a version of the pop tune "Sunny." The recording was done live, and that alone was exciting enough, but when I realized what this guy was playing, I had to find a way to get out of bed to turn up the stereo. Pain or not, this was most important! I was taken by what a powerful and poignant linear player he was—thoughtful, concise, and laser-like. He became an influence immediately. About a year later, I met a friend who was Pat's student, so I was able to get his number and take some lessons. At the time, most everything he talked about musically was way over my head. But just to spend some time with him, sitting and listening to him talk and play and him sharing his Wes Montgomery Trio records with me, was an invaluable experience. A few years ago I went to see Pat and we reminisced about the time of my lessons back in the mid-1970s. I hope he knows what an impact he had on me and so many others. He will always be one of our heroes and among the elite few who have a major and unique jazz guitar voice.

Ben Monder

I've never had the honor of meeting Pat Martino, but I've been listening to him since I first became interested in jazz. One of the first solos I ever transcribed was "Impressions" off of *Consciousness*. That record blew me away when I first heard it and still does. Standout records for me in the past were that one, *Live!, Starbright, Joyous Lake,* and *We'll Be Together Again,* as well as Willis "Gator Tail" Jackson's *Bar Wars*. I found that just by listening to a Pat Martino record I would play better afterward. He set an unprecedented standard with his drive, swing, and linear conception. He is a true original whose influence can be detected in just about everyone playing jazz guitar today.

Jimmy Bruno

In the 1970s, Pat was an original voice. Nobody played the guitar like that. And now, in 2011, Pat is still an original voice. And nobody can play the guitar like that. I first saw Pat play in 1969. I was sixteen when my father took me to Grendel's Lair to see him. He had dark glasses on. He was just a major force . . . not only his music, but his presentation. And you know what? He just got better and better and better. What can I say? He's a genius.

Dave Stryker

Pat Martino was one of the first guitarists I got into once I got bit by the jazz bug when I was around seventeen (along with Wes Montgomery, Grant Green, George Benson, and Jim Hall). Coming from rock music, I was struck by the fire in Pat's lines. His driving eighth notes and burning approach made me realize that jazz didn't have to be sedate. I remember being blown away by Pat's *Live!* as I listened over and over (on my eight-track!) driving around in my van during high school. "Sunny" and "The Great Stream" remain classics. I spent many hours taking Pat's solos off his records, and I wore out *Conciousness*. Later I had to quit listening to his music, as I realized I wanted to have my own sound and there was only one Pat Martino. But I owe a lot to Pat for bringing me into jazz. The first time I heard Pat live was at Fat Tuesday's when he made his comeback after his brain surgery. I introduced myself and laid one of my CDs on him with a tune I wrote for him called "Azzara." Since then, it's always a great feeling getting a nod and a smile at one of his shows in New York, knowing what an inspiration he's been to not only me, but to so many other guitarists. I recently heard him at Birdland play a solo on one of his B♭ blues that was so nasty and burning with ideas flowing that I just left walking down the street shaking my head. Pat is the baddest. Thanks, Pat!

Ed Cherry

I grew up listening to James Brown, Kool and the Gang, Jimi Hendrix, et cetera, but I also knew a lot about Wes Montgomery and Grant Green, as my dad had their recordings and played them constantly in our home. Even back then when I was still copying Hendrix and Jimmy Page licks, I was attracted to Grant Green's style. And I knew that if I ever wanted to play jazz guitar, it would probably be sounding more like him. Later on, around 1973 or so, I was turned on to Pat by a friend of mine who was an advanced student of jazz guitar. He was copying Pat's licks and transcribing them and told me to check him out. I was already just introduced to George Benson's recordings and had gone to New York to see him a couple of times at the Village Gate and also caught him at the Jazz Workshop in Boston. I was into Larry Coryell's flashy, fast-fingered style, as well (like most eighteen- or nineteen-year-old guitar players back then, faster was better). I'd bought Pat's *Live!* at some point and was blown away by the endless streams of notes seemingly pulling the band along. The intricate melodies on the original tunes and the burning version of "Sunny" were some great stuff. I learned (after many repeated listenings) the melody to "The Great Stream" and was pretty proud of myself for that. I then bought everything I could find that Pat was on. From the Don Patterson recordings *Holiday Soul* and *Funk You,* I learned a lot about comping with an organ player and tried to use what I heard on my first jazz gigs with B-3 playing brothers Bobby and Eddie Buster. Also, the recordings Pat did with Charles McPherson, Eric Kloss, and his own early Prestige records, especially *Strings!* and *Baiyina,* were my faves. I knew even back then that to try and play like Pat was not in my musical DNA, but I sure did enjoy listening to him for a long while in my early development. Pat is still playing great, looks healthy and grounded. Peace to you, Pat Martino.

Greg Skaff

Pat Martino is one of the gods in my personal pantheon. He's among the few guitarists who, when I first heard them, made me think, "That's what

I want to do." Where I grew up, in Wichita, Kansas, there was a club that brought in national jazz acts for a week at a time. I used to go there, and I developed a special affinity for organ-based groups because that's what the bookings at the club leaned toward. I heard Jack McDuff, Lou Donaldson with Lonnie Smith, Jimmy McGriff, Groove Holmes at this place and would try to meet the musicians after their sets to talk to them and pick their brains. I never heard or met Pat with those groups, but I remember that his name was constantly mentioned when the musicians spoke about what guitarists were happening or who I should be checking out. So around that time I narrowed my listening focus to four guitarists—Wes Montgomery, Grant Green, George Benson, and Pat Martino. All four of them played and recorded in the context of the organ group, which is still my favorite context in which to play. I remember I transcribed Pat's solo on the song "Lazybird" from a record called *East!* And even though he had *beaucoup* technique, I remember being more impressed by the drive in his playing and that he seemed to be able to go on and on, chorus after chorus, with new ideas and constant inventiveness, seemingly never repeating himself. I was also blown away by his records like *El Hombre* and particularly *The Visit!* . . . man! Such feel . . . such drive in his playing . . . so amazing! I'm also thankful that we're still able to go and see Pat play today. He is still sounding great.

Jonathan Kreisbreg

Pat Martino's *Conciousness* had a strong impact on me when I was first exposed to it in high school. Of course, then I immediately sought out other stuff and found *El Hombre, Live!* and his incredible work with Don Patterson. The swinging drive that he provides with his time feel was something I aspired to as soon as I first heard it. I'm still aspiring to it! I always felt that his sound possibly came from working with organists and growing up in Philly. He is one of the few guys that can get the punchiness of an organ on the guitar . . . just listen to "Just Friends" on *El Hombre.* It's a perfect example of someone who has completely amazing technical facility but uses it in the spirit of making folks tap their feet and jump out of their seats. I love that! Pat also has his own brand of chromaticism that he applies to various harmonies that I always felt was unique among guitarists. It creeps around the chords in a surprising, snaky way, yet always seems so clear and resolves so perfectly. There is and will always be just one Pat Martino!

Julian Lage

As a player and a person, Pat is my hero. I remember going with my guitar teacher to see Pat at Yoshi's in Oakland, California, when I was about twelve years old. It was one of the concerts that became part of Pat's record *Live at Yoshi's*. I was absolutely blown away that evening. It was one of the most defining moments in my life as a guitarist. To see a player so incredibly fluid and tasteful and soulful all at once, making the guitar sing, was something that changed my perception of what is possible on the guitar forever. After the performance, my teacher and I had the privilege of meeting Pat, and I was so touched by his warmth and generosity as a person. Not only was this the most amazing guitar playing I've ever seen, it was being played by such a kind and loving person. Pat's wife Aya took a photo of us together, and I remember a few weeks later receiving a signed copy of the photo in the mail. This completely knocked me out! I owe so much to Pat and am forever grateful to him for all that he has shared with us.

Jack Wilkins

Pat and I are about the same age. Actually, I'm a couple of months older than him, but we were both born in the same year. We never actually played together, but I've always admired him. I think I first heard Pat on record on his Prestige album *El Hombre*, but *Consciousness* was my favorite. I transcribed a couple of those solos and played them . . . the best I could. It was amazing—remarkable chops and technique, and a great sound. Pat is just one of the all-time great players. I had a record-release party in 1977, and he was gracious enough to come to that, and it was great to see him there. That was around the time he had recorded *Joyous Lake,* and he was living in Manhattan on Jane Street, I believe. Then when he had his brain operation and came back some years later, I heard him play at the Bottom Line. That was incredible, unreal! It was such stunning playing. I had never heard anything like that. It was, for me, the best playing Pat ever did . . . ever. Because it was so emotional. That particular night, he was pure emotion, and it was really wonderful to hear that. I'll never forget that evening.

Rik Jonna

I feel extremely fortunate to have met Pat in 1972 while he was performing at Baker's Keyboard Lounge in Detroit. Witnessing his extraordinary technique, Cadillac tone, quick reflexes, and boundless imagination—live for the first time—was an incredible experience. His gliding over difficult passages and execution of what seemed impossible just blew me away. Many of us celebrate achievements and worship celebrity while at the same time virtually ignoring where they came from. Because of his precise and virtuosic abilities on the guitar, some watch in awe, thinking Pat must have been a "natural." I mention this because it is far from reality. Early on, Pat developed a passion for the instrument and tallied hours upon hours of extensive and deliberate practice. It wasn't some "God-given talent." Pat never settles for mediocrity and always demonstrates great originality.

In 1976, while I was attending the Berklee College of Music in Boston, Pat visited the school to audition and assemble band members for his *Joyous Lake* project. With my plans to leave Berklee the following year, Pat invited me to join the band on tour. I recall engagements at the Berklee Performance Center in Boston, the Bottom Line in New York, and the Detroit Music Hall. That music was electrifying and far from predictable. It was complex and challenging, and the band members Pat had assembled were consistently brilliant in form . . . as was Pat, of course. He was continually stretching himself on that tour. It was on the *Joyous Lake* tour that Pat introduced me to his "diminished and minor conversion concepts," which were later released in full detail in his enlightening two-volume series "Creative Force, Parts 1 and 2." Pat has always remained passionate when it involves sharing his love, his knowledge, his life, and his approach to the guitar with others, whether it be a fellow guitarist, student, music journalist, or book publisher. He is warm and sensitive to everyone and has often been quoted saying that "it is the people that the instrument brings to him that is of true significance and importance. The guitar itself is just an apparatus."

In 1985, Pat wanted me to have his custom Ovation Adamas acoustic guitar. It was a double-neck guitar with two nylon six-string necks, which were a mirror image of each other—basically, a right- and left-hand neck on the same side of the guitar. It was made so that Pat could play a line, then immediately switch to the other neck and play the retrograde inversion of the line by repeating the finger pattern. I am not sure why Pat was steadfast on disassociating himself from this instrument. Apparently, he didn't have an interest in its odd nature at that particular moment in time and felt comfortable keeping it with me. Only Pat, with his exceptional capacity of intellect and continuous working over and over the many aspects of the instrument, could appreciate such a fantastic guitar.

The guitar remained in my possession for about a year. In 1987, I sent it to Ovation/Kaman Music Corporation for storage and display purposes. I was told that it is likely the only one that will ever be built incorporating that particular design.

In early 1996, I received an invitation from Pat to be his guest at his induction to the Philly Walk of Fame, which was held on May 9, 1996. I am blessed for the fulfilling moments Pat and I have shared over the past forty years, and those moments have helped me grow and evolve. His guidance, support, and friendship are invaluable, and it is always an honor when he refers to me as his little brother.

William Jesset

Thank you for sending me your *Fundamentals: A Broader Interpretation of the Guitar.* My opinion is this is the best insight to the "mystery" of the spatial parameters of the guitar available, that is, the relationship between the "parental" forms and the chords they produce. Also, my opinion is that the majority of instructional material is so convoluted that the only result is utter confusion for the student, who becomes focused on only "scales" in relationship to the sounds produced. I have on order your DVDs *Creative Force* and *Quantum Guitar,* which are a great way to introduce you and your music to my younger students here in Liuzhou, Guangzi, China. And with your permission, I hope to share your *Fundamentals* to further inspire a deeper understanding.

(From the Guestbook at www.patmartino.com)

Pete Townshend

When I hear Pat in free flow, that's what I feel. It's just that he's . . . he's not adrift, he's not awash, he's not on a highway, he's just flying and swooping. And that's a delightful thing to be able to do as a musician.

Martino Unstrung: A Brain Mystery
Interviews with Pat Martino, Film Director Ian Knox, and Neuropsychologist Paul Broks

By Victor L. Schermer

In 2008, British filmmaker Ian Knox produced the documentary *Martino Unstrung: A Brain Mystery* (Sixteen Films), which focused on Pat's brain aneurysm, emergency surgery, profound memory loss, and miraculous musical and personal recovery. With British neuropsychologist Paul Broks acting as narrator/investigative reporter, Knox embarked on a journey of discovery about the legendary guitarist and his lifelong struggle with AVM (arteriovenous malformation). Psychologist-journalist Victor L. Schermer conducted interviews with Martino, Knox, and Broks for publication in *All About Jazz* (AAJ). Excerpts from the three interviews are reprinted here with permission from the author and from AAJ.

Interview with Pat Martino

What prompted you to participate in a film which is deeply personal and is focused on your memory loss and recovery as such rather than the music?

Pat Martino: That's a really interesting question in that normally what leads me to do anything that takes place prior to its fruition was the very thing that led me to want to interact with Ian Knox when I first saw his presence in the room I was sitting in at Ronnie Scott's in London. I was relaxing between shows, and in walked a very interesting individual whose aura was attractive and attracted attention. We turned and looked at each other, greeted each other's presence, said hello, and then sat down and talked. I asked him what he did, and his qualities were very magnetic and exciting. And it moved from there. And the film was no different from that moment. To me, the outcome is what is left behind compared to the very moments of filming when it's been enjoyed as life itself. So, for me, each and every moment on the film is not what I see on the film, even though it's a replica. It has been "captured," very much like a photograph of a loved one in a catalog. There's no life in it to me personally. I'm more interested in the enjoyment of my life, and that's what the film is all about. And that went from moment to moment to moment. Even now it still continues, and I enjoy what I'm doing. Now I live.

The film was stimulated by a friend of Knox, the neuropsychologist Paul Broks, who became fascinated by your story. So once you discussed the film and started fleshing it out with Knox and Broks, the central focus of the film became your aneurysm, surgery, and subsequent recovery and restarting your career.

PM: Yes. It leaned towards Broks's interests as a neuropsychologist, and I shared his interest in terms of the events that took place in my life. It was interesting to me personally as a former patient.

Beyond your personal interest, do you have a reason for wanting the public to know about what happened to you medically?

PM: Not necessarily. I'm a very simple human being. To me the most valuable thing is action, to be active. Automatically it's as creative as it can be because it's my top priority. No matter what I do, if it's in action, if it's happening, it's a creative act, it's my life. Therefore, anything that takes place that triggers that productivity in any shape or size—it doesn't have to be music, it can be just social interaction—I enjoy the same way as a musical performance. I'm into action.

In other words, you approach living the way you might approach jazz.

PM: However it manifests, whatever masks it wears, it's the same thing, it's a moment of my life.

Did you do much deliberation about the message you wanted to get across about your illness and recovery?

PM: Absolutely not!

But in any case, the film does end up taking a hard look at the medical side. Many of your fans surely already know about your recovery from the aneurysm and memory loss—the story has been publicized widely, and many of us stand in wonder at how you were able to take up the guitar again and restart your career after such a trauma. But this film goes into much greater detail. It offers a microscopic analysis of many details of the aneurysm, the surgery, and the impact on your memory. There is actually one scene where a woman psychologist does standardized memory testing with you. There's even a scene where an updated MRI of your brain was made by the hospital specifically for the film. Not many people would agree to have a brain MRI for a movie! So my question is: What made you agree to let the filmmakers take such an intense look at your medical condition? Most people would prefer to keep these things private. In fact, that's one of the reasons for laws of confidentially regarding medical records. So what led you to undergo this scrutiny?

PM: That's an excellent question. And what comes to mind is rather profound for me, and I'll tell you what just occurred to me about this. To me, privacy is something that must be protected, and as such the weight of it will only remain private as long as you carry it and protect it. It's like baggage. Since that operation, I've been deeply interested in freedom, freedom of all the things that until that point were carried by me as an individual. Today, I find it unnecessary to protect the truth. The truth is what it is, and it will always be what it is. It cannot be protected or hidden. So once a person reaches a point, in my opinion, that he evaluates what hampers him, he begins to make changes. Definition. Changes of the very things that used to necessitate my protecting and hiding from others because that was my privacy—that became redefined. And by redefining it, I didn't have the weight of my privacy. It was as if I had a post-office box where I would get all my mail and wouldn't have to worry about anyone else seeing it. I no longer had to pay the price of that PO box, because I gave it up.

There's a moment in the film where you're looking at an MRI of your own brain. And both you and Paul Broks, the neuropsychologist, express anxiety. You ask Paul, "Have you ever looked at your own brain?" And he becomes quite flustered. And it's obvious there's a big hole on one side where the diseased tissue was removed. What was it like to look at a graphic representation of your own brain?

PM: I would say that there was actually one thing that was very valuable about it. And that was the similarity between looking at an item that is a tool that is very demanding to use, and the condition that it's in. The brain is simply a tool, an instrument, like the guitar. And because of that, it was similar, for me personally, to looking at a guitar as another tool that I use if it's in bad condition. The feeling that I get prior to the creative act is one that is difficult, anxious because of its condition. But that is not me, it's a tool that

I use. So to look at the MRI of the brain and see these deficits revealed was not about me, but about a tool.

One of the stars of the film, so to speak, was the surgeon who performed your operation.

PM: Frederick Simeone.

Not many people have a chance to meet their surgeon ten or twenty years later and talk with them.

PM: And then to go out and have dinner and spend the entire evening with him enjoying ourselves!

So what's it like to get to know your surgeon, who usually is behind that mask, as a person?

PM: It was a special moment, the enjoyment of mutual respect for one another. It was the pleasure of living, just as it would be with any other person.

I know that Dr. Simeone loves jazz. So when you were flown in from Los Angeles for this emergency operation, did he know you were a jazz icon?

PM: He told me that he was fully aware of my career. I'm sure that it was brought to his attention, because when I called my parents from Los Angeles about the diagnosis and the warning that I had only two hours to live at that time, they contacted Dr. Simeone here at Pennsylvania Hospital, and I'm sure they filled him in on all of the details about me.

If they felt you were at such immediate risk, why didn't they find the best neurosurgeon in L.A. to do the operation instead of taking the further risk of a long flight back here to Philly?

PM: I myself had already made that decision, for personal reasons.

The movie discloses many things about you, and one thing in particular startled me—namely, a time when you angrily chastised Matt Resnicoff, a recording producer [for the All Sides Now *session on Blue Note]. To your credit, you later tried to apologize to him. I know you as such a loving and gentle person that it is hard for me to imagine you getting so angry. But, then, everyone has a dark side.*

PM: Well, I don't know if it's a dark side. I would say it's a weak side on my part. I was upset with the futility of having been such a nice person, again and again and again. Finally, when it didn't work, I literally lost control and literally turned the table over! Things were going wrong with the production, and I just couldn't take it anymore! I exploded. Later, I told a mutual friend to apologize for me to Matt. This morning, I received a letter from a prisoner who asked for a photo and an autograph, and in my response, one of the things I told him by way of advice was, "Give to others what you ask of them, and never look back." With Matt, I failed to follow that advice.

So it was something you regret having done, but it was inevitable in view of all that had been building up inside you.

PM: Yes. That thing with Matt was something I carried around and felt badly about for a long time, and I wanted to get that across. But so far, Matt hasn't responded to my apology, which I conveyed to him through a mutual friend, and I hope to meet him face-to-face at some point.

A number of people who see the new film will have undergone their own personal traumas, whether medical, divorce, natural disaster, and so on. What would you like those people to learn from the film? More specifically, and I know you've given talks at hospitals on this subject, what would you like to say to those who have suffered memory loss?

PM: Something very simple: Definition. How we define what we like or dis-like. If we could see "like" and "dislike" from a distance, we'd no longer be subject to either of them. And that allows us to consider our suffering in a different light. Try to remember a time when you wanted to change the color of your complexion, and you went to the beach, and you prepared to put on suntan lotion, lie down on your blanket or towel, and consciously suffer to become what you wanted to be, namely get a tan. If you could suffer like that to reach any of your goals in recovery, you will achieve them.

You don't see a difference between intentional suffering to achieve an end and the suffering that is brought on by traumatic events?

PM: No suffering should be intentional. If you are brought into a situation that requires professional or medical assistance, get another opinion as to alternatives. But any way that you go is going to be difficult. Accept the difficulty, and do it from the bottom of your heart. That's called courage.

And there's something healing about it. Self-esteem is healing. To do the best you can and be proud of yourself in the process. Plant seeds, let them grow, and move forward.

Interview with Ian Knox

In *Martino Unstrung,* the stories, personalities, and audio-visual images come at the viewer with the relentless rapidity of some of Martino's runs on the guitar. The result is a driving, honest, and moving narrative that could only have been made by a director who loves jazz, humanity, and filmmaking with equal passion and dedication. Such is Ian Knox, the prime mover of what is perhaps the finest documentary about a jazz musician ever made. I had the privilege of meeting and talking with Knox when he came to Philadelphia to offer a private screening of a preliminary "cut" of the film to Martino, his wife Ayako, and some of his close friends and associates. Far from the flamboyant, demanding individual that I always assumed movie directors to be, Knox turned out to be relaxed, warm, friendly, and open. That may be one what gave him such relaxed directorial rapport with Martino and the other personae who weave their way through this marvelous film.

You're a noted film director, and like Clint Eastwood and Martin Scorsese, are you also a jazz fan?

Ian Knox: I listen to all sorts of stuff. At Edinburgh College of Art, I played bass in a jazz quartet called Jobsworth. Wes Montgomery's "Four on Six," which Pat has made his own, was in our repertoire. We were pretty good, though deeply unfashionable, as everybody else was in punk bands at the time. I love great guitar players. It's a complex, soulful instrument with incredible range. I love the clean, mercurial lines of Pat Martino and, at the other end of the spectrum, Ali Farka Touré, with his rough-hewn African blues. I don't really understand why, but they both move me deeply. I think Pat and Mr. Farka Touré would have hit it off.

How did you become a film director?

IK: Serendipity. As an art student, I spent a lot of time in the photography department preparing silkscreens and found a Bolex camera in the cupboard. I was going out with a girl who was a drama student, so we just started shooting films over weekends with her friends. Also, I was seeing the best of world cinema on my doorstep at the Edinburgh Film Festival and had the chance to meet some great filmmakers. I was very inspired by the work of Hungarian director Miklós Jancsó, who sparked in me a lifelong love affair with Hungarian cinema. [His son Nyika is the director of photography on *Martino Unstrung.*]

IK: One hot summer's day in 2005, whilst painting the house we had recently moved into, I read a newspaper review of Pat Martino's gig at Ronnie Scott's. I didn't know Pat's work, but this review said get down there and hear one of the jazz guitar greats who, furthermore, had "forgotten more music than most musicians learn in a lifetime," alluding to Pat's experience of amnesia. I went along that night with my wife, Sarah. The first set was amazing—Pat was on fire. Between sets I said hello to him at the bar and thanked him for the beautiful set. He bought me a beer, and during a brief conversation I asked him if, on returning to the guitar, he had "studied himself." He roared with laughter: "No, man, I stayed well away from myself, that was the point!" I was hooked. I asked him if we could meet again to talk about the possibility of making a film based on his story. We exchanged numbers and arranged to meet for lunch at his hotel the following day. In fact, we very nearly didn't meet; London was paralyzed by the terrorist bombings of 7/7, but by midafternoon I was able to find a way around the police cordons by bicycle and we had a very long chat, way into the night, as Pat's gig at Ronnie's was canceled. I'd been thinking for some time about how to write a movie based on Pat's story when a friend recommended that I read a book called Into the Silent Land by a neuropsychologist called Paul Broks. As I read Paul's stories, a thrill of recognition passed through me. Here was a great writer who could not only describe, seemingly from the inside and with compassion, the place where Pat had been, but could also make accessible the science of the human brain, its shortfalls and the challenges it faces in understanding the human condition. I wrote to Paul, and he responded enthusiastically to my proposal that we write a dramatized film together. On meeting, we hit it off and we seemed to be interested in making the same sort of film. After spending a long afternoon with Pat in London, we somewhat changed our ideas. The chemistry between the three of us felt great. Pat and Paul were clearly fascinated by each other. We felt that we'd be missing a trick if we failed to get Pat himself on film and decided to make a documentary.

What audience is the film intended to reach?

IK: I hope the film will satisfy the most avid jazz fan, curious for insight to this brilliant and iconic player, but the extraordinary nature of the human interest story will, we hope, reach further to a general audience. In addition to the eighty-two-minute running time of the film, we have cut a further seventy minutes of DVD extras, which includes extended concert footage, interviews, master-class footage, and a taste of Pat's "Sacred Geometry" musical theory.

Did you conceive the film more as an inspirational story, or as a realistic "slice of life"?

IK: The film was very much conceived as an inspirational piece. Pat is an unlikely and inspiring hero whose remarkable survival holds hope and wider meaning for us all.

From working so closely with him on the film, what are your impressions of Pat as a person and a musician?

IK: It is impossible to separate the man from the musician. Pat is an artist to his very core. It's a cliché, but he really does live and breathe music. He's very curious and open to all opportunities that life puts in his way. His discipline and stamina are formidable. He exercises his brain like a muscle, and his short-term memory seems better than mine. When filming, he would work until we dropped. We'd work him fourteen- to sixteen-hour days, requiring great concentration from him and often in unbearable temperatures. Then at the end of the day he'd unwind for an hour or so playing duets with his wife Aya, before taking us out to dinner. He's a witty and charming man, and I miss him now that the film is completed. We became great friends.

The film is done compassionately, yet it is brutally honest in some ways. What made you decide to dig in so deeply into Martino's personality and character rather than portray him as a "matinee idol" of jazz, so to speak?

IK: Our love and respect for Pat were a given from the outset, so we didn't really view the material in terms of "negative" or "positive"; rather it was about trying to chart the symptomatic shifts in his mood and behavior over the years. The idea was for Paul to make a forensic interrogation of Pat's brain to see what conclusions, if any, we could draw about Pat's remarkable recovery. To unravel this complex mystery, we needed to be scientifically accurate in presenting the evidence. The film takes the form of a series of neurological tests, which open up the biographical highways and byways of Pat's memory. Pat is the gentlest, most spiritual person, adored and admired by most of those who come in contact with him, but we did encounter some very oddly diverse opinions from the past. According to one aggrieved producer, he's the devil incarnate! Pat's illness and recovery took him to the furthest emotional and psychological extremes, and we have charted that in the film, as far as possible, through people's testimonies. The brain surgery was performed back in 1980, so no records existed. His brain surgeon, Dr. Fred Simeone, could recall a good deal about the operation, but we needed to do an MRI brain scan in order to fully understand what had been done to him.

What made the diverse elements of Pat's story come together into a unified whole?

IK: The underlying theme of the film is about the brain and "the self" and what it is that makes each and every one of us who and what we are. That's a universal question, which we have tried to deal with in an entertaining and humorous way. That is what hopefully gives the film unity.

What prior filmmaking experiences were useful to you in making the film?

IK: My background is in fiction filmmaking. I'm used to working with actors and being able to hold and construct the film in my head. The experience of making *Martino Unstrung*, my first documentary film, could not have been more different. The lack of crew and equipment was enormously liberating. We started with a clear structure for the film, but we were very improvisational and spontaneous in shooting. We'd just follow the moment as it occurred and see where it took us. But the same rules of dramatic storytelling apply—it's just that you don't necessarily understand what the story is until much later in the process. We shot 120 hours of material, and I initially felt swamped by it. Jonathon Morris, the editor, is a seasoned documentarist, and he gave me confidence through a prolonged editing process. He was brilliant.

How did you help your nonactor subjects to get comfortable in front of the camera?

IK: Well, Joe Pesci can hardly be described as a nonactor! But seriously, musicians are performers; they love being in front of the camera, and once they were started, it was almost impossible to stop them. Townshend and Santana are total naturals. Also, we were a tiny crew—only Paul, myself, and Nyika—and frankly, we were such rank amateurs as documentarists that our subjects were more amused by us than intimidated!

Did anything unexpected happen as you were making the film?

IK: Almost everything was unexpected and surprising, but two characters stand out—both somehow characteristically "Pat." Pat received an email from a gentleman in Toronto called Stan who had heckled him at a concert in 1976. He said that he'd carried the guilt of that act for thirty years and needed to apologize. I invited him to attend a gig that Pat was playing at the Iridium in New York, with the intention of keeping them apart until the end of the gig, when we'd film the big "I forgive you." Of course, as we were setting up, Pat came right across the club, walked up to Stan, said,

"Hey Stan, I'm so glad you could make it," and gave him a big hug. After the gig, we shot them meeting, but it was awful. The moment was lost, and they couldn't act it. We had Stan's quest threaded through the film through most of the edit, but it proved too great a distraction from the main storyline, so we cut it. It was a fascinating insight into how a seemingly insignificant incident can end up being an overwhelming part of somebody's life. [The story of "Stan: The Toronto Heckler" is included in the DVD extras.] On another occasion, Pat wanted me to interview his friend who is a kind of alternative health guru, who had played a key role in his recovery from a life-threatening condition. This impressive whirlwind of a lady arrived at Pat and Aya's place one afternoon, took one look at Paul, and set about treating him for a painful problem that was afflicting him. As she worked on him, she was observing Nyika the cameraman's posture as he set up the lights, noting, correctly, that he had a back problem. She laid Paul out on the floor and set about giving Nyika treatment! At a certain point, I looked at my watch and realized that two hours had passed, we had not shot anything, and my interviewer and cameraman were both incapacitated. So I picked up the camera, switched it on, and said, "So, tell me about how you first met Pat." We did the interview whilst she worked on Nyika on the floor, but her words were gradually drowned out by deep, sonorous snores from Nyika. (To be fair, he was exhausted from jet lag.) Of course, we deleted all this from the final version of the film.

In the film your use of cityscapes to convey meaning and emotion is marvelous. What led you to emphasize urban imagery in the way that you did?

IK: We wanted to tell the medical story without resorting to men in white coats and gratuitous medical footage. We used the city as a metaphor for the human brain. The film merges these three cities on two continents into a generic whole. I loved shooting in New York, because people were, on the whole, very helpful in their brusque New York way. They were curious and seemed to like us being around doing our thing in their space, whereas Londoners just don't want the hassle. They're not interested unless you're going to pay them, which doesn't work too well in low-budget filmmaking. Pat lives in South Philly, so we spent a lot of time there. Home was the Holiday Inn next to the Eagles ground. It's a big-hearted blue-collar town, and it felt like coming home each time we returned.

Can you tell us a bit about the film's composer and what qualified him for the specifics of this movie?

IK: Milton Mermikides is an English guitarist and composer whom Paul and I met through the Wellcome Trust, right at the beginning of the project. He was pioneering interesting experimental music, writing his own computer software to capture human brain waves to trigger musical sequences through midis. He's a great fan of Pat's and offered his services with the suggestion that he could hook Pat up to his rig. This led to one of the most lyrical musical performances in the film, which we filmed in his London studio with Pat. I knew that I wanted a score for the film, independent of Pat's own stuff, that would accompany the brain journey. Pat has experimented with symphonic music in the past, and we talked about the idea of his composing the score, but his busy schedule was clearly going to leave him little time to work on it. At the back of my mind, I'd been thinking of Milton for the job, but it was in fact Pat who said that in his opinion there was somebody already involved with the film who would be right for the score. He had listened to Milton's stuff and was impressed by it. It seemed organically the right way to go. That's how the score came about. It was a very fertile and happy collaboration.

What have you learned about human beings in the course of your life and work?

IK: Mainly that there is no objective truth or reality. That's not to say that people are dishonest. Everybody has a unique story to tell, but the contradictions and paradoxes that occur when you start looking at any story from multiple points of view are fascinating. That is the stuff of drama and art, and maybe the clearest way to tell a story is through fiction. Paul Broks, who trained as a scientist, understands that very well, which is why I initially went to him with this project.

What do you have in mind for future filmmaking projects?

IK: If you want to get to the truth, do fiction! Paul and I are working on the fictionalized movie version of the Martino story, as well as an anthology of shorter neurological tales, which will be presented in the manner of a latter-day *Twilight Zone*. With Rebecca O'Brien, our brilliant producer at Sixteen Films, I'm preparing a movie adaptation of an epic Scottish novel set around World War I, called *Fergus Lamont*. Making *Martino Unstrung* was a wonderful, liberating experience, so, given the right subject (probably musical), I'd hope to do another documentary film before too long.

What does Ian Knox do when he's not making films?

IK: Outside of film I play music, ride motorcycles and bicycles, but mostly I change nappies and go to the park with my two gorgeous little girls—Kita, aged three, and Anna-May, aged one.

Interview with Paul Broks

Paul Broks is a prominent British neuropsychologist who is featured in the film *Martino Unstrung* and conducted a study of guitarist Pat Martino's memory loss and recovery as documented in the movie. He conceived the entire project with director Ian Knox, and they made the film with the help of a grant from the Wellcome Trust. In the film, Broks uses psychological testing, an updated MRI scan of Martino's brain, and other data to arrive at tentative conclusions about Martino's well-known medical condition and his miraculous comeback as a jazz musician. This is the most in-depth study of Martino's memory disorder and its implications yet to be done. In the process, it seemed to me that Broks conducted himself with a rare combination of scientific objectivity and humanistic compassion.

Briefly, what is the history of your friendship and association with film director Ian Knox?

Paul Broks: Ian wrote me a letter sometime in 2004. He set out Pat's story, which I didn't know, and invited me to join him on the project. I didn't take much persuading. We became friends along the way. I admire Ian's vision and energy. He can do things I can't, and I think it's good to recognize that in an artistic collaboration.

How did you and Ian Knox first get the idea for the Martino Unstrung film?

PB: It was Ian's idea. We talked first about developing a fictional treatment, but it was the availability of funding that tipped us toward documentary. It was my idea to approach the Wellcome Trust for funding. It seemed to me the Pat Martino story was perfect material for their "Sciart" program—which encourages collaborations between artists and biomedical scientists. So we applied to Wellcome, and here we are. They've been hugely supportive.

When and under what circumstances did each of you first meet Martino?
PB: I first met Pat when he played at the Pizza Express Jazz Club in London in January 2006. Ian and I got together with Pat for a postshow beer, and then we all met for lunch in Soho the following day.

The film is done compassionately, yet it is almost brutally honest in some ways, for example with a CT scan of Pat's brain made explicitly for the film and a disclosure of Pat's rage attack with a recording engineer. What led to such honesty, as opposed to what could have been an idealized or softened portrait of Pat?

PB: Pat was courageous in allowing us to make the film the way we did. We were clear right from the start that we saw the project as a three-way collaboration— four-way for the times that the brilliant cinematographer Nyika Jancsó was working with us. But it required a degree of trust on Pat's part that neither Ian nor I had to invest. We were not interested in doing a hagiography—which would have been an artistic disservice to Pat— nor was there any temptation to sensationalize. Pat's story is sensational enough. He knew the kind of film we wanted to make, and if at any stage he'd said he wasn't happy with the way things were going, we would have listened and taken stock. But the question never came up. Pat's approach to the film, I think, was somewhat like his approach to his music. Integrity is the word.

What about the MRI?

PB: I saw the MRI scan as part of the continuing story. We really didn't know the extent of the surgery that Pat underwent. The original surgical records and CT brain images no longer exist, and, in any case, brain imaging has moved on enormously since 1980. It seemed important—dare I say histori-cally important—to establish definitively the condition of Pat's brain. What exactly was it that he'd recovered from?

From your close working relationship with Pat on the film, what are your impressions of him as a person and a musician?

PB: I got on well with Pat from the start. I'd taken a serious interest in his music in the year before we first met and had grown to love it. It also helped, I think, that he'd read my book *Into the Silent Land*. Ian had sent him a copy. I was nervous about his reaction. It's a disturbing book in some ways, challenging our deepest intuitions about what it means to be a person. I wrote, among other things, about people who—like Pat—have undergone the severest possible challenges to their selfhood. But Pat grasped it straight away. He'd been there. He understood what I was trying to say. Over the course of the days and weeks we spent together making the film, Pat and I had many conversations on matters of psychology and philosophy, and much else besides. He has a sharp mind and is relentlessly inquisitive. I get the sense it's that aspect of his personality that drives him as a musician: plain curiosity. He is constantly in search of creative insight. In another life maybe he would be a neuroscientist or a philosopher—but thankfully for those of us who love music, not in this one! Pat has remarkable energy and stamina. As a musician he is incredibly disciplined and professional. When he last came over to London to play Ronnie Scott's, I went to see him backstage before the show. He had a chest infection and looked so frail and ill he could have been at death's door. I was seriously concerned for him. And yet he went out and gave one of the finest performances I've seen him give. The guitar seemed to have a life of its own that night.

Did you experience Martino's wry sense of humor along the way?

PB: Yes, that aspect really was contagious. There was a lot of laughter on this journey. Here's just one example. Pat had just played the Iridium, and afterward we were sitting in a bar. There's a keyboard player, and people are getting up from the floor to sing their party pieces—mostly old musical-theater stuff. It's a good atmosphere. Then a guy with the most astounding voice starts to sing. It's a deep, wobbly voice, getting deeper and wobblier as he goes. It's so weird it could be an acoustic weapon designed to destabilize the rhythms of your internal organs. People start to look at one other in disbelief. I look at Pat; he looks at me. It's a question of who's going to give in first. Then the accompanist stops playing and says to the singer, I think with genuine curiosity, "Are we doing the same song?"—at which point Pat and I are simultaneously just helpless with laughter.

What further impressions of Martino occurred to you?

PB: Pat is the consummate professional, dedicated to his art, perfectionist, obsessional even, but with a capacity to totally let go and wind down once he's done the business. There is a darker side, too, no doubt—the volcanic temperament that the film hints at; the moment, as Pat puts it in the film, "when the ego steps forth." But I honestly never saw any hint of that, even though at times we must have really tested his patience—long, long days of filming and psychological testing. Invariably, at the end of the day Pat was ready to go out and eat and share a bottle of wine and talk late into the night.

Pat's emphasis on living in the moment seemed to help him turn his memory loss into an asset. Do you think he acquired that attitude from Buddhism and other religious studies prior to the memory loss, or that the latter led him to such a philosophy?

PB: I think Pat is an original thinker. By that I don't mean he is a great intellectual or guru. But let's say he has a "turn of mind" which can be truly impressive. Perhaps that's what he expresses in his music. If I can make a sports analogy—I watch a lot of soccer—elite players are all super fit and super skillful. They are capable of remarkable things in terms of technique, agility, and stamina. What separates the great from the merely remarkable is "turn of mind": invention and originality, a certain way of anticipating moves and patterns, a unique way of seeing things. Pat seems to have had a very "spiritual" outlook well before his illness and surgery. How much of that was shaped by the underlying brain disorder we can never know. I would very much like to look further into Pat's "in the moment" philosophy—and what, incidentally, is more "in the moment" than musical improvisation? The focus on "the now" is something that is very much a genuine part of his experience, it seems to me. I recently gave a talk about Pat at a neuroscience meeting. Professor Richard Gregory, a senior statesman of neuropsychology and a very distinguished neuroscientist, was in the audience. He immediately picked up on the question of Pat's perception of time, and that's something I'd like to look at experimentally.

Pat told me that his ability to play the guitar was completely lost. What is your professional opinion about this?

PB: The Pat Martino story is a wonderful legend. I didn't believe for a moment that Pat had literally forgotten how to play the guitar. If that had been the case, we would have to radically revise our current understanding of the organization of brain function and I'd now be on my way to a Nobel Prize. It seems extremely unlikely that he "completely lost" the memory of the guitar, if by that we mean a total loss of skills and knowledge. There are cases of musicians with dense and persisting amnesia—perhaps most famously the British musician Clive Wearing—who nevertheless retain their musical skills, even whilst denying they have any. In neural terms, musical skills—as procedural knowledge—are laid down in phylogenetically old structures of the brain such as the basal ganglia and cerebellum. These regions were not affected in Pat's case. Other, cortical, areas are involved in the execution of musical skills, notably the motor regions of the frontal lobe, but these, too, were not directly affected in Pat's case. Clive Wearing has been studied for many years, and his wife, Deborah, published an account of their story a couple of years ago. It is entitled *Forever Today*. Most recently, Oliver Sacks has written about him in his book *Musicophilia*. Pat certainly seems to have experienced a period of significant amnesia post-surgery, and it may be that, like Wearing, he had no knowledge of having played the guitar. Certainly by all accounts he had no interest in picking up the instrument and seems to have been quite alienated from it—so, yes, "seemed foreign to him" would be an apt description. His father's well-meaning but emotionally intrusive efforts to encourage him to play were probably counterproductive.

What enabled Martino to resume his guitar artistry after his virtually complete lack of recall for this part of his past life?

PB: At this distance in time, it's hard to establish exactly when the amnesia began to resolve and when Pat picked up the guitar again, or indeed whether these phases coincided. I put these questions to guitarist John Mulhern, perhaps our most reliable witness, who spent time with Pat immediately before the surgery and during the weeks and months that followed. John couldn't say for sure what the tempo of recovery was, but I got the sense it was certainly weeks and possibly a number of months before Pat started playing again. It is even harder to establish the point at which Pat reestablished a continuous sense of his old identity. As John describes it, when Pat finally did pick up the guitar again, he seemed to rediscover his passion for the instrument and was playing and transcribing music almost maniacally. So I would say it was a resurgence of motivation and a rediscovery of skills rather than a relearning. This makes complete sense neuropsychologically. Musical skills are represented diffusely throughout the brain and include, as I've already mentioned, subcortical areas not directly affected by Pat's AVM and the surgical procedure to remove it.

How does amnesia of Martino's type relate to brain structure and function?

PB: That is a most interesting question about the neuropsychological nature of Pat's postoperative amnesia. Why should he have become amnesic? After all, the key episodic and procedural memory structures are unaffected. In particular, our MRI scan shows the hippocampus to be intact left side and right. There are various possibilities we might speculate on, although his surgeon, Dr. Fred Simeone, would be better placed to offer a comment on the medical and surgical aspects here. One possibility is that the surgery had nonspecific physiological effects on certain key brain regions involved in recall of episodic/autobiographical memory, which subsided as the brain readjusted physiologically post-surgery. There is no clear suggestion that Pat's new learning and recall abilities were affected postoperatively, which would tend to suggest that the hippocampus was functional. In any case, severe amnesia (at least of the sort associated with temporal-lobe damage) typically requires damage to the hippocampus bilaterally. In Pat's case it was only structures adjacent to the left hippocampus that might have been affected. My hunch—and it's only a hunch—is that there were relatively temporary dichotic effects in the frontal lobe in areas important for both motivation and autobiographical recall.

It is also difficult to disentangle genuine recall of remote memories from new learning acquired since the surgery. As Pat says in the film, he worked hard to relearn and assimilate names of family members and to reconstruct his autobiography through the accounts that others were giving him. I'm inclined to think that his autobiographical recall comprises a combination of the two to some extent, though I'm also confident that a good deal of genuine memory from childhood and early adulthood has been reestablished. Again, this is what you'd expect given the pattern of brain damage. Semantic ("fact recall") memory is one area where Pat does seem to have some subtle problems, which is in line with damage to the left temporal lobe. There's a neat illustration of the difference between semantic memory and episodic ("event recall") memory in the film. Poring over a photo album, Pat speaks animatedly, and in detail, about being in Boston in 1963 on the day JFK was shot (episodic memory). But then on another occasion when asked to give the date of the assassination, he struggles (semantic memory).

Neurologically speaking and otherwise, what would explain Martino's ability to relearn guitar playing, especially since jazz requires not only rote learning, but improvisation, creativity, and a feeling for the music, all of which are usually based on the sorts of experiences which Martino forgot?

PB: For reasons I've already given, Pat wouldn't have lost his amazing dexterity on the guitar. Nor would one expect him necessarily to lose the ability to improvise and imbue feeling—his emotional systems may have been recalibrated to some extent given the loss of adjacent brain tissue, but the basic brain structures of emotion remain in place. There is evidence to suggest that fluent improvisation depends upon dynamic interaction between different regions of the frontal lobes—which were not structurally affected in Pat's case. It's interesting, however, that when he started playing again he lacked the confidence for a long time even to play familiar jazz standards without the crutch of having the chord sequences written out in front of him. So he quite likely suffered a loss of musical knowledge (semantic memory again) rather than basic skills. This would be consistent with the temporal-lobe damage he suffered. So in some ways it's perfectly true to say that he had to learn his craft again—but not all aspects of the craft. What I'm saying in no way diminishes Pat's achievement in returning to the peak of his art. Given the knowledge we now have, Pat's return seems to me all the more heroic. This was an extraordinary recovery, believe me.

More generally speaking, on the face of it, music seems to be a luxury or pastime rather than an ingredient of the evolutionary imperative of "survival o –the fittest." Can you tell us something about what you see to be the role of music in brain function and human evolution? (Dr. Simeone told me that musical processing occurs in a wide swath of the human brain.)

PB: Ethnomusicologists point to the collective functions of music, its use in ritual and ceremony, its contribution to the continuity and stability of cultures. Singing and dancing draw people together, synchronizing emotions, bonding the group in empathy and reflection or in preparation for action. The power of music lies beyond language and intellect. It comes from an emotional need for communication with other human beings. But I think there is something prior even to that. Music goes deeper; it perfuses the body. It fuels our most primitive mental machineries—the systems of emotion, bodily sensation, and action that constitute the "core self"—the embodied self of the present moment. Without coherence at this level, there is no possibility of developing a stable personal identity or social relationships. Perhaps that's one of the basic functions of music: to tune up those engines of self-awareness. I don't believe, as Steven Pinker seems to, that music is mere "auditory cheesecake" with no primary adaptive function.

How would you compare and contrast your own interests as a neuroscientist with those of Oliver Sacks?

PB: We share similar interests to the extent that we both write about neurological disorder and are drawn to unusual, striking cases.

Oliver Sacks is a neurologist, and I'm a neuropsychologist by training, so we have taken rather different career paths in terms of clinical work. I've also spent time in basic research posts, including in the pharmaceutical industry. We share similar interests to the extent that we both write about neurological disorder and are drawn to unusual, striking cases. Of course, I am following his lead on that, as he had followed the pioneering Russian neuropsychologist, A. R. Luria. But there are differences in the way Sacks and I write about these things. My writing style veers more to the quasi-fictional and, as well as writing about "real cases," I sometimes make excursions into speculative fiction. Sacks writes inspiringly about human survival. My vision is darker, though I hope with shafts of illumination and inspiration.

In the film, you become self-admittedly anxious when Martino asked you if you ever saw your own brain scan. What was triggered for you?

PB: First, it just hit me that this was a very unusual situation, like giving a clinical consultation but in front of the camera. I felt conflicted because I would have preferred to discuss Pat's MRI in private, yet here we were by mutual consent making a film, and it was important for the film that we captured the moment on camera. And then into this unusual situation Pat flings a perfectly reasonable but unexpected question, one that I would have welcomed in the privacy of the consulting room and perhaps used as an opportunity to talk about different personal reactions to brain imaging but which now put me under the spotlight. The answer I give was true. I have never been that much involved with brain imaging for research and have never sought out opportunities to be scanned, in common with most people who do this sort of work. Again, honestly, this is for no particular reason, though scans are still relatively expensive and researchers have budgets to watch so are not inclined to do such things purely for fun. Maybe if Pat agrees to take part in some further brain imaging for us, I'll take my turn in the scanner and give him a picture of my brain to hang on his wall.

Pat is a very spiritual person. By contrast, you are a neuroscientist and thus are basically "materialistic" in your work in terms of linking behavior and mentation to causes or correlates in the brain. What, if any, is the place of spirituality in your understanding of the personality and life itself?

PB: Spirituality and materialism are not mutually exclusive. I consider myself a spiritual person, too—the spiritual intangibles of love, awe, inspiration, beauty, mystery, and elevation are as important to me as to anyone else. I'm a materialist—"naturalist" is better— in the sense that I just don't believe in the spooky stuff of supernaturalism!

Now that you've made a film, in addition to your many other accomplishments, what do you see as your career path from here on?

PB: I still teach and have some involvement in clinical work, but my aim now is to devote more time to writing. There's plenty to keep me busy. I'm working on a second book entitled *The Laws of Magic*, which explores imagination, memory and identity, and I've just been commissioned to write a regular column for the *London Times*. I also have a new play opening in London later this year, *On Emotion*, co-written with the brilliant director Mick Gordon. In addition, one hopes there might arise opportunities to develop Pat's story in other ways—who knows!

Appendix III

Pat Martino Master Class
Sacred Geometry

Simplifying the Fretboard with Pat Martino

By Jude Gold (*Guitar Player* magazine, April 2004)

If there's one common misconception people have about geniuses, it's the notion that these stellar intellects engage only in the most strenuous of thought; that in order to even hold a conversation with one of these brainiacs you need an Ivy League PhD, an IQ of 200 or more, and a bulbous cranium that makes you look like a character from *Star Trek*. In reality—as brilliant inventions such as the wheel, the light bulb, the magnetic guitar pickup, the TV dinner, and the Pet Rock all so vividly prove—the most ingenious ideas are often the simplest. And if the mark of true genius is the ability to find simple, head-slapping, gosh-why-didn't-I-think-of-that solutions to complex problems, then Pat Martino is truly one of the guitar's cleverest minds. In this lesson, the jazz legend shares with you an inspiring remapping of the fretboard that is radically different from what is typically taught in private lessons or at music schools.

"The guitar is structured like no other instrument," states Martino, "and it unveils itself in a unique way. Like the piano, it has its own fully unique temperament. But the communal language of music that all musicians share—that is, the language of scales, theory, and intervals that we all use when explaining or communicating music—really has nothing to do with any instrument other than the piano."

But guess what, guitarists: It's now finally time to describe music from our point of view. And there's probably nobody more qualified to step up to the podium and demonstrate a guitar-centric vision of the musical universe than Martino, because he has written a mesmerizing treatise called "The

Nature of Guitar" that may forever change how you visualize the way harmony, melody, and improvisation all function on the fretboard. And yes, Martino's genius ideas are almost childishly simple.

Abandoning the Piano

"Here's the piano," says Martino, playing the C-major scale in Example 1.

"These seven notes are the white keys. And the piano's black keys are here" (Example 2).

"These five black keys spell a D♯ pentatonic minor scale, starting on the 7, C♯. Combine those two groups of notes and you get all twelve notes of the octave—in other words, . . . you get the chromatic scale" (Example 3).

"That's seven plus five. It's a system of addition—a horizontal system based on the fact that the piano goes from left to right, from lower in pitch to higher in pitch. This is where scales come from, which are part of the community language you use to function with other musicians so that you can discuss modes and scale forms, et cetera. But scales really have nothing to do with how the guitar works. The guitar does not work horizontally."

Meet the Parents

The guitar, like the piano, does have horizontal properties, at least in the sense that as you ascend horizontally from left to right on a given string, the notes get higher in pitch. What makes the guitar inherently different, though, is that it also has a vertical nature, because it allows you to move up and down—which is exactly what you do when moving from a higher string to a lower string or vice versa. This means that the fretboard is an x–y axis. "It's a matrix," adds Martino. "By being both horizontal and vertical, you have latitude and longitude. It's like a compass—north, east, west, and south."

We're about to enter the heart of Martino's unique vision of the fretboard—but fear not: Although Martino plays some of the most ferocious, angular modern jazz lines you'll ever hear from a guitar player, all you'll need to grasp the concepts that follow is a basic knowledge of music theory, because, in Martino's mind, there are only two basic shapes you absolutely must know to unlock the secrets of the fretboard. One of them is the augmented triad (a major triad with a raised 5) such as C aug 5 in Example 4.

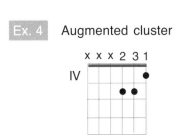

Ex. 4   Augmented cluster

"This augmented cluster is one of two parental forms on the guitar," explains Martino. By "parental," Martino means that the augmented triad—in this case a C aug 5 spelled C–E–G♯—produces multiple chordal offspring. Specifically, it's a harmonic gateway to three major chords. Just lower any one of its three tones and you get a major triad. As shown in Example 5, if you drop the lowest note, C, a half step, you get an E-major triad. Or lower the middle note, E, the same distance, and you have a G♯-major triad. Or, finally, knock the highest pitch, G♯, back one fret to hear a C triad. Slick!

Augmented cluster's offspring

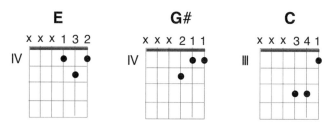

"Also, be sure to try raising any note in the augmented cluster a half step," encourages Martino. "That's how you'll get minor chords. For instance, raise the lowest note in our C aug 5 chord a semitone to C♯, and you've got a C♯-minor triad. Sharp just the middle note, and you'll hear an F-minor triad. Or raise the highest note, and you've got A minor."

The other parental shape that Martino deems crucial is the diminished-seventh chord, which is represented by the E dim 7 in Example 6.

Diminished cluster

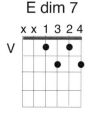

"The diminished cluster has a different set of siblings," notes Martino, playing the shape's four offspring chords in Example 7.

"Lower any one of its notes by a half step and you get the root of a dominant 7 chord. For example, drop the lowest tone and you get G♭7. Or, drop the second-lowest note and you get C7. Drop the second-highest note and you get E♭7. And if you lower the highest note, you'll hear A7. To me, this is the guitar. These two parental shapes—the augmented and diminished clusters—are the fastest way to learn the instrument, provided you have a basic command of chord theory and scale spellings."

Diminished cluster's offspring

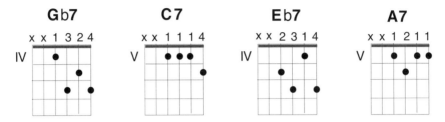

Symmetry in Motion

The most beautiful aspect of the two parental forms has to be their perfect symmetry. The augmented triad, for example, divides the octave equally into three intervals of a major third. For that reason, if you move the shape up or down the fretboard a major third (or four frets), as shown in Example 8, the chord doesn't change in any way except for the fact that its tones become rearranged (with one shifted an octave). We're playing the same shape at the fourth, eighth, and twelfth frets, yet the harmony, note names, and fingering remain exactly the same.

Symmetrical Inversion

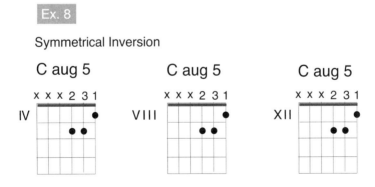

"It gives you automatic inversions of itself with no necessity of memorizing new fingerings," observes Martino. "If you arrange the twelve notes of the chromatic scale like the face of a clock, you'll see that the augmented cluster forms a perfect triangle" (Example 9).

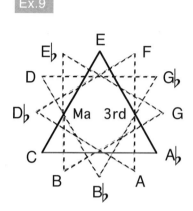

Due to its perfect symmetry, there are only four different augmented triads, as shown by the four triangles in Example 9. Our C aug 5 triad is in bold, spelled enharmonically C–E–A♭. Similarly, the other parental shape—the diminished cluster—is perfectly symmetrical, as well. Dividing the octave equally into four minor thirds, a diminished chord repeats itself every three frets, as shown in Example 10. Again, the only thing that changes in these four identical grips is the arrangement of the notes.

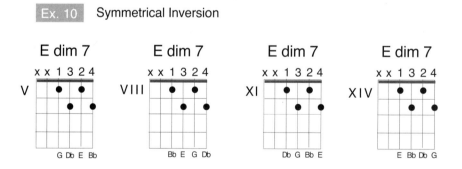

"The diminished cluster forms a square," says Martino, referring to Example 11. "Unlike the piano, which uses a seven-plus-five system of addition, the guitar uses multiplication. With both of our parental forms, we cover all twelve notes of the chromatic scale by multiplying three times four."

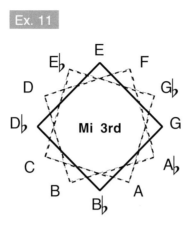

Ex. 11

Movin' On Up

When it comes to inverting chords, the portability of Martino's two parental forms proves very convenient. Take the augmented cluster, for example. Remember how, in Example 5, a fourth-position C aug 5 triad yielded a different major chord each time we lowered one of its tones? Well, if you move C aug 5 up to its first inversion at the eighth fret, it still produces the same three major triads (though you'll find the trio of triads has swapped fingerings). For instance, in Example 5 we dropped the lowest note of the chord, C, a half step and our C aug 5 became an E-major triad. But in Example 12, the augmented cluster is at the eighth position, and C appears on the first string. Now lowering the highest note yields E major, as shown.

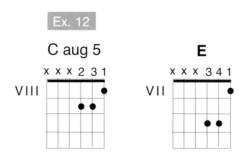

Ex. 12

Example 13 shows the same process as it relates to the diminished cluster. Here, by lowering G to G♭, E dim 7 still becomes G♭7 , but because we're at the eighth position, the dominant chord is now achieved by lowering the second-highest note in the diminished form, not the lowest note (as was the case with the fifth-position E dim 7 in Example 7).

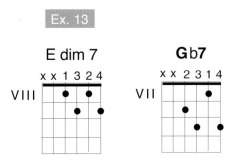

The Big Bang

"These clusters are great for generating chord progressions," shares Martino. "By lowering one note here, raising another there, you have a very efficient way of generating complex harmonies—and with the smoothest of voice leading." Martino demonstrates the approach in Example 14, taking the diminished parental form (in this case, C♯ dim 7) and expanding it one note at a time. First, he drops C♯ to C, yielding C7. Next, he raises B♭ to B. ("That gives you a beautiful form of C maj 7.") Adding an open-A pedal tone to the C maj 7 chord creates a chimey Am9 voicing. Raising G a half step produces the tendon-twisting Am9 (maj 7), which, when you raise E to E♯, relaxes into the ear-twisting Am9♯5 (maj 7) that closes the progression.

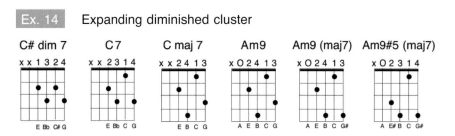

Ex. 14   Expanding diminished cluster

"It's a whole different approach to shifting harmony from the standard method, which involves creating chords from scale tones and applying complex alterations," says Martino. "And again, it's so portable. Shift our original C♯ dim 7 up to its next inversion—which is simply the exact same fingering moved up to the fifth fret—and you can easily generate a new inversion of the entire progression" (Example 15). "Just as we did in the previous example, we're expanding one note at a time, but this time the same notes are on different strings."

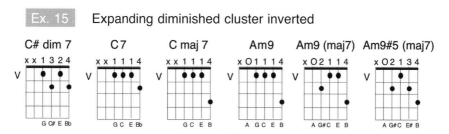

Ex. 15 Expanding diminished cluster inverted

Branching Out

The next step toward conquering the fretboard using Martino's two parental forms is to place the clusters on different groups of strings so you can take advantage of the many timbres and pitch ranges that the guitar offers. Example 16 displays seven ways of fretting the augmented cluster using unique string groups, while Example 17 shows five ways of doing the same with the diminished cluster. In each example, the chord remains the same throughout, but the inversion and timbral character changes with each new grip. And yes, with any of Example 16's augmented voicings, if you lower any single chord tone, you'll get a major triad, and similarly, if you flatten any note in one of Example 17's diminished forms, you'll hear a dominant 7 chord.

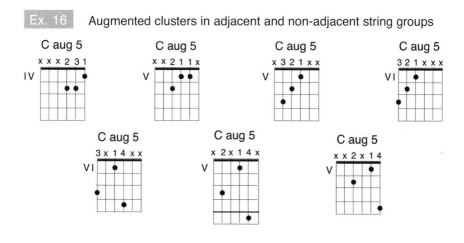

Ex. 16 Augmented clusters in adjacent and non-adjacent string groups

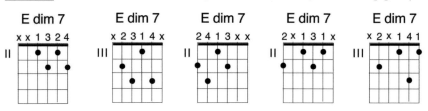

Ex. 17 Diminished clusters in adjacent and non-adjacent string groups

Martino especially likes the open-voiced sound you get by placing the parental forms on nonadjacent string sets—and the offspring they produce. Example 18 shows one of Example 16's shimmering open-voiced C aug 5 chords with its offspring (not counting the minor chords you get when you raise any one of C aug 5's tones), and Example 19 shows one of Example 17's open-voiced E dim 7 clusters with its offspring.

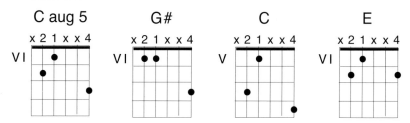

Ex. 18 Open-voiced augmented cluster and offspring

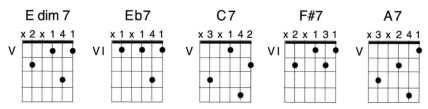

Ex. 19

Diminished cluster

Chromatic Attack!

Now that you've seen how the two parental shapes act as key centers and yield dozens of colorful, closely related chords, it's time to start thinking of them as launching pads for melodic improvisation—which is exactly what Martino does. That means putting aside notions of scale patterns and really learning to visualize the fretboard as a network of shapes connected by neighbor tones and passing tones. "Chromatic intermediates intertwine across the entire fretboard," says Martino, demonstrating this fact with one of his trademark chromatic runs in Example 20.

    While there are a ton of chromatic notes in this long descending line, the blazing riff somehow makes the entire neck seem to scream "C7." "You can use chromatic notes to weave the whole fretboard into one given topic."

Ex. 20

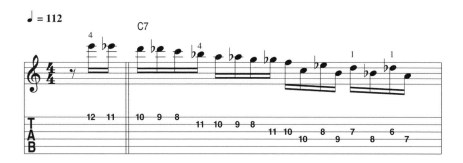

Encore

It's one of the most inspirational stories in jazz: Pat Martino learning to become a master guitarist—twice. "The first time around, I was a dead-serious youngster who was tuned in to the competitive nature of our culture and was fully motivated to achieve success," says Martino, who in 1980, at the peak of his form, suffered a catastrophic brain aneurysm that caused him to forget all he knew about playing guitar. "My second relationship with the instrument began in a much more intimate, innocent kind of way. The guitar became a playful resting place during a period of intense therapeutic recovery. It allowed me to take my attention away from my ordeal. I was able to enjoy the guitar in a pure and almost childish way—like a child does with a toy. I think we're ultimately chosen to be childish. That's exactly how we come into this world and exactly how we leave it. The guitar just happens to be my favorite toy."

[For a more purely theoretical analysis of Pat's methods, read Guy Capuzzo's academic treatise "Pat Martino's *The Nature of Guitar:* An Intersection of Jazz Theory and Neo-Riemannian Theory," which appears in Volume 12, Number 1, of Music Theory Online: The Online Journal of the Society for Music Theory at http://www.mtosmt.org/issues/mto.06.12.1/toc.12.1.html.]

Appendix IV

Pat Martino Discography

As a Leader:

1967—*El Hombre*, Prestige

Recorded May 1, 1967, with Trudy Pitts, organ; Danny Turner, flute; Mitch Fine, drums; Abdu Johnson, percussion; Vance Anderson, percussion.

1967—*Strings!*, Prestige

Recorded October 2, 1967, with Cedar Walton, piano; Joe Farrell, tenor sax, flute; Ben Tucker, bass; Walter Perkins, drums.

1968—*East*, Prestige

Recorded January 8, 1968, with Eddie Green, piano; Ben Tucker, bass; Tyrone Brown, bass; Lenny McBrowne, drums.

1968—*Baiyina (The Clear Evidence)*, Prestige

Recorded June 11, 1968, with Bobby Rose, guitar; Gregory Herbert, alto sax, flute; Richard Davis, bass; Charlie Persip, drums; Reggie Ferguson, tabla; Balakrishna, tamboura.

1970—*Desperado*, Prestige

Recorded March 9, 1970, with Eddie Green, electric piano; Tyrone Brown, electric bass; Sherman Ferguson, drums; Eric Kloss, alto sax, soprano sax. (Pat plays twelve-string guitar throughout. Liner notes by Les Paul.)

1972—*The Visit!*, Cobblestone

Recorded March 24, 1972, with Bobby Rose, guitar; Richard Davis, bass; Billy Higgins, drums. (Reissued on Muse Records as *Footprints*).

1972—*Live!*, Muse

Recorded September 7, 1972, with Ron Thomas, electric piano; Tyrone Brown, electric bass; Sherman Ferguson, drums.

1974—*Consciousness*, Muse

Recorded October 7, 1974, with Eddie Green, electric piano; Tyrone Brown, electric bass; Sherman Ferguson, drums.

1976—*Exit*, Muse

Recorded on February 10, 1976, with Gil Goldstein, piano; Richard Davis, bass; Billy Hart, drums.

1976—*We'll Be Together Again*, Muse

Recorded February 13–17, 1976, with Gil Goldstein, electric piano.

1976—*Starbright*, Warner Bros.

Recorded July 1976 with Gil Goldstein, keyboards; Warren Bernhardt, synthesizer; Will Lee, electric bass; Mike Mainieri, synthesizer; Michael Carvin, drums; Charles Collins, drums; Alyrio Lima, percussion; Marty Quinn, tabla; Albert Regni, flute; Joe d'Onofrio, violin. (Pat introduces guitar synthesizer here.)

1977—**Joyous Lake**, Warner Bros.

Recorded September 1976 with Delmar Brown, Fender Rhodes, synthesizer; Mark Leonard, electric bass; Kenwood Dennard, drums.

1989—**The Return**, Muse

Recorded February 1987 with Steve LaSpina, drums; Joey Baron, drums.

1994—**Interchange**, Muse

Recorded March 1, 1994, with James Ridl, piano; Marc Johnson, bass; Sherman Ferguson, drums.

1995—**The Maker**, Evidence

Recorded September 14, 1994, with James Ridl, piano; Marc Johnson, bass; Joe Bonadio, drums.

1996—**Night Wings**, Muse

Recorded May 27, 1994, with James Ridl, piano; Bob Kenmotsu, tenor sax; Marc Johnson, bass; Bill Stewart, drums.

1997—**All Sides Now**, Blue Note

Recorded June 1, 1996–January 15, 1997, with Mike Stern, guitar; Tuck Andress, guitar; Charlie Hunter, guitar; Kevin Eubanks, guitar; Michael Hedges, guitar; Joe Satriani, guitar; Les Paul, guitar; Lou Pollo, guitar; Cassandra Wilson, vocals; Scott Amendola, drums; Ben Perowsky, drums; Jeff Hirshfield, drums; Scott Colley, bass; Paul Nowinski, bass.

1998—**Stone Blue**, Blue Note

Recorded February 14–22, 1998, with Delmar Brown, keyboards; James Genus, bass; Eric Alexander, tenor sax; Kenwood Dennard, drums.

1999—***Fire Dance***, Mythos

Recorded August 18, 1998, with Peter Block, flute; Habib Khan, sitar; Zakir Hussain, tablas; Ilya Razman, violin.

 2001—***Live at Yoshi's***, Blue Note

Recorded December 15–17, 2000, with Joey DeFrancesco, organ; Billy Hart, drums.

 2003—***Think Tank***, Blue Note

Recorded January 8–10, 2003, with Joe Lovano, tenor sax; Gonzalo Rubalcaba, piano; Christian McBride, bass; Lewis Nash, drums

 2006—***Remember: A Tribute to Wes Montgomery***, Blue Note

Recorded August 9–10, 2005, with David Kikoski, piano; John Patitucci, bass; Scott Allan Robinson, drums; Daniel Sadownick, percussion.

 2011—***Undeniable: Live at Blues Alley***, High Note

Recorded with Tony Monaco, organ; Eric Alexander, tenor sax; Jeff "Tain" Watts, drums.

As a Sideman:

With Willis "Gator Tail" Jackson

 1963—***The Good Life***, Prestige

Recorded May 23–24, 1963, with Jackson, tenor sax; Carl Wilson, organ; Leonard Gaskin, bass; Joe Hadrick, drums; Frank Robinson, trumpet.

1963—*Grease 'n' Gravy*, Prestige

Recorded May 23, 1963, with Jackson, tenor sax; Carl Wilson, organ; Leonard Gaskin, bass; Joe Hadrick, drums; Frank Robinson, trumpet.

1963—*More Gravy*, Prestige

Recorded October 24, 1963, with Jackson, tenor sax; Carl Wilson, organ; Sam Jones, bass; Joe Hadrick, drums; Frank Robinson, trumpet.

1964—*Boss Shoutin'*, Prestige

Recorded January 9, 1964, with Jackson, tenor sax; Carl Wilson, organ; George Tucker, bass; Joe Hadrick, drums; Frank Robinson, trumpet.

1965—*Jackson's Action!*, Prestige

Recorded March 21, 1964, with Jackson, tenor sax; Carl Wilson, organ; Frank Robinson, trumpet.

1965—*Live! Action*, Prestige

Recorded March 21, 1964, with Jackson, tenor sax; Carl Wilson, organ; Frank Robinson, trumpet.

1964—*Tell It . . .*, Prestige

Recorded March 21, 1964, with Jackson, tenor sax; Carl Wilson, organ; Frank Robinson, trumpet.

1974—*Headed and Gutted*, Muse

Recorded May 16, 1974, with Jackson, tenor sax; Mickey Tucker, organ, piano, electric piano; Bob Cranshaw, electric bass; Frederick Waits, drums; Sonny Morgan, percussion; Richard Landrum, conga.

1978—***Bar Wars***, Muse

Recorded December 21, 1977, with Jackson, tenor sax; Charles Earland, organ; Idris Muhammad, drums; Buddy Caldwell, conga.

1978—***Single Action***, Muse

Recorded April 26, 1978, with Jackson, tenor sax; Carl Wilson, organ; Jimmy Lewis, bass; Yusef Ali, drums; Idris Muhammad, drums; Buddy Caldwell, conga; Ralph Dorsey, percussion.

1980—***Nothing Butt***, Muse

Recorded 1978 with Jackson, tenor sax; Charlie Earland, organ; Grady Tate, drums; Buddy Caldwell, conga. (Dig the multiple images of backside nudity on the cover!)

With Don Patterson

1964—***Holiday Soul***, Prestige

Recorded November 24, 1964, with Patterson, organ; Billy James, drums.

1967—***Four Dimensions***, Prestige

Recorded August 25, 1967, with Patterson, organ; Houston Person, tenor sax; Billy James, drums.

1968—***Boppin' and Burnin'***, Prestige

Recorded February 22, 1968, with Patterson, organ; Charles McPherson, alto sax; Howard McGhee, trumpet; Billy James, drums.

1968—***Opus de Don***, Prestige

Recorded June 5, 1968, with Patterson, organ; Junior Cook, tenor sax; Billy Mitchell, tenor sax; Billy James, drums.

1969—***Funk You!***, Prestige

Recorded September 24, 1968, with Patterson, organ; Sonny Stitt, alto sax, tenor sax; Charles McPherson, alto sax; Billy James, drums. (Reissued on CD as *Dem New York Dues.*)

1969—***Oh Happy Day***, Prestige

Recorded June 2, 1969, with Patterson, organ; Virgil Jones, trumpet; Houston Person, tenor sax: Frankie Jones, drums. (Reissued on CD as *Dem New York Dues.*)

1973—***These Are Soulful Days***, Muse

Recorded September 17, 1973, with Patterson, organ; Jimmy Heath, tenor sax; Albert Heath, drums.

With Jack McDuff

1966—***Walk on By***, Prestige

Recorded February 1966 with McDuff, organ; Red Holloway, tenor sax; Joe Dukes, drums.

1967—***Hallelujah Time!***, Prestige

Recorded June 1966 with McDuff, organ; Red Holloway, tenor sax; Joe Dukes, drums.

1967—***The Midnight Sun***, Prestige

Recorded June 1966 with McDuff, organ; Red Holloway, tenor sax; Joe Dukes, drums.

1967—***Soul Circle***, Prestige

Recorded June 1966 with McDuff, organ; Red Holloway, tenor sax; Joe Dukes, drums.

2001—***Brotherly Love***, Concord

Recorded March 6–8, 2000, with McDuff, organ; Frank Gravis, bass; Red Holloway, tenor sax, alto sax; Grady Tate, drums.

With Eric Kloss

1965—***Introducing Eric Kloss***, Prestige

Recorded September 1, 1965, with Kloss, alto sax, tenor sax; Don Patterson, organ; Billy James, drums.

1967—***Life Force***, Prestige

Record September 18, 1967, with Kloss, tenor sax; Jimmy Owens, trumpet, flugelhorn; Ben Tucker, bass; Alan Dawson, drums.

1968—***Sky Shadows***, Prestige

Recorded August 13, 1968, with Kloss, alto sax, tenor sax; Jaki Byard, piano; Bob Cranshaw, bass; Jack DeJohnette, drums.

1969—***To Hear Is to See!***, Prestige

Recorded July 22, 1969, with Kloss, alto sax, tenor sax; Chick Corea, piano, electric piano; Dave Holland, bass; Jack DeJohnette, drums.

1970—***Consciousness!***, Prestige

Recorded January 6, 1970, with Kloss, alto sax, tenor sax; Chick Corea, piano, electric piano; Dave Holland, bass; Jack DeJohnette, drums. (Pat plays twelve-string guitar on a couple of tracks.)

1972—***One, Two, Free***, Muse

Recorded August 28, 1972, with Kloss, alto sax; Ron Thomas, electric piano; Dave Holland, acoustic bass, electric bass; Ron Krasinski, drums.

With Others

1967—John Handy, ***New View***, Columbia

Recorded March 19, 1967, with Handy, alto sax; Bobby Hutcherson, vibes; Albert Stinson, bass; Doug Sides, drums.

1967—Trudy Pitts, ***Introducing the Fabulous Trudy Pitts***, Prestige

Recorded February 15–21, 1967, with Bill Carney, drums; Abdu Johnson, conga.

1967—Trudy Pitts, ***These Blues of Mine***, Prestige

Recorded September 21 and 25, 1967, with Bill Carney, drums.

1967—Richard "Groove" Holmes, ***Get Up and Get It!***, Prestige

Recorded May 29, 1967, with Teddy Edwards, tenor sax; Paul Chambers, bass; Billy Higgins, drums.

1968—Charles McPherson, ***From This Moment On***, Prestige

Recorded January 31, 1968, with Cedar Walton, piano; Peck Morrison, bass; Lennie McBrowne, drums.

1969—Charles McPherson, ***Horizons***, Prestige

Recorded August 27, 1968, with Cedar Walton, piano; Walter Booker, bass; Nasir Hafiz, vibraphone; Billy Higgins, drums.

1969—Sonny Stitt, ***Night Letter***, Prestige

Recorded October 27, 1969, with Gene Ludwig, organ; Randy Gelispie, drums.

1972—Barry Miles, **White Heat**, Mainstream

Recorded 1971 with Miles, keyboards; John Abercrombie, guitar; Victor Gaskin, bass; Lew Tabackin, tenor sax, flute; Terry Silverlight, drums; Warren Smith, percussion.

1973—Stanley Clarke, **Children of Forever**, Polydor

Recorded December 26 and 27, 1972, with Chick Corea, keyboards; Joe Farrell, soprano sax, flute; Airto Moreira, drums, percussion; Lenny White, drums; Art Webb, flute; Stan Webb, flute; Flora Purim, vocals; Andy Bey, vocals; Dee Dee Bridgewater, vocals.

1974—Jimmy Heath, **The Time and Place**, Landmark

Recorded June 24, 1974, with Heath, tenor sax, alto sax, soprano sax; Curtis Fuller, trombone; Stanley Cowell, piano; Sam Jones, bass; Billy Higgins, drums; Mtume, percussion.

1998—Joe Pesci, **Vincent LaGuardia Gambini Sings Just for You**, Columbia Recorded in 1997.

2000—Eric Alexander, **First Milestone**, Milestone

Recorded November 3 and 4, 1999, with Alexander, tenor sax; Harold Mabern, piano; Peter Washington, bass; Joe Farnsworth, drums.

2001—**The Philadelphia Experiment**, Ropeadope

Recorded June 21, 2001, with Uri Caine, keyboards; Christian McBride, bass; ?uestlove, drums; Larry Gold, cello; John Swana, trumpet.

2002—Charles Earland Tribute Band, **Keeper of the Flame**, HighNote

Recorded June 6, 2000, with Joey DeFrancesco, organ; Eric Alexander, tenor sax; James Rotondi, trumpet; Bob DeVos, guitar; Vincent Ector; drums, Kevin Jones, percussion.

2002—Joey DeFrancesco, ***Ballads and Blues***, Concord Jazz

Recorded September 4 and 5, 2001, with DeFrancesco, organ; Papa John DeFrancesco, organ; Gary Bartz, alto sax; Paul Bollenback, guitar; Byron Landham, drums.

2003—Joey DeFrancesco, ***Falling in Love Again***, Concord Jazz

Recorded May 29 and 30, 2002, with DeFrancesco, organ; Jeff Hamilton, drums; Kevin Eubanks, guitar; Ron Eschete, guitar; Elijah Davis, trumpet; Red Holloway, tenor sax; Ralph Moore, tenor sax; Ramon Banda, conga; Byron Landham, drums; Joe Doggs, vocals.

2003—Elio Villafranca, ***Incantations—Encantaciones***, Universal Music Latino

Recorded June 2002, with Villafranca, piano; Jane Bunnett, soprano sax, flute; Terrell Stafford, trumpet, flugelhorn; Carlos Henriquez, bass; Wilson "Chembo" Corniel, bata; Pedro Martinez, bata, vocals; Dafnis Prieto, drums.

2004—Royce Campbell, ***Six by Six: A Jazz Guitar Celebration***, Moon Cycle

Recorded May and June 2004, with Campbell, guitar; Larry Coryell, guitar; John Abercrombie, guitar; Dave Stryker, guitar; Bucky Pizzarelli, guitar; Essiet Essiet, bass; Ugonna Ukegwo, bass; Lynn Seaton, bass; Marcello Pellitteri, drums; Joe Cocuzzo, drums; Billy Drummond, drums.

2006—Various Artists, ***Viva Carlos: A Supernatural Marathon Celebration***, Tone Center

Recorded 2005 with Robben Ford, guitar; Eric Johnson, guitar; Eric Gales, guitar; Mike Stern, guitar; Frank Gambale, guitar; Albert Lee, guitar; Vinnie Moore, guitar; Coco Montoya, guitar; Jeff Richman, guitar; Peter Wolf, keyboards; Abe Laboriel, bass; Dave Weckl, drums.

2008—Joey DeFrancesco, ***Estate***, Zucco

Recorded November 19, 2008, with DeFrancesco, organ; Massimo Farao, piano; Aldo Zunino, bass; Byron Landham, drums.

2008—Andreas Oberg, *My Favorite Guitars*, Resonance

Recorded April 8, 2008, with Oberg, guitars; Marian Petrescu, piano; Kevin Axt, bass; Harish Raghawan, bass; Kuno Schmid, keyboards; Vic Stevens, drums.

2009—Jermaine Landsberger, *Gettin' Blazed*, Resonance

Recorded May 2008 with Landsberger, organ; Gary Meek, tenor sax, flute; Andreas Oberg, guitar; James Genus, bass; Harvey Mason, drums.

2010—Lee Ritenour, *6 String Theory*, Concord Jazz

Recorded December 2009–March 2010 with Ritenour, George Benson, Mike Stern, John Scofield, B. B. King, Keb Mo', Slash, Robert Cray, guitars; John Beasley, keyboards; Larry Goldings, keyboards; Melvin Davis, bass; Nathan East, bass; Vinnie Colaiuta, drums; Simon Phillips, drums; Paulinho Da Costa, percussion.

Index

Index

Index

Index

Index

Index